PI-BSF-897

D0122981

JUN 2015

Spinster

Washington Square Arch, New York City

"A lady who used to walk through the park forty and thirty and twenty and ten years ago could have walked there the other morning and found that, after all, nothing had really changed very much," wrote Maeve Brennan in 1966 about Washington Square Park.

Spinster

MAKING *a* LIFE *of* ONE'S OWN

KATE BOLICK

CROWN PUBLISHERS
NEW YORK

Published in the United States by Crown Publishers, an imprint of the Crown Publishing Group, a division of Penguin Random House LLC, New York.
www.crownpublishing.com

CROWN is a registered trademark and the Crown colophon is a trademark of Penguin Random House LLC.

Grateful acknowledgment is made to the following:

Edith Konecky: excerpts from diary entries by Edith Konecky about Maeve Brennan, copyright © 1974 by Edith Konecky. All rights reserved. Reprinted courtesy of Edith Konecky.

Houghton Mifflin Harcourt Publishing Company: excerpt from "Her Kind" from *To Bedlam and Part Way Back* by Anne Sexton, copyright © 1960 by Anne Sexton, renewed 1988 by Linda G. Sexton. All rights reserved. Reprinted by permission of Houghton Mifflin Harcourt Publishing Company.

Houghton Mifflin Harcourt Publishing Company and the Society of Authors: excerpt from "Professions for Women" from *The Death of the Moth and Other Essays* by Virginia Woolf, copyright © 1942 by Houghton Mifflin Harcourt Publishing Company. Copyright © renewed 1970 by Marjorie T. Parsons, Executrix. All rights reserved. Reprinted by permission of Houghton Mifflin Harcourt Publishing Company and the Society of Authors as the literary representative of the Estate of Virginia Woolf.

Russell & Volkening: excerpt from a letter by Maeve Brennan to William Maxwell, 1965 and excerpt from a letter by Maeve Brennan to Tillie Olsen, from Edith Konecky's folders, c. 2003, both excerpts copyright © The Estate of Maeve Brennan. All rights reserved. Reprinted by permission of Russell & Volkening as agents for the author.

Portions of this book have been adapted from material by the author that first appeared in *The Atlantic, Elle, The New York Observer, Poetry,* and *Slate.*

Library of Congress Cataloging-in-Publication Data
Bolick, Kate.
Spinster: a life of one's own / Kate Bolick.—First edition.
1. Bolick, Kate.   2. Authors, American—21st century—Biography.
3. Single women—United States—Psychology.   I. Title.
CT275.B583136A3 2015
973.932092—dc23
[B]   2014037871

ISBN 978-0-385-34713-6
eBook ISBN 978-0-385-34714-3

PRINTED IN THE UNITED STATES OF AMERICA

Book design by Elizabeth Rendfleisch
Illustrations by Heather Gatley
Jacket design by Christopher Brand
Jacket photograph by Peter Yang
See page 309 for interior photography credits.

10 9 8 7 6 5 4 3 2 1

First Edition

To my father, my brother,
and the memory of my mother

Author's Note

In writing about my life and the lives of others, I sought to be personal without being confessional. I faithfully adhered to factual information (names, places, chronology, dates), but to protect the privacy of those still living I occasionally changed identifying details, used initials instead of names, and sometimes told only part of the story.

You have won rooms of your own in the house hitherto exclusively owned by men. You are able, though not without great labour and effort, to pay the rent. You are earning your five hundred pounds a year. But this freedom is only a beginning; the room is your own, but it is still bare. It has to be furnished; it has to be decorated; it has to be shared. How are you going to furnish it, how are you going to decorate it? With whom are you going to share it, and upon what terms? These, I think are questions of the utmost importance and interest. For the first time in history you are able to ask them; for the first time you are able to decide for yourselves what the answers should be.

       —*Virginia Woolf*, *"Professions for Women,"* 1931

This is our little while. This is our chance.

       —*Susan Glaspell,* The People, 1917

Contents

FOR SEVERAL SUMMERS WHEN I WAS A CHILD MY FAMILY VACA-
tioned on a tiny island off the coast of Maine. Barely a fleck on
the map, it's a mile at the longest point, a scruffy bramble of fir
trees and rocky beaches, no hotels or stores or restaurants, not
even cars, only a scattering of forty or so once-grand summer
homes sagging on their foundations. While the adults read or
played tennis on the dusty clay courts, we children disappeared
into an alternate universe, sprinting in bathing suits along gritty
dirt roads and across wide green lawns, the salt air noisy with
foghorns and birdcalls.

To reach the beach we raced down a path cut between hedges
so tall that it felt like a chute bursting forth onto the sand and
sea, catapulting us into yet another dimension. When the tide
was low, rather than leap into the surf with the others, I'd break
away to an isthmus of tidal pools and boulders to "play Karana."
She was the heroine of my favorite children's novel, *Island of the
Blue Dolphins,* based on the true story of a Native American girl
who'd been left behind on an island off the coast of California in
the early 1800s and who survived on her own for eighteen years.

First, I'd gather driftwood "whalebones" to stake in the damp sand in the shape of a circle—my "hut." There was always some plastic container washed up onshore to serve as my "woven basket." These basic preparations secure, I'd set about hunting snails. The little beasts were beyond plentiful, studding the giant rocks all around me, suctioned so tightly I had to hack at them with a stone until they clattered off. Briskly, before they could reattach themselves, I'd sweep their hard, round bodies into my "woven basket" and hurry to my "fire pit"—a hollow worn into a boulder— to "cook" them in seawater, then brutally smash their shells, pluck their dark, slimy selves from the broken shards, and pretend to "eat." That my make-believe meal was so revolting sweetened my sense of conquest.

I built, then, my own kingdom according to my own laws, and when the sun beat down, it beat down only on me, and when my feet acclimated to the freezing water, it was my resilience that made this so. My experience of being alone was total.

Spinster

There, Thought Unbraids Itself

The Bolick family home, Newburyport,
Massachusetts

WHOM TO MARRY, AND WHEN WILL IT HAPPEN—THESE TWO QUES-
tions define every woman's existence, regardless of where she was
raised or what religion she does or doesn't practice. She may grow
up to love women instead of men, or to decide she simply doesn't
believe in marriage. No matter. These dual contingencies govern
her until they're answered, even if the answers are nobody and
never.

Men have their own problems; this isn't one of them.

Initially the question of whom to marry presents itself as play-acting, a child pulling a Snow White dress from a costume box and warbling the lyrics of "Someday My Prince Will Come" to her imaginary audience of soft-bottomed dwarfs. Beauty, she's gleaned, is her power and lure, a handsome groom her just reward.

Next she deduces that a flammable polyester gown with tulle underskirts does not an actual princess make, and that beauty is in the eye of the beholder—which is to say, she discovers her market value. For me it was the morning in second grade when I understood with a cold, sharp pang why I disliked gym class, even though I was the fastest runner and could do the most chin-ups. As our gym teacher, a man, led us toward the playground, I saw that he didn't playfully tease me the way he did my friends—the pretty ones. And so I learned, *I am not pretty*.

With puberty comes yet another opportunity for self-inventory. In fourth grade, I was second in my class to develop breasts, which I hid by wearing two heavy wool sweaters simultaneously all through an exceptionally warm spring—intuiting, rightly, that when the world saw what my body was up to I'd be thrust into a glare of visibility I wasn't prepared to meet.

Fifth grade: buck teeth. Sixth grade: braces. Seventh grade: popularity. I'd always found friendship easy, with boys and girls both; now I was also getting romantic attention and the two beams of social approval wove themselves into a crown. During class, my friends and I traded intricately folded notes about our crushes and practiced writing our someday surnames in fancy cursive letters. When I saw the high school girls' soccer team circled for warm-ups, one girl at center leading the stretches, I decided that some-day I, too, would be team captain.

Eighth grade brought with it hourglass proportions, which I learned while swimming in the pool at my grandparents' re-tirement complex in Florida. Two college boys appeared out of nowhere, cannonballed into the water, then shot to the surface, wet heads gleaming. "Gotta protect that one," they leered, loudly enough so that my mother, reading on a lounge chair, could hear. I blushed with pleasure and shame—and the shame of pleasure. What did it mean? Later she explained my "nice figure."

And so the approach of ninth grade made me mournful and agitated. I suspected that thirteen was the last, outermost ring of the final stage of childhood, and that those idle diversions I'd never thought to question—long hours paging through picture books trying to spot an overlooked arm reaching out from the rubble of Pompeii, or "praying" to the Greek gods (the most plausible deities, I'd decided)—would soon seem immature, unsuitable. When I turned fourteen and began my freshman year in high school, I'd have to cede the private kingdom of my imaginary life to the demands of that larger empire, where the girls who were already drinking beer and having sex were writing new laws I didn't want to play by but couldn't ignore.

Braces and breasts—and so a girl becomes, if not one of the pretty ones, attractive. To boys, I mean. College sees a few more adjustments—baby fat melts away; the late bloomer sprouts curves; the blandly pretty cultivates envy for the beautiful's chiseled bones—and then the real games commence, carrying on from campus through her twenties and thirties.

Some get the matter over with as quickly as possible, out of love or duty or fear. I've had friends who consider themselves plain tell me they seized the first husband they could get, leaving the playing fields open to the pretty and the hot. Others postpone the inevitable as long as possible, each passing year more thrillingly uncertain than the last. Their evasions are inscrutable to the romantics, who lie in wait, expectant, anxious.

It's hard to say which is more exhausting: the sheer arbitrariness of knowing that her one true love could appear out of anywhere, anytime, and change her fate in an instant (you never know who's just around the corner!), or the effortful maintenance (manicures, blowouts, bikini waxes, facials) that ensures she'll be ripe for the picking when it happens.

Eventually, whether you choose or are chosen, joyously accept or grudgingly resist, you take the plunge.

You are born, you grow up, you become a wife.

But what if it wasn't this way?

What if a girl grew up like a boy, with marriage an abstract, someday thought, a thing to think about when she became an adult, a thing she could do, or not do, depending?

What would that look and feel like?

In 2012, I read that modern America's first iconic single woman and my favorite girlhood poet, Edna St. Vincent Millay, had lived in my hometown in the early 1900s. Obviously, Google Earth wouldn't do. I rented a car and drove the five hours north from my studio apartment, in Brooklyn, New York, to the house I grew up in, on the coast of Massachusetts.

The news had astonished me, both the exciting nearness of a woman I admire, and that I hadn't known it already. We the people of the historic seaport (so heralds a sign on the highway) of Newburyport put great stock in our civic past; it's how we compensate for having no contemporary relevance. Every schoolchild is taught that George Washington once spent a night in what is now the public library. John Quincy Adams slept everywhere, apparently. Yet we don't stake our rightful claim to one of the twentieth century's most famous poets.

Admittedly, it wasn't Millay's poetry that had inspired me to make the trip. When I was twenty-three my mother died unexpectedly, and in the months that followed I'd been gutted to discover that without our conversations, which I'd always assumed would be there for the having, I had absolutely no idea how to make sense of myself.

Unconsciously at first, and eventually with something resembling intention, I began the very long process of re-creating our conversations—not with other, real, live women, who could only ever be gross approximations of the mother I missed, but with real, dead women, whom I could sidle up to shyly and get to know slowly, through the works they left behind and those written about them.

By now, including Edna Millay, there were five such women: essayist Maeve Brennan, columnist Neith Boyce, novelist Edith Wharton, and social visionary Charlotte Perkins Gilman.

I'd come to consider them my "awakeners," a term I'd borrowed from Wharton, who used it in her memoir, *A Backward Glance,* to describe the books and thinkers who'd guided her intellectual studies. Granted, mine was a more sentimental education. I'd encountered each awakener at a different stage in my own coming-of-age as an adult, which, I could no longer deny, I finally was. I'd just turned forty.

I'd made a very big deal of the birthday. Those of us who've bypassed the exits for marriage and children tend to motor through our thirties like unlicensed drivers, unauthorized grown-ups. Some days it's great—you're a badass outlaw on the joyride that is life! Other days you're an overgrown adolescent borrowing your dad's car and hoping the cops don't pull you over. Along the way I decided to take as faith Erik Erikson's famous theory of psychosocial development, which maintains that age forty is when "young adulthood" ends and "middle adulthood" begins, and I vowed that when that day came, I'd properly celebrate my place in the order of things, no matter how unsettling it felt to accept I was no longer young.

For six months my friend Alexandra and I planned a seaside clambake for forty of our mutual friends and closest family, to be held several towns south of Newburyport the first weekend in July. Alexandra is married, with two children, and, possibly because of this, handled our wedding-like preparations with more sangfroid than I, who had never hosted a big event and fixated on every last detail, most fanatically, the exact-right motif.

It should be simple, I decided, and nautical (an anchor, a clipper ship, a crab) yet also . . . iconic, representative of transition, one door opening as another closes (Janus), or perhaps straddling two worlds (a centaur, a minotaur) but female obviously (not a harpy; a Valkyrie?).

That it took me so long to arrive at the obvious made my final preparations all the more manic. The night before the party I stubbornly carved a mermaid into a linoleum block—a skill last deployed as a YWCA camp counselor the summer before college—poured a pan of black ink, and doggedly printed her shapely silhouette onto forty red-striped cotton dishtowels, one for each guest, while my new boyfriend, S, gamely affixed homemade mermaid stickers to matchboxes, somewhat alarmed, he later admitted, to witness what happens when, as my family has long put it, I get a bee in my bonnet.

My heart hummed. Hadn't I wished as a girl to be a mermaid, and wasn't I a mermaid now? Never before had I been so liminal: astride the threshold between young womanhood and middle adulthood; in love but living alone; half invisible, half statistical reality*—as in, over the course of my own lifetime the ranks of unmarried women (and men) had grown so swiftly that the num-

---

* Statistics vary by age and are therefore difficult to pin down. In September 2014, the Census Bureau reported that in 2013, 105 million people age eighteen and older were never married, divorced, or widowed, 53 percent of whom were women. Also that month, the Bureau of Labor Statistics reported that in August 2014 there were 124.6 million single Americans, or 50.2 percent (up from 37 percent in 1976) of the population, enabling news outlets to claim that single Americans now outnumber marrieds, but they were counting those sixteen and older.

ber reached a record high, turning what had felt, in my twenties, to be a marginalized status into a demographic so enormous it was no longer possible to question our existence.

The next morning the caterer, my childhood friend Martha, who'd reinvented herself as a feast-maker, arrived with buckets of lobsters and clams. Our friend Alison, an antiques dealer, laid the rented tables with black-and-white gingham cloths and silver candelabra. Like me, they were both unmarried mermaids, as were all but one of my female guests.

Without a doubt I was forcing myself toward epiphany, come hell or high water, but it worked. The night itself was clear and warm. Watching my family mingle with friends from every stage of my life, some they'd known forever and others they'd never met, I began to sense a shift in my perception, a growing awareness that I was now in possession of not only a future, but also a past. It was almost a physical sensation, as if everything I'd ever thought or done had been embroidered onto the long train of a gown that now trailed behind me wherever I went.

When I looked over my shoulder to inspect this feat of silken wizardry, there they were, my five ghostly awakeners, holding it aloft.

I'd never regarded all five women together before, as a group, and in the weeks following the party I found that I couldn't stop. The oldest was born in 1860, the youngest in 1917. One was from Ireland, but they'd all spent their adult lives in America (at least through young adulthood; one decamped to France in her forties). Though all were writers of various stripes, none had been friends in their lifetimes.

These women had been with me for over a decade, and yet still they were mostly abstractions, spectral beings confined to the invisible sanctum that exists between the reader and the page, as if they weren't once real people who'd walked this same earth, negotiating their own very different personal and historical circumstances.

Discovering that Edna Millay had actually walked the streets of Newburyport, the only place to which I feel an intense, visceral attachment, as if it's not merely my hometown but a phantom limb, ignited a desire to bring all five of my awakeners back to life, so to speak. Getting to know them, *really* know them—visit their homes; read their letters; smell their perfume—was a task long overdue. I wasn't sure what I'd learn by seeing Edna's house, for example, but given how sensitive I am to my own surroundings, I knew it would somehow deepen my understanding of who she'd been.

I drove the first hour of the trip in silence; the snarl of exits and on-ramps that quarantines New York City from the rest of the state requires militant attention to the GPS. But once I'd hit the highway, I turned on the radio and toggled through the stations, a baggy American songbook.

I'd chanced upon my five awakeners with a similar hopscotch of happenstance and instinct, and until well past New Haven I suffered a variant of commitment phobia, or buyer's remorse, tallying up all those who might have been, musicians and artists and thinkers just as interesting as the ones I'd chosen.

This ad-hoc approach had discounted scores of perfectly acceptable candidates. For instance, Mary McCarthy, many a bookish girl's imaginary avatar, even though one morning I found myself looking in the bathroom mirror thinking a passage from her *Intellectual Memoirs* as if it were my own: "It was getting rather alarming. I realized one day that in twenty-four hours I had slept with three different men. . . . I did not *feel* promiscuous. Maybe no one does."

But crossing from Connecticut into Massachusetts, I remembered that McCarthy a) had been a touch too coolly imperturbable at the exact moment I needed warmth and b) grew up in Seattle and Minneapolis, two cities I know nothing about.

All four of my native-born women had strong ties to New England.

Besides, I decided, isn't that how falling in love so often works? Some stranger appears out of nowhere and becomes a fixed star in your universe. My susceptibility to the seeming poetry of random chance is both blessing and curse.

By now it was late evening. I took the exit for Newburyport and continued along High Street, a wide boulevard of pretty eighteenth- and nineteenth-century houses, toward the center of town. As always, the buildings of my youth were exactly where I'd left them. The deceptively dignified-looking Newburyport High School. The tiny, shingled Lynch's Pharmacy, where I was always greeted by name. St. Paul's Church, home of my Montessori kindergarten and later my mother's funeral. The sweet red-brick façade of my grammar school.

Four of my five awakeners were redheads.

Not until I was driving through my blindingly white hometown did I realize that the only characteristics all five women had in common were a highly ambivalent relationship to the institution of marriage, the opportunity to articulate this ambivalence, and whiteness—each of which, arguably, was inextricable from the rest. During the period I was drawn to—primarily, the turn of the last century—vanishingly few women of color were given the privilege to write and publish and, therefore, speak across the decades.

And then thinking ceased and muscle memory took over and I turned left onto our street, pulled into the driveway, and parked the car.

The house was dark; it's not exactly a home anymore. In 1990 it began to empty out—first me, then my grandmother, then my little brother, and finally our mother. After she died, my father easily could have sold this vestige of his former existence—a three-story "double house" built by two brothers in the early 1800s, it has ye olde New England appeal—and for a long while I braced myself for that eventuality, one I had no control over and desperately didn't want.

So I was relieved if slightly horrified when, instead of unloading it, he quit his small law firm downtown, colonized what had been the dining room, living room, and my late grandmother's bedroom into an office suite, and launched his own private law practice on the first floor. He even hung a plastic IN/OUT sign on the front door, beneath the original doorbell that still issues a throaty trill when you twist its brass handle. That was in 2000.

Nighttime in that house always seems to fall grayish, never pitch-black; I know every last inch so completely, I can see the wallpaper and furniture even when I can't. Upstairs, when I switched on the little peach-colored lamp with its dented shade, my bedroom blinked awake: small white space with a low, sloped ceiling; makeshift valance of torn lace at the window (tacked there circa high school); messy stacks of books and old journals; wide, old floorboards dulled with dust—not much of a room.

But when I set my suitcase on the floor and started to undress, my ears adjusted to that seductive hush unique to libraries and childhood bedrooms—a busy, almost trance-inducing silence, a noiseless hum, as if all those abandoned books and journals buzzed on an alternate frequency straining to be tapped—until slowly the hush itself became real.

I've come to think that, much as neglect in infancy scars the eventual adult, so our first experiences of pleasurable solitude teach us how to be content by ourselves and shape the conditions in which we seek it. For me it was being alone up in that bedroom, reading or lazing about, one ear forever tuned to the orchestra of family life. As I slipped beneath the sheets, that lost din echoed in all its comforting familiarity. By the time I turned off the lamp, it seemed incomprehensible that anything of consequence had ever existed beyond this tiny pinnacle.

To set sail on the black unknown of sleep in a room that's been "mine" nearly my entire life is one of the greatest luxuries I know. As Edna Millay once put it about an island she loved: "There, thought unbraids itself, and the mind becomes single."

When I set out for Edna's house the next morning, it was almost noon, the streets empty and hot; a small town at midday is nearly as quiet as at night, everyone shut indoors at their jobs.

The distance between my childhood home and the one Edna lived in is barely a ten-minute walk, so before I knew it, there it stood: classic federalist, white with green shutters, three stories, flat roof. The way it's set flush to the sidewalk, without even a strip of front yard, gives it a looming quality, like someone who stands too close when he talks.

I walked across the street to get a better view. I used to be embarrassed to gawk at the homes of the famous; it seemed like watching the movie version of a novel without ever reading the book. But now I know that a house is a book, just not the kind we're accustomed to reading.

This one told a story of borrowed finery. Edna's mother, Cora Buzzell, was born in Belfast, Maine, in 1863, met and married Henry Millay in 1889, and quickly bore three daughters—after which the couple's differences (she was responsible and industrious, he was not) grew too obvious to ignore. By 1901, when she was thirty-eight, Cora had deemed him more trouble than he was worth, and she brought her brood to Newburyport, where her own siblings lived. Edna, the oldest daughter, was eight. Of the several houses they bounced among in town, this is the only one that remains. It was the nicest Edna had ever known, or would again until she was an adult.

Ah, I thought to myself, *this is the purpose of my trip.*

Newburyport was founded in the 1600s where the Merrimack River empties into the Atlantic Ocean, and prospered as a clipper shipbuilding center in the 1850s; that original boom-time class system is writ into the architecture. At the top is High Street, the main thoroughfare, a parade of grand, cupola-topped mansions erected by wealthy ship captains. Between that and the river is the crowded middle—these are the streets I'd walked from my house to hers—a latticework of small and large clapboard houses built by rope-makers and blacksmiths, merchants and distillers. The lowest class—longshoremen and stevedores—was sequestered along the waterfront in a rat-infested village of seamy boarding-houses (since razed and developed as parkland).

I knew from my reading that as adults Edna and I had little in common, but as children we were very similar, highly sensitive to what we did and did not like, imaginative though not dreamy, as that adjective often implies—more like bossy, in the best sense of the word. If I learned how class works by walking the streets of this town, then she did, as well. Her house, like mine, is just off that main thoroughfare, attractive without being showy, a house to be proud of—and grandeur proximate.

The longer I looked at Edna's old house, the more I saw: the template for the one she'd go on to buy in 1924, and the distance she would traverse as a person; that house, also, would be a federalist, also white with green shutters, though on seven hundred acres in New York State, near the Massachusetts border. The resemblance was striking, right down to the delicate, semicircular fanlight window capping the front door.

After a while I stopped gawking and turned back. Making my way along the ancient brick sidewalks, buckled by tree roots and warped by cold snaps, I wondered what my childhood home might reveal about me to a stranger. It never ceases to astonish me how readily we presume to know ourselves, when in fact we know so little.

Each of us is a museum that opens for business the moment we're born, with memory the sole curator. How could a staff of one possibly stay abreast of all those holdings? No sooner does a moment occur than it's relegated to the past, requiring that it be labeled, sorted, and filed into the appropriate cabinet. Given this ceaseless deluge of paperwork, it's no wonder we have such a tenuous handle on the present. And so the curator toils alongside us in the dark, bereft of the information needed to truly understand who we are; the individual is inseparable from context.

Take the topic at hand: the Single Woman. In the museum of your mind, your conscious ideas about her are on prominent display. It's a very smart exhibit, with an auditorium for viewing old film and television clips (*Ally McBeal, Living Single, The Mary Tyler Moore Show, Murphy Brown, Sex and the City*), a collection of yellowed magazine advertisements mounted on the walls, headphones for listening to audio recordings of all the relevant conversations you've had with friends, and (once you've read this book) a neat row of glass cases in which facts and figures are typed on placards set beside diaries and letters that date all the way back to the founding of America. Impressive!

Except the curator forgot to check the vault in the basement, the one where all the cultural attitudes about single women you've inherited from everyone you've ever known, particularly your parents, are spilling out of the cabinets and papering the floor. And that's not all. On the front desk is an unopened report that just arrived from a think tank collating all the current statistics about single women in America,* which means you need a new glass display case.

The graph depicts a V, with the year 1890 sitting atop the left arm and the year 2013 atop the right. The overall number of single women in America starts at a high of 34 percent in 1890, slides down one percent per decade, all the way to the bottom point of the V—17 percent in 1960—and then climbs back up and up, 2 percent per decade, to 53 percent in 2013.

Every year I try to reread Doris Lessing's slim 1987 polemic (originally a lecture series), *Prisons We Choose to Live Inside.* In the book, this "epicist of the female experience," as the Swedish Academy put it when awarding her the Nobel Prize in Literature in 2007, reminds us how difficult it is to detach ourselves from the mass emotions and social conditions of the age we're born into; all of us, male and female, are "part of the great comforting illusions, and part illusions, which every society uses to keep up its confidence in itself."

A few pages later she writes, "Very few people indeed are happy as solitaries, and they tend to be seen by their neighbours as peculiar or selfish or worse. Most people cannot stand being alone for long. They are always seeking groups to belong to. We are group animals still, and there is nothing wrong with that. But what is dangerous is not the belonging to a group, or groups, but not understanding the social laws that govern groups and govern us."

To further thwart self-knowledge, there's a theory that we as humans lack the imagination to "remember" any further back than the generation or two that directly precedes us, limiting our historical memory to the eras of our parents and grandparents. This may be why the so-called "golden years" of the 1950s and

---

* The graph is not actually from a think tank—my research assistant and I came up with it by combining census reports; the most recent finding is from the Census Bureau's 2013 American Community Survey.

early 1960s loom so large in our contemporary consciousness, bullying many of us into believing that the institution of marriage was always thus, and will be evermore. We simply can't see through that dense hedge of norms and expectations to the decades that came before.

The flip side of this collective assumption is that the single woman has always been stigmatized as a lonely old spinster with too many cats, for example. Certainly she was reviled in the 1950s, in the way all minorities are stigmatized, to ratify the choices of the majority. But that was just one of the spinster's iterations in her constantly evolving reputation. Perceptions of her have fluctuated so wildly across the decades that she's never merely a living, breathing being, but is also a lightning rod for attitudes toward women in general. She's selfless: Lady Liberty, Florence Nightingale, Mother Teresa. She's charmingly eccentric: Mary Poppins, Holly Golightly, Auntie Mame. She's powerful: Rosie the Riveter, Wonder Woman, Joan of Arc.

Which is also to say that in spite of her prevalence the single woman is nearly always considered an anomaly, an aberration from the social order. Piece together all her guises and you get a Lernaean hydra, bristling with countless projections and assumptions. (In 2006, social psychologist Bella DePaulo, PhD, coined the word *singlism* to mean "the stereotyping, stigmatizing, and discrimination against people who are single.")

As I thought about Edna Millay and her mother, I found I wasn't even sure what a single woman is, exactly. Unmarried, obviously. But we were three unmarried women (including myself), in one neighborhood, in different eras, at various ages and life stages—were we all single women?

Not young Edna, of course; by the time she left Newburyport, she was only twelve, just a girl—though, hold on. In Shakespeare's time reproductive ability equaled maturity; Juliet was thirteen when she married Romeo. At what age was a girl considered a woman in America at the turn of the last century? For this I turned to marriage historian Stephanie Coontz: throughout the 1800s the legal age of consent in most states was ten, eleven, or twelve—seven in Delaware—but, mercifully, by century's end social reformers had pushed that number to between sixteen and eighteen.*

Edna's mother and I were both around forty, but unlike her I'd never been married or, therefore, divorced. Is a divorcée a single woman? And what about widows—do they count?

Because single women and married women have historically had different rights, I asked my father to consult his *Black's Law Dictionary,* the most widely used law dictionary in the United States. There's no entry for "single woman," but there is the very glamorous-sounding Latin term *feme sole*: "a single woman, including those who have been married but whose marriage has been dissolved by death or divorce, and, for most purposes, those women who are judicially separated from their husbands." (Note that even the law defines a single woman by what she lacks.)

DePaulo elaborates on that definition of a single woman. She argues that you're "socially single" if you're sexually or emotionally involved with someone but the two of you don't consider yourself a couple, or don't meet society's definition of coupledom (which ranges from exclusivity to cohabitation). Further, you're "personally single" if you *think* of yourself as single, even if you're coupled.

That her definitions apply to men and women alike might seem to suggest that the single experience is the same regardless of gender. But the old-fashioned synonyms that remain in circulation indicate otherwise. *Bachelor* originally referred to men of

---

* Today the federal age of consent, which applies to sexual acts that involve travel between different states or countries, is sixteen, which also holds in thirty-one states; of the remaining states, eight set the age at seventeen, and ten at eighteen.

inferior status in professions so demanding, they precluded marriage. In thirteenth-century France this meant, for instance, a theological candidate who held merely a bachelor's degree instead of a master's. Around 1300 the word crossed into English to describe low-ranking knights. Much later, Victorian matchmakers appropriated the term and added *eligible,* for an unmarried man blessed with financial and social inducements, and *confirmed,* for any who wanted to remain that way. By the late nineteenth century the term had neutralized to simply mean "unmarried man," as it still does today.

The term *spinster* follows an inverse trajectory. It originated in fifteenth-century Europe as an honorable way to describe the girls, most of them unmarried, who spun thread for a living—one of very few respectable professions available to women. By the 1600s the term had expanded to include any unmarried woman, whether or not she spun.*

Not until colonial America did *spinster* become synonymous with the British *old maid,* a disparagement that cruelly invokes *maiden* (a fertile virgin girl) to signify that this matured version has never outgrown her virginal state, and is so far past her prime that she never will. At a time when procreation was necessary to building a new population, the biblical imperative to "be fruitful and multiply" felt particularly urgent, and because only wives, of course, were allowed to have sex, the settlers considered solitary women sinful, a menace to society. If a woman wasn't married by twenty-three she became a "spinster." If she was still unwed at twenty-six, she was written off as a hopeless "thornback," a species of flat, spiny fish—a discouraging start to America's long evo-

---

* When servants became common, so did neologisms that likewise doubled for occupation and marital status: the German *magd,* the British *maid.* In the nineteenth century, when single women recently immigrated from Ireland dominated America's domestic workforce, the popular Celtic girl's name Bridget became the generic term for any Irish female servant.

lution in getting comfortable with the idea of autonomous women. During the Salem Witch Trials of 1692, of the nearly two hundred people accused of witchcraft—all of them from the little farming villages and seaside towns I grew up among—the majority were adult women at the fringes of society, whether poor single mothers or widows whose wealth inspired jealousy.*

Indeed, I was raised in spinster territory. Throughout the nineteenth century, New England harbored more single women than anywhere else in the country, with the highest proportion in Massachusetts, which had more than double that of the American population as a whole. This was largely because of the massive losses sustained by the Civil War, which of course ravaged the whole country; historically, wars create a radical spike in the single female population. (In ancient Rome, repeated military campaigns so drastically depleted the pool of marriageable freemen that some single women tried to marry slaves, to much public resistance.) But other factors—the bruised postwar economy, which made it difficult for men to professionalize and marry early; a regional commitment to intellectual and literary pursuits, which extended to women—created a social atmosphere in which single women were allowed, a little bit, to flourish.

Few people, if any, seriously use the term *spinster* today, and yet we all agree on what she is. *Oxford English Dictionary*: "An unmarried woman, especially an older woman thought unlikely to marry"; *American Heritage Dictionary*: "Often offensive. A woman, especially an older one, who has not married"; the dictionary on my MacBook Air: "An unmarried woman, typically an older woman beyond the usual age for marriage. Usage note: In modern everyday English, 'spinster' cannot be used to mean

---

* Of the tens of thousands executed for witchcraft in central Europe from 1450 to 1750, three-quarters were widows over fifty who lived alone. Which is to say: their crime was the audacity of existing without a husband.

simply 'unmarried woman'; it is now always a derogatory term, referring or alluding to a stereotype of an older woman who is unmarried, childless, prissy, and repressed." Only *Black's Law Dictionary* offers a neutral definition: "The addition given in legal proceedings and in conveyancing to a woman who has never been married."

I'd made my trip home the month I turned forty—my era's version of the hopeless thornback.

In ancient Rome, there were several Vestal Virgins at any given time guarding the sacred fire of Vesta, goddess of the hearth. Each was tapped for the priesthood before puberty and sworn to celibacy for thirty years. Once she'd fulfilled her service—usually by her mid-thirties, and no later than forty—she was given a pension and was free to do whatever she wanted, even marry. Marriage to a former Vestal was a coveted status symbol.

My five awakeners had brought me all this way. Maybe it was time I set down on paper everything they'd taught me, then progress into this next decade by myself.

2

The Spinster Wish

Nancy O'Keefe Bolick, 1968

THE STORY OF HOW I FOUND MY FIVE AWAKENERS IS A TRUE STORY about a series of fictions—the genuine desires and received expectations, confused yearnings and cagey half-truths—that go into making a life, and the ways in which fantasy and reality coexist. When I set out to write it, I assumed I'd start with my first awakener and proceed from there, only to discover a prelude leading up to that main event, an antechamber of wishes, both my mother's and my own, which is where the story actually begins.

My mother once told me that as a young girl she'd lie in bed conjuring the man she would someday marry. Where was he at that exact moment? What was he thinking about? What did he look like? When would they meet? Sometimes she'd sneak into the backyard and wrap her arms around a tree, for practice.

She met her fate in February 1968, the month she turned twenty-four, at a Pennsylvania ski resort. They spied each other in line for the chairlift: a cute guy with curly hair and an adorably wrong white silk scarf (he grew up in North Carolina and had never been skiing); a curvy brunette in a kelly-green snowsuit (from New England, she was used to the slopes). Later, back at the lodge, they flirted over hot cocoa and discovered that they both lived in Washington, DC, where she worked for the just-founded Job Corps, and he was an Army intelligence officer, studying Mandarin Chinese. He asked for her number. She told him she was in the phone book. He liked her sass. Eleven months later they married in a small chapel just outside of Newburyport—frighteningly fast, from my adult perspective, but common then.

Growing up, I thrilled to stories of their genuinely romantic newlywed years, and I asked to hear them so often that eventually I could repeat the details verbatim, from dialogue to costume changes.

When I started thinking about my five awakeners in earnest, however, I came to see that, demographically speaking, my parents had made a series of very ordinary decisions at an extraordinary moment in history—providing me with a convenient example for understanding marital trends in the second half of the twentieth century.

They were a good match: she gave him the stability he craved while also sharing in his adventures; he was caring and communicative, the opposite of her gruff, cigar-smoking father. Immediately after the wedding he was dispatched to Okinawa to fill a Chinese-language position in Special Action Force Asia; framed and hung on the wall at home in Newburyport is the telegram he sent a month or so later:

```
HAVE SNUG BUNGALOW SEND POWER OF ATTORNEY
LOVE DOUG.
```

They lived off base in an Okinawan neighborhood until he shipped out to Vietnam. She moved back in with her parents, got a job in Newburyport teaching English (at the same school Edna Millay had attended as a child, now long demolished). As my father put it to me later, those were "exciting, heady times. Winds of war, leave-takings, R & Rs, anguish."

In July 1971 he finished his one-year tour of duty, and they returned to Washington, DC, so he could start law school on the G.I. Bill; she found work at the Council for Exceptional Children, a professional advocacy group. In July 1972 I was born, followed four years and one day later by my brother, Christopher; in 1977 we moved back to Newburyport, where my father established his private law practice downtown, and my mother returned to teaching school.

Every time I see the numbers, I'm amazed all over again. In 1890, only 54 percent of all households were married couples. By 1950, that number had grown to 65 percent. By the time my parents were getting married, so were 80 percent of their peers.

Completing school, leaving home, starting a career, getting

married, having children—until very recently this lockstep progression was taken for granted as the fast track to the American dream. But as Betty Friedan famously revealed in 1963 with *The Feminine Mystique,* even then there were cracks in the pavement. In one particularly telling 1962 poll, the majority of wives claimed that they were happy, but only 10 percent wanted their daughters to follow suit. *Wait a little longer to get married,* they whispered. *Live a little; go to college.*

Which is exactly what happened. By 1970 the number of married households had plummeted to 61 percent. Between 1966 and 1979 divorce rates doubled.

By the time my mother was raising me, whispering was no longer necessary. The second wave of the women's movement that flared into being in the late 1960s had gone mass by the early 1970s, swiftly spreading beyond urban centers all the way out to small towns. Newburyport wasn't exactly a feminist hotbed, but my mother found a certain sisterhood with the local chapter of the League of Women Voters, and in 1980, when she was thirty-six, became its president. *"If* and when you decide to have children," she would say as soon as I was old enough to start thinking such thoughts.

She once surprised me by confiding that one of the most blissful moments of her life had been when she was twenty-one, several years before she'd met my father, driving down the highway in her VW Beetle, with nowhere to go except wherever she wanted to be. "I had my own car, my own job, all the clothes I wanted," she remembered wistfully. Had she been born just a little later, she could have spent an entire decade enjoying that unfettered lifestyle.

Instead, she pushed aside her own ambitions, raised two children, and in her mid-thirties began finding her way toward work she enjoyed, only to discover that she had an awful lot of catching up to do. She was deeply happy with us, her family, but she was also frustrated, and this tension had an enormous influence on the adult I became.

----◄▌►----

When I was a teenager, my mother wrote a short essay about the time a neighbor had spied me walking along the street, and she gave it to me as part of my high school graduation present. "Kate has your bearing," the gentleman had said, "the same narrow shoulders held erect." My mother was delighted with the comparison and concluded that, long after she was gone, she would live on through me, there in my very deportment. I told her I loved the piece, but inwardly I cringed. *Really? Was I doomed to look like her forever?*

If you're a daughter, your mother's face is your first mirror, and if you share her features—in our case hazel eyes, brown hair, a serious amount of freckles, a small frame with those "narrow shoulders held erect"—odds are you'll unconsciously adopt her attitude of self-regard. My mother considered herself to be plain, if not homely, and so I believed her, and so I considered myself. She'd spoken so vividly about her awkward adolescence that I could conjure that mousy girl in a heartbeat—in my mind's eye she was always slumped against a wall of lockers at Newburyport High School (along with our looks we shared the same alma mater), hair dull and limp, painfully alone in an ill-fitting plaid dress. I carried this phantom twin wherever I went, no matter that I couldn't have been more different myself, outgoing and athletic. A favorite family story was of the time her college admissions counselor, dismayed by my mother's lousy grades, advised that she apply to beauty school. "I don't even like brushing my *own* hair!" my mother had moaned.

The joke's extra punch was how successfully she'd outgrown that sad, hapless girl to become a woman whom others looked up to and described as strong. All through her teens and twenties she was racked with self-doubt and insecurity—and then, at thirty-four, she did an about-face: she quit her job teaching middle-school English and convinced *The Newburyport Daily News* to hire her as its features editor, despite not possessing a single professional credential. Two years later she quit her full-time job and reinvented herself as a freelance journalist, contributing travel stories to national magazines and newspapers. Because my father worked for himself, he was able to keep the household running as she flew to Greece or Germany on assignment.

When she was thirty-nine (I was ten), my mother found a lump in her breast and underwent a mastectomy. The surgery was a success, and the scare inspired her to live more fully and bravely than before. During her recovery she redoubled her freelance efforts, taking on more challenging topics, reporting on important social issues, and publishing history books for the young-adult market. Her true ambition was to someday publish fiction; in her rare free time she worked on short stories and joined a writing group.

In 1990, my senior year of high school, she ran for the school board in our small town. Sometimes I joined her as she marched up and down the streets of Newburyport, knocking on doors and leaving behind fliers. Everyone commented on how much we looked alike in person. In her campaign photo, she was a tougher, more polished version of the warm, generous mother I knew: short hair brushed into a no-nonsense coif; mascara brightening her eyes; full lips closed in a resolute line. Her real self she saved for real life: after she won, she didn't merely revel in her victory but shared it, holding a public meeting encouraging other women to run for office, then teaching them how to do it.

Deep down, though, we all knew the cancer could strike again at any moment.

We were a family of people who loved and lived to talk, and

we openly discussed seemingly anything. Every night when I was a very small child, as my mother or father tucked me into bed, I'd snuggle deeper into the blankets and croon my favorite (albeit ungrammatical) phrase: "Let's talk about." Let's talk about the books we just read, or the walk we took after dinner, or what we're eating for breakfast tomorrow. You tell me; I tell you. Anything. All of it! Every close relationship since, friendships included, had coursed along this river of conversation. For me, closeness was talking.

But the only time of year we'd truly acknowledge the ticking time bomb in our midst was Valentine's Day, when my mother first learned she was in remission. It was her event—we three were her chosen guests. She'd set the dining table with our best finery and put a small, special gift on each of our plates—I distinctly recall a red-and-blue Siamese fighting fish in a plastic sack fat with water—and before we ate, she gave a sort of secular grace about how grateful she was to still be alive, doing work she cared about, married to a man she loved, watching her children grow up.

I'd look down at my hands in my lap, willing her to hurry up and finish, ashamed of my impatience. I preferred not to talk about this particular topic.

My sports-obsessed public high school proved a welcome distraction. I'd always loved to run and was very good at it; little in life since compares to the intense pleasure of winning a half-mile race. By senior year I was co-captain of the track and soccer teams.

Where my mother had been a teenage misfit, I was a social butterfly, flitting between school dances and Friday-night football games. Our worst battles during my teenage years were over clothes. Oh how I longed, circa 1989, for a pair of white Guess jeans with ankle zippers. Her objections started with cost and impracticality, then shot straight to my character: How had *her* daughter become so superficial, heart set on such frivolities? I'd glare at her—in my mind's eye she is forever frozen in her uniform of fat white running shoes, loose khaki pants, off-brand polo shirt, a crewneck sweater around her shoulders—and wish she'd get off her high horse and care about what she looked like for once.

My romantic life was equally anodyne. Freshman year I fell in love with B, a junior (his sports were baseball, hockey, and football). He was smart and funny and kind; my parents made him part of our family. We stayed together all four years, until I graduated.

At my small liberal-arts college in Maine I fell in love again, with W. When a friend introduced us in the dining hall our sophomore year, we shook hands, and a bolt of electricity shot up my arm. One night not long after we met, he ran over to my dorm room and knocked. When I opened the door, he wasn't standing there so much as pausing, like a hummingbird hovering in place. He'd come to tell me the moon was incredible. I must come see it. I threw my winter coat over my pajamas, and we ran outside.

Our first summer together we spent our spare time in the converted barn behind his family's home outside Boston, painting and writing (him), reading and writing (me), having sex, taking long walks through the orchard, picking blackberries for our morning cereal. His mother owned a little flock of bedraggled sheep and a peacock named Dick, who screamed like a woman tied to railroad tracks (as peacocks do). I wanted to quit my plans to study abroad in Ireland that fall, but I didn't, and we ended up seeing quite a bit of each other anyhow; that October my mother's cancer reemerged, and when I flew home for her second mastectomy he picked me up at the airport and stayed with me for the duration. Back on campus that winter we were that couple that is rarely apart.

But this was the 1990s, not the 1960s. I loved W for all the obvious reasons—his curious mind and dry humor and enormous blue eyes—but also because we were both trying to be artists, and as we neared the end of college, I began to sense a friction between the intimacy we shared and the autonomy required to become the people we wanted to be.

Or that I wanted to be; he was pretty sure of himself already.
I had a long way to go.

After graduation, W and I moved to opposite coasts—he to his
family's summer home on Martha's Vineyard, me to Portland,
Oregon—and maintained our relationship long distance, through
phone calls and visits and letters (dial-up Internet access having
yet to reach the masses). While apart, we decided, we were free to
see other people, as long as we didn't tell each other.

I remained in constant touch with my family, as well. My
brother was enjoying his first year of college in New York. My
parents were working and seeing friends and tending to Newburyport's civic life; rare was the night they weren't out saving the
waterfront or debating zoning laws. Now that my mother's second
bout of cancer had finally come and gone, there was nothing to
worry about. She'd even run for reelection the year before, so infu-
riating the opposition—who'd discovered during her first term that
she didn't truckle to the entrenched good ol' boy regime—that she
received actual death threats in the mail. Take that: she won with
the biggest landslide in the town's electoral history.

I'd found a room in a huge falling-down house full of aspiring
artists on the worryingly named Failing Street, and to make rent
I acquired four part-time jobs: three days a week as the events
coordinator at a Barnes & Noble bookstore; four mornings helm-
ing the register at a Japanese takeaway eatery in a strip mall; four
evenings waiting tables at a Mexican restaurant; ad-hoc weekends
at a tiny literary journal that paid me in martinis and copyediting
lessons.

On my days off I tried to write poems—I wanted to be a poet;
my plan was to apply to an MFA program and eventually teach—
and when the trying got too torturous, I'd bicycle on a blue three-

speed I'd found at a yard sale to one of the city's countless coffee shops to read. My banking system was to cash my paychecks and divide the currency among separate envelopes. When I'd depleted the one marked *coffee,* I'd forgo the cafés and read and write at home.

In fourth grade I'd set out to complete all the biographies on the shelf in my classroom, two rows of squat mustard-colored hardbacks. There were a lot of presidents (my favorite was Abraham Lincoln, with his long, craggy face and soulful eyes), and Benjamin Franklin, and Betsy Ross (though I didn't get why someone who'd sewn a flag warranted an entire book). Their accomplishments were inscrutable and beside the point; the intrigue was in watching a fellow child grow up into an Important Person. Taken together they were a dynasty of adopted uncles and aunts—adults who weren't my parents who opened portals to lives I couldn't have imagined until they showed me how.

Now I was reading biographies of my favorite poets, in order to learn how to be one: Elizabeth Bishop, Robert Lowell, Sylvia Plath, Anne Sexton. The vocation, I felt, came with its own set of concerns, that only its practitioners could answer: Was a poet born, or made? How did you get a poem published? Could I support myself by writing? When the time came, how would I balance the demands of creative work with those of being a wife and mother?

Cross-country expatriation aside, the coincidence of all four poets being from my same little northeastern corner of Massachusetts didn't even register, though I trust it gave me unconscious comfort.

I hadn't expected the lives of poets to be as straightforward as those of presidents, but the futility of my quest for answers did come as a surprise.

In college, my vague impression of the grown-up worlds of Plath and Sexton had seemed perfectly ordinary: they were married women with children and houses. It was remarkably easy to imagine myself out of my derelict surroundings and into a very specific fantasy of the East Coast: relaxing in an Adirondack chair on a wide, freshly mowed lawn, pleasantly tired from a rigorous day of writing, icy gin and tonic in one hand, cigarette dangling from the other—all this even though I can't stand the taste of gin, don't smoke, and could hardly tolerate two uninterrupted hours of writing poetry.

But now that I was twenty-three, to realize that Plath was my same age when she'd married, and Sexton only nineteen, gave me pause. I adored W, but marriage was the last thing on my mind. My objectives were purely vocational: figure out how to be a writer; become financially independent. Then marriage.

That isn't to say, given the chance, I wouldn't have crashed into love with a "singer, story-teller, lion and world-wanderer" with "a voice like the thunder of God," as Plath once described Ted Hughes. I'd possibly even be fool enough to marry him. But surely having two children by thirty (Sexton had hers by twenty-seven) while also trying to be a serious poet and devoted spouse was a catastrophe I'd have sense enough to avoid—or so I told myself rather smugly, not yet fully aware I had the second-wave women's movement to thank for such sagacity.

One of the first things I'd done when I'd moved into the Failing Street house was take a book of Sexton's to Kinko's and repeatedly enlarge the cover—a black-and-white portrait of her looking straight at the camera—on a photocopier, until her face was larger than life, over which I stamped a poem she'd written in the late 1950s, "Her Kind," in cobalt ink. I taped my DIY poster to the wall above my bed. The first stanza:

I have gone out, a possessed witch,
   haunting the black air, braver at night;
dreaming evil, I have done my hitch
   over the plain houses, light by light:

lonely thing, twelve-fingered, out of mind.
A woman like that is not a woman, quite.
I have been her kind.

Even I didn't understand why I'd chosen this, of all poems, to be my bedroom manifesto. But after the restaurant had closed, and my co-workers and I had mopped the floors and prepped the tables for the following day, then migrated to the bar next door to drink beer and play darts into the early hours, I'd bicycle home through the dark, silent streets, a little drunk, wide awake, a thick stack of tip money bulging my coat pocket, aloft on a freedom almost shocking in its purity, and recite those lines to myself.

The far-off security of a boyfriend was almost better than having him nearby. I busied myself furnishing my little room, set up a bank account so I could write checks to my landlord and the utility companies, and started to pay off my student loans. Most extraordinary was waking alone, into my own thoughts. I'd replump the pillows and stretch my legs until my body spanned the entire mattress, and I'd lie suspended in that gauzy dreamscape between sleep and real life for as long as it lasted. Once the spell broke, I'd get up and dress and follow the day wherever it went.

Soon enough I started exercising my right to see other people, which turned out to be problematic. Far from feeling even more self-sufficient, I became ensnared in complications of my own making. I'd wake up, rue the day I was born, stuff the pillow over my head, and try to will myself back into the sweet obliteration of sleep.

This is when reference to a mysterious "spinster wish" first appears in my journals—shorthand for the extravagant pleasures of simply being by myself.

The journals: I opened a whole box of them recently, fifteen slim hardcover books chronicling my first half decade out of college, 1995–2000. Reliving those years was not unlike watching an overwrought performance from standing-room-only at the back of an opera house, but without the liberty to cut out at intermission.

My frantic, slanted scrawl smothers hundreds of pages (you'd never guess handwriting was in its final throes), analyzing every last hiccup of my newly melodramatic romantic life, faithful to fact as a car manual, and just as tedious to read.

But every thirty or forty pages a clear, calm voice pops to the surface, a life preserver bobbing on my own stormy sea.

OCTOBER 3, 1995: Ah, finally, W has left; back to my little spinster ways.

OCTOBER 18, 1995: We all know how a body in the bed can be so much lonelier. Still, I can't believe I'd actually want nothing over him. It makes no sense.

NOVEMBER 12, 1995: A long, perfect spinster wish of a Sunday, read all day, took two naps.

In my mind's eye, the spinster wish was the shape of that small, steel sylph gracing the nose of a Rolls-Royce, arms outstretched, sleeves billowing, about to leap from her earthbound perch and soar.* Itself an incongruous image: culture tells us that a spinster is without future—no heirs to bear, nobody to remember her when she's gone—not a woman racing toward it.

---

* This sylph was modeled on a real-life single woman: Eleanor Thornton, mistress to the married editor-in-chief of *Car Illustrated,* who convinced Rolls-Royce to create a "mascot" in her image. "The Spirit of Ecstasy" debuted in February 1911, fated to become the most recognizable hood ornament of all time. Critics called her "Ellie in Her Nightie." Four years later, Thornton died in a shipwreck.

I was going through my Milan Kundera phase, so snippets from his work pepper the pages. From *Immortality*:

> Of course, these were only dreams. How could a sensible woman leave a happy marriage? All the same, a seductive voice from afar kept breaking into her conjugal peace: it was the voice of solitude.

This moved me. Why must women always be leaving marriages to find what they want? Why couldn't they find what they want first?

I was taken, too, by this line—"That calm was in her soul and it was beautiful; let me repeat: it was the calm of silent birds in treetops"—which, on a fall afternoon, inspired some long journal philosophizing. "Exactly," I'd scrawled after the quote. "Something especially peaceful in the quiet of the potential for noise—like a drawer full of silverware just before it's opened, or just after it's shut? Yes, that is the more solitary way, just shut, alone in the drawer until it's opened again—and when will the hand come, and whose will it be? And this question is the excitement."

But like a nineteenth-century diarist, rather than address my attraction to being alone head-on, and behave accordingly, I concealed it, if not in calligraphy, then in the privacy of my journal.

In my actual life, the one beyond those pages, my spinster wish manifested itself as a confused and confusing ambivalence and, ultimately, a sort of double existence.

> DECEMBER 9, 1995: Really? You've been boy crazy since middle school. Isn't it time you stop squandering your energy and direct it toward something more—dignified?

I even turned on the spinster. About a tryst with a crush:

APRIL 13, 1996: I did it because I was curious, I felt excited
by the unfamiliarity of the evening, the blackness of the
graveyard, the electric of the moment, felt self-righteous that I
<u>should</u> be able to experience other things, not lock myself into
a spinster's dry, unfeeling tower. And yet I regret it already. I
regretted it halfway through.

Meanwhile, I was engineering all sorts of passive-aggressive
fiascos, telling W we needed to "take a break" one week and changing my mind the next; falling hard for L, a broody philosopher-
musician who kept me on a string; applying heretofore unknown
powers of detection to cracking the mystery of whom W had been
with when we'd been apart, in spite of our mutual pact to "do
whatever you want as long as you don't tell me about it."

At that point I'd been coupled for one-third of my life. Actually
being alone was proving to be genuinely incomprehensible.

One afternoon a strange thing happened. It was February or
March of 1996, eight months since I'd moved to Oregon. I was on
the curb, struggling to wrest a used bookshelf I'd just bought at
Goodwill from my rusty Toyota hatchback to haul it upstairs to
my room, when out of nowhere my vision began to blur and time
slowed down and I was suddenly overcome by the blinding realization that everything I considered so important—my new jobs,
friends, the bookshelf—would be rendered instantly meaningless
should the phone ring with news my mother was sick again, that
I'd leave the bookshelf standing there on the sidewalk, get into the
car, and drive the three thousand miles back across the country
to help her get well.

I'd blinked, seen the snow on the roof, blinked again, and the snow was gone. My mother was in perfectly fine health. There was nothing to worry about.

The moment was so uncanny that I didn't take it seriously. For years afterward I told myself that I had no idea what was about to come next, but that isn't exactly right. It was that I hadn't learned to decipher the mysterious ways of the undermind, how occasionally it erupts into an avalanche of clarity, a sheet of snow shearing off the roof and thundering to the ground, leaving the shingles exposed—knowledge issuing a messenger to announce its arrival.

The phone call came several months later, in May. It was very early on a Saturday morning, an odd time for the phone to ring. My father: "Her cancer has spread everywhere." By Tuesday I'd broken my lease, quit my four jobs, and pushed all my furniture and appliances—even that crummy Toyota—onto whoever would take them. Wednesday I packed my remaining possessions into six cardboard boxes, and that night I boarded a red-eye flight to Boston.

When I arrived at Massachusetts General Hospital on Thursday morning, my mother was a deflated life raft in a sea of white sheets, more pale and tired than I'd ever seen her. Her hazel eyes lit up when she saw me. I didn't know how to hug her through the tangle of IV sacks and tubes.

"Oh, honey," she said. "You're finally here. What's the latest with W, and with L?"

I cringed, embarrassed by my months of histrionics, some of which she'd kindly talked me through. Could she possibly think that I cared about them now?

"Oh, God, Mom, who cares! They don't matter!"

"Sure they do," she said.

I steered the conversation toward other topics, and very soon after she drifted away into a morphine haze.

My father and brother and I spent the next five days at the hospital, driving home to Newburyport at night. She wandered in and out of consciousness, and when she spoke, it was about things the rest of us couldn't see, or comprehend.

We remained very hopeful, along the lines of, *None of this should be happening; therefore, it isn't.*

On Tuesday afternoon the doctors pulled us into an empty room and told us she wouldn't last.

"It's hard to say how long. A few weeks. Maybe even a few months," they said.

Did we cry? All I remember is explaining to my father that, even though I knew Mom wasn't going to die that very night, I couldn't leave her alone, knowing now what I did.

The nurses set up a cot for me by the window. The Charles River snaked below. I fell asleep.

Wednesday morning I was woken by a familiar voice, resonant and warm.

"Honey, is that you?"

I turned over. My mother was sitting up in bed, wide awake, smiling. I got out of my cot and climbed over her bed rail and snuggled in, IV sacks and tubes be damned.

"I thought I saw something red!" She laughed. "And it was you!"

We talked and talked.

It felt like an actual, honest-to-God miracle.

Neither of us acknowledged that she was dying.

I knew for sure. Did she?

Her rings glinted on a string around her neck; the nurses had removed them before her fingers had swollen into puffy pink sausages, useless.

When breakfast came, I peeled the foil lid off the tiny orange-juice carton, and shook salt onto the eggs, but neither of us felt like eating.

Same with lunch.

We talked and talked. I have no idea what we talked about.

Talking was just what we did, always. It wasn't an activity; it was our shared condition.

That night she slipped away again.

She slept all through the next day.

Thursday evening the doctors told us: tomorrow.

Did we all spend the night in the hospital? All I know is that at seven o'clock the next morning the three of us were sprawled on her bed, holding her hands. She didn't breathe so much as gurgle, as if drowning. She actually was drowning.

The sound was unbearable.

We stroked her arms, told her over and over how much we loved her, as if our words could penetrate her unconscious state.

Her breathing rattled and slowed until each pause seemed like the very last. Eventually my father whispered, "It's okay, Nancy. You can go now."

She died almost immediately. She had heard him. She had heard us.

We stood silent. A terrible unknown nurse none of us will ever forgive barged in and asked how things were going. My father bellowed at her to get out.

My brother leaned down to close our mother's eyelids, the way he'd seen people do on television. They wouldn't stay shut.

My father reached over and unfastened the string around her neck, slipped her wedding and engagement rings into his pocket, and handed the other two to me. The stones were lavender—one amethyst, the other glass. I put them on and didn't take them off for a decade.

We collected her things and found the car in the parking garage and drove home.

It was the last day of May. I couldn't cry or think or read. The weeks piled up.

Nothing in Oregon to return to, I stayed in Newburyport, sleeping all day, or fighting on the telephone with W. Our already strained relationship groaned beneath my grief. I hated him for not knowing how to take care of me. And then I hated my friends for that, too.

The days disintegrated into a gummy torpor.

W and I broke up, got back together.

My torpor mobilized into a mania.

I'd seen a posting online about an unpaid internship program at my favorite magazine, *The Atlantic Monthly*. A plan snapped into shape: if I was accepted, I could live at home rent-free and intern for a few months, use the time to apply to MFA programs, and the following year move to wherever I'd gotten into school.

When I went in for my interview, I was told that the assistant to the senior vice president had just been promoted—rather than apply for the internship, would I like to apply for the job? I wanted to think I was hired for my literary proclivities, but really it was my experience waiting tables. My new boss liked that I could juggle a lot of things at once.

In the mornings my father drove me to the bus terminal, and I made the hour-long commute to Boston. In the evenings, there he'd be again, waiting for me in the parking lot in his red truck. After dinner we'd walk the dog to the public pond at the top of our street, the still water indistinguishable from the night. This pond had been the beloved locus of my youth, where we went to ice-skate and picnic, but since I'd left home, the city had ignored its upkeep until it sagged into something more like a swamp, tall weeds and rushes choking the edges, the majestic swan fountain at its center as dry as bone. I grew terrified that I would never leave my little childhood bedroom, that little town.

"Childhood is the kingdom where nobody dies," Edna Millay once wrote. I was twenty-three when my mother died, long past childhood, but, like most progeny of the middle class, I'd indulged an unthinking helplessness about my parents longer than I should have, an entitlement to what I felt I was owed, a willful blindness to their lives as individuals with needs of their own.

There had been a fluke telephone conversation a few months before her death when it struck me that though my mother and I spoke candidly and often, there was a part of herself she held in reserve, that she was waiting for me to get just a little older—a few years, maybe by the time I was thirty, I hazarded, married and with my own family—to talk to me frankly about herself, woman to woman, and the two strands of our lives, necessarily divided by my growing into my own person, would twine back together into one long rope, and she'd unburden herself of the secrets she carried, and I'd learn things about her I'd never known.

And so I couldn't shake the conviction that we'd been robbed. She'd raised me in her image to be the one true friend she'd never had, and now neither of us would ever know the conversations we'd waited for all our lives. There was a sickening symmetry to her losing her first breast just as I began to wear a bra, and then exiting her adulthood at midlife, at the moment I embarked on mine, as if I were still a parasitic fetus leeching her of blood and calcium.

You are born, you grow up, you become a wife.

You delay your ambitions, you raise a family, you're struck down by cancer at midlife.

It was resolved: I had my own aspirations to live out, but also hers.

If you're lucky, home is not only a place you leave, but also a place where you someday arrive. Sometimes I wish I'd never left Newburyport, or at least that I'd stayed a little longer. Certainly it was the last time I'd feel at home in the way I'd first known, where every familiar teacup and chair triggered the ongoing conversation that had been my relationship with my mother, which would soon fade to a whisper and then threaten to vanish outright. The literary critic in me resents her role in this book the way I would a sentimental plot twist in a movie. We all have had mothers; few among us want to lose them; I wish my experience had transcended such an obvious bid for your sympathy, and I could have become a different writer. But I can't erase the fact that the first day of my adult life was that morning in May my mother took her last breath.

3

The Essayist: Part I

Maeve Brennan, 1948

BOSTON, I'D DECIDED, WAS A JOKE. WHETHER MY SCORN WAS A PRO-
jection of my interior state or a legitimate critique, I still can't
decide. I'd spent a lifetime immersed in New England's monotony
of white faces, khaki pants, and little painted placards commemo-
rating a colonial this or that, and I began to feel suffocated. Once,
out with W, to make the point that everyone in the city looked

like someone from my hometown, I gestured at a group of guys in Red Sox caps and Bruins jerseys across the bar, who, when they got up to leave and I saw their faces, actually turned out to be a group of guys I'd grown up with. At least they made sense to me in a way the people I worked with did not.

I was acutely aware of how lucky I'd been to land my job at the magazine, but it was a while before I actually liked it. *The Atlantic* was founded in 1857 by a group of progressive intellectuals and poets; by the time I appeared on the scene, it was a hushed temple to WASP decorum, equal parts Henry James's *The Bostonians* and standard-issue Ivy League: nobody ever spoke too loud or too much, the men wore bow ties and played squash, the women looked sternly down their noses, or so it felt. In college I'd unconsciously befriended fellow work-study students; here, even the interns carried an air of privilege and entitlement I'd never encountered before.

My boss was frosty and inscrutable, the work tedious. When I wasn't booking her flights and managing her incredibly complex schedule, I was painstakingly encoding archival material into HTML, for "content" to post online. For instance, all seventeen thousand words of the first five chapters of Henry James's classic coming-of-age novel, *The Portrait of a Lady,* which first appeared in the magazine's pages in November 1880. I did not appreciate the irony.

At six o'clock I'd ask if she needed anything else, then take the subway home to Jamaica Plain, where I shared an apartment with three college friends. My bedroom was a Japanese tearoom our landlord had salvaged from a local museum—one room rebuilt inside another, like nested boxes. To enter, I'd turn a cut-glass doorknob on a paneled wood door, duck beneath the low bamboo opening, and hunch around, my own madwoman in the attic.

All this time I'd thought poetry a gift handed down by the ancients—a transcendent, elusive medium with which to try to capture every moment of being, and that the poet's greatest good fortune, perhaps the only one, was that, when bereaved, she could funnel her grief into elegies, and that these elegies would immortalize whatever was distinct about the beloved before all memory vanished into the cold black immensity of time, irretrievable.

But whenever a promising image burbled to mind, I'd take out my notebook, write it down, and then recoil in disgust. Nothing remotely conveyed what I actually felt. Every phrase was, in fact, a lie. I'd glare back at the page, then chastise myself for being so stupid and utterly without talent. I couldn't believe that language was completely failing me exactly when I needed it most. Or was it me, I wondered, who couldn't rise to the rigors language demands?

Despairing, I'd tear out the page and toss it into an old wooden fruit crate I kept on the tatami floor, beside my mattress. Very deep down there was a kernel in me that thought maybe someday far in the future I'd want to read these failed attempts—as if they weren't trying to be poems after all, but cryptic letters to a version of myself I'd yet to meet.

My problem, I decided, was that I didn't know where to picture myself next—a failure of imagination, you could call it, though it felt more like a flailing response to an unseen adversary, or a refusal of the options as I saw them presented. How do you embark on your adulthood when you don't know where you're headed?

Everywhere I looked women were leading lives I didn't want for myself. There was the Childless Executive, my boss, the most ambitious woman I'd ever met, who'd raised herself up from nothing to the top of the business side of this venerable institution, and stormed around the office with a constant scowl, only seeing her husband on weekends.

There was the Ex-Wife, a friend's mother, whose husband had left her for a younger woman; she'd never worked, and her struggle to find an identity now that she was no longer married was painful to witness, her loneliness and desperation a void she couldn't figure out how to fill.

Then there was Having It All, the neighbor I passed every morning on my walk to the subway, hurrying from her beautiful house in a visibly uncomfortable state of chaos, hair still wet from the shower, papers trailing from her briefcase, yelling instructions to the nanny about what to feed the children for dinner because she wouldn't be home until very late.

She wasn't much older than I was; I could be her if I wasn't careful.

Once upon a time all of these women had been young like me, with a fantasy of how their futures would go. Something didn't add up.

The only example that seemed even remotely appealing was an elderly widow who worked at the magazine. Phoebe-Lou Adams was trim and athletic and made all her own clothes—chic sleeveless sheaths, slim tailored pants. During the summer she topped herself off with outrageously broad-brimmed straw hats. She'd been hired as an assistant in 1944, when she was twenty-five, and started writing her own book-review column in 1952; for the centennial issue in 1957 she was dispatched to Cuba to wrangle a story from Ernest Hemingway (he gave her two).

Three days a week she'd drive in from her home in Connecticut, shut the door of her office, and bang out her reviews on a loud old electric typewriter, chain-smoking all the while. Her voice was gorgeously raspy and brusque in person, pithy on the page (regarding *On the Road*: "Neither of these boys can sit still"; her full summation of *Sabbath's Theater*: "As a protest against inevitable death, sexual excess is as futile as any other. Mr. Roth's latest novel makes it tiresome as well.") In 1971, when she was fifty-two, she'd married for the first time, to the magazine's former editor-in-chief, Edward Weeks; every year they went salmon-fishing in Iceland or New Brunswick, and after he died in 1989, she carried on their tradition by herself.

That, I thought, seemed like a very good life.

I was alone with her once. It was fall, and we were both waiting for the elevator. I decided to ask her about the blazer I'd just bought at Filene's Basement, not from the sale rack, a bit of a splurge. Was it all-season, I hoped? Assembling an office wardrobe was an enduring challenge. She reached out her tanned, wrinkled arm and fingered the hem. "No," she said, "that's linen." When the elevator arrived, we rode down in silence.

In the spring of 1997, an editor slated to interview the novelist and essayist Cynthia Ozick for a Q&A to be published online had come down with the flu, and she suggested I take her place. The assignment literally changed my life. For a week of evenings and stolen workday minutes, I read as much of Ozick's writing as I could and labored intensely over my questions. I conducted the interview over the phone. For an hour I hardly breathed, I was so nervous about missing a word. I loved every second.

After that I published an interview with the author of a new book every six weeks or so—Nadine Gordimer, Edna O'Brien, Annie Proulx. My boss didn't mind, as long as I took care of her stuff.

By now, my father was seriously involved with a woman who

lived in Newburyport. He'd started seeing her several months after our mother had died—insultingly, heartlessly soon, my brother and I thought. We were righteous with rage.

You are born, you grow up, you become a wife.

You delay your ambitions, you raise a family, you're struck down by cancer at midlife, your husband moves on without a second thought—or so it seemed to us.

At the end of the summer, W left for Iowa to pursue an MFA in poetry, and we finally broke up. Though it had been ages in coming, I hadn't anticipated how lost I'd feel without him. When he told me not long after that he was seeing someone new (indeed the woman he eventually married), I writhed with jealousy and self-loathing. She'd gone to college with us; like my father's new girlfriend, she was very pretty and soft-spoken—the antithesis of women like my mother and me. Since finishing *The Portrait of a Lady,* I'd developed a Henrietta Stackpole complex: feisty, overly talkative journalists were all well and good, but you only secure a man's heart if you're as pretty as Isabel Archer (an instance of revisionist literary history: I'd decided to forget that Henrietta marries in the end). I hung up the phone and cried so hysterically that my common sense had no choice but to snap awake and intervene:

Kate, I said to myself, *the only place this horrific jealousy exists is inside of you. If you stop feeling it, it will disappear.*

At the time, I was lying on my bed. I'd moved again, to the dreary outskirts of North Cambridge, and I shared an apartment with two men, both friends, all of us gleefully not keeping house. I opened my eyes and looked at the ceiling and realized I'd never talked to myself this way before. Now that my mother was gone, my father subsumed by his new family, W out of the picture, I could no longer outsource my problems to intimates, and I had to learn to keep my own counsel.

It was not a pleasant realization. I felt very tired, like someone who'd been struck mute and now had to set about learning American Sign Language.

———◄█►———

"There's your next boyfriend," Michael said.

It was fall, and Michael, a college friend, was in town for the weekend and wanted to see the office. We'd met our freshman year, in an early-morning class on Ancient Greek Civilization, before he'd come out. He'd introduced me to W, and then to L when I lived in Portland, and he liked to claim himself the puppet master of my romantic life.

"What? Where—?" I turned just in time to see a co-worker vanish around the corner, a flash of oxford blue and khaki. "Him? R? Preppy R?"

Michael nodded with maddening confidence. "That's the one."

R was an editor at the magazine, two years older, handsome, compact, with a gentle manner I found incredibly calming and a face that reminded me of that famous photograph of Kafka: dark shining eyes, high cheekbones, ears that stick out just a little too far (Obama-style, as I think of it now). Once or twice a week we'd take our sandwiches to the conference room and talk as expansively as we could in an hour.

Our conversations had a limitless quality that I loved. It was a relief to embark on a simple friendship with a man, free to talk about anything we wanted, without the roller coaster of emotions and confusion over roles and expectations.

"Please," I groaned. "The last thing I need is another relationship." Taking his arm, I hurried Michael out of the office and down the elevator to go find lunch.

———◄█►———

That winter I came home from the office Christmas party and devoted an entire journal entry to Phoebe-Lou Adams. It reads like something you'd see in an old society column:

> DECEMBER 12, 1997: Phoebe-Lou Adams was a knockout
> tonight in a long black dress with an empire waist, a long
> necklace of clear glass beads wrapped around and around her
> neck, white hair teased, and subtle black makeup on her old
> eyes. She brought something called a Tipsy Cake—petite,
> snowy whipped-cream frosting, it looked of another era.

By now I'd been at *The Atlantic* for a year and a half, and single for six months. I continued to obsessively record everything I did and thought.

> DECEMBER 17, 1997: Bought my first pair of "synthetic pants"
> (there is spandex woven into the fabric). Finished reading Joan
> Didion's *Play It As It Lays* and Edith Wharton's *The House of
> Mirth*.

> DECEMBER 18, 1997: I feel that I could fall for R, but resist.

My connection with R had continued to be a source of great pleasure. Whenever Michael called he'd say, "So, are you seeing R yet?" and I'd growl at him to stop sullying a perfectly good friendship with his sordid romantic agendas.

How quickly the plot thickens.

> DECEMBER 22, 1997: Feeling very fond of R, but know it's
> because he's a force of good, and cute. We shouldn't be
> together. I'd make him unhappy. I'm still too much of a wreck
> to be with someone else.

The next day we took a walk after work, along the twisty cobblestone streets of Boston's North End. It was dusk. R mused aloud that sometimes he felt he was getting to know me really well, and other times was "hitting up against a wall."

A gust rushed through me—I hadn't known what I was about to say until I heard myself say it: "That's because I have a little crush on you!"

I laughed. The notion was so ridiculous that I wasn't even embarrassed to admit it.

R stopped walking and looked at me, smiling. "Me, too."

I shook my head at the predictability. Seriously. You put a man and a woman together, and what do you get?

"Thank God all that boy-girl stuff is out of the way," I said. "Now we can *really* be friends."

Back home that night I was far less sanguine.

DECEMBER 23, 1997: The recent flirtation with R is unnerving. I am fond of him, attracted to him, he is incredibly sweet and kind, but to be involved would bring out all the impatience and resentment in me. He represents a tenor of safety I am not presently interested in. What a luxury, to be twenty-five and unattached; here's hoping I can use it.

I actually wrote that phrase, "not presently interested."

A week later, New Year's Eve, R stopped by my desk on his way out, to say good-bye, as he usually did. I was rushing to fin-ish some paperwork so I could get home and change; I was going to a bathtub-gin party that night with a friend. But as usual, once we started talking, I didn't feel like stopping, and then, when it really was time for him to leave and me to wrap up, and he rose from the chair, I was overcome with a sensation so powerful that I asked him to hold on a minute. He sat back down.

"I don't know what's happening," I said.

He was concerned. "Where does it hurt? Your head? Your stomach?"

I could hardly look him in the eye, because when I did, the sensation got worse.

"It's like I'm dizzy and light-headed and moving in slow motion all at once," I explained. "It's like I just can't bear for you to leave."

"Do you want to come out with me tonight?"

Before I could say yes, I had to say no. Instantly I saw why: this was the last night I'd be single, and I wanted to savor it.

The next day we kissed on my sofa.

Initially we kept our relationship secret at work, but eight months later, when we decided to move in together, I figured I should tell my boss (who simply looked up from her paperwork and said, "I don't care. Just don't fuck on my desk.").

The week before our move, I was promoted to junior editor.

My head spun with the speed of it all.

Our apartment was the top floor of a three-unit house in Somerville built in the 1910s. We turned the sunlit front room into a shared office, with desks on opposite walls. The bedroom was just big enough to hold R's queen-size bed; its substantial cherry headboard made even the act of sleeping feel grown-up. A close friend sewed us a silky rose and lavender duvet cover as a housewarming present, and I found curtains that flowed to the floor.

Much later, Michael admitted that the first time he visited he felt as if he'd stepped onto a stage set. He was particularly taken aback by a pile of empty gilded frames stacked like mousetraps in a corner—readymade templates waiting to be filled with photographic evidence of our coupledom.

Unconsciously I patterned our relationship on that of my parents. Both had grown up in traditional 1950s families, with breadwinner fathers and mothers who kept house, but by the time they married, that template was transitioning into the egalitarian model my generation inherited.

And so it was with R and me, and every other young couple we knew. I'd just turned twenty-six and he was twenty-eight, and though we weren't married, we might as well have been; we split our expenses down the middle, provided mutual emotional support, discussed every decision, spent holidays with each other's family, shared friends.

At work we kept our distance, but in the evenings, back home, we'd make a big salad or vat of pasta and talk about the day. Talking—about what we were reading, feeling, thinking—was our highest form of intimacy, and glue. He asked me questions about my mother and gave me the space to grieve her; I cried a lot, to be sure, too much. His patience was astonishing. Little by little I started to return to myself.

For two years we lived very happily this way.

And because we were happy, neither of us noticed as I very slowly started to wander off, down the two flights of stairs and past the soft, mowed pelt of front lawn, to the street, which I followed to another, and then another, not paying attention to where I was going, until one day I looked up and saw that I was nowhere near where our life was taking place, but at the edge of some huge unknown expanse, and when I looked behind me, I saw that I had no idea how I'd gotten there, that the path of return had disappeared, and so, like a sly child who doesn't know what's good for her, I stood gaping at the strange, wide openness, wondering what it held, instead of turning around and finding my way back the way I'd come.

It was that drowsy stretch between Christmas and New Year's, when everyone is working, but only barely. R and I had commuted together to work, as we always did; our subway ride had been eerily empty. The building was, too. At the reception desk he turned right and I turned left. I switched on the lights and hung up my parka, still amazed that I finally had my own office: a big desk, a bookshelf, and a burgundy leather armchair illuminated by a floor lamp.

I worked quietly through the morning. Along with conducting author interviews I oversaw the website's poetry section, commissioning essays from poets about their favorite poems and recording their readings. I loved everything about the job—coming up with ideas, assigning projects, the close, careful work of copyediting, which I was still learning how to do. It eased my mind to know that I was acquiring real, practicable skills that I could take with me anywhere in the English-speaking world, as if I were a hairdresser or a mechanic.

At lunch, I settled into the armchair with a peanut-butter sandwich and the latest issue of *The New Yorker*, ostensibly our competition, though I suspected that the glossy upstart (it was founded in 1925) didn't worry much about our fusty selves.

In my mind's eye the magazine springs open of its own accord to an enormous black-and-white portrait. The picture is of . . . me.

Rather, a woman who resembles a grown-up version of me. The same narrow shoulders, the same Irish features, slightly pointed without being angular. There is glamorously pale skin, the kind that inspires comparisons to alabaster or cream, and then there is my kind, the kind that's merely without color and freckles easily, and I thought maybe this was her skin, too.

In the photograph she is sitting at a desk, in front of a grand fireplace, back straight, collar up, dark hair pulled into a tight, high bun, looking over her shoulder though not directly at the camera.

Her expression reads somewhere between indifference and glower. Amid the low stacks of books on the desk is a vase of long-stemmed roses, an empty glass tumbler, and a slim silver box of cigarettes, one of which she holds between her fingers. The scene radiates an austere, prideful autonomy that I suddenly, desperately wanted to inhabit.

It was like looking into the future and discovering that my unremarkable self had somehow become a person of consequence.

At twenty-six I couldn't have been less like the woman in the picture. For my office wardrobe I scoured the sale racks of Banana Republic and Filene's Basement for the most inexpensive and nondescript pants and collared blouses I could find (collars, for some reason, I deemed nonnegotiable), presuming that if you have no idea how to present yourself, you might as well aim for inconspicuousness.

After absorbing every last inch of the photograph, I turned to the article that ran alongside. Her name was Maeve Brennan. A publisher had just reissued an expanded version of her essay collection, *The Long-Winded Lady*. She was born in Dublin in 1917 and had moved to the United States as a teenager. The portrait was shot in Manhattan in 1948, when she was thirty-one, just before she joined the staff of *The New Yorker*. She'd been married once, very briefly.

"For most of her life Brennan lived alone," the article explained, "moving restlessly about the city."

A life like that couldn't have been easy, but at least it was interesting.

The article went on to report that in 1954 she assumed the sobriquet The Long-Winded Lady and published her first essay under that name, launching a column that would run in the magazine intermittently for the next two decades. At the top of each installment the magazine's editors would note, with dry mischievousness, "We recently received a letter from the long-winded lady. She wrote as follows."

I looked again at the photograph.

A thrill took hold: the spinster wish made manifest. This is who I wanted to be.

Later that afternoon I made my daily pass by the "free table," where extra books were tossed for anyone who might want them, and I was surprised to see hers among the offerings. My habit was to linger for a while, killing time, but now I grabbed the book and hurried back to my desk and began, hungrily, to read.

Once again, there I was—in her pages and not just her face. Not the me who rode the subway to work with R each morning or made dinner with him at night. It was the me beneath all that, the solitary self I hadn't been able to access or articulate ever since—well, ever. I'd written one or two poems that got within shouting distance of that self, and certainly I'd felt her power when competing in a race. Mostly, though, it was an amorphous form of consciousness, sensed but never spoken. Reading Brennan's words, this inner self flickered to the surface.

You know how a text message can impart an uncanny sense of intimacy merely by arriving at the most mundane moment— while you're shopping for new sneakers or waiting for a friend in a restaurant? This is how Maeve's essays reached me, though in reverse: dispatches from one woman's private experiences of public places. By recording her observations from that shoe store, or restaurant table, she disclosed the significance of seemingly fleeting experiences, the way a poem can, but with a clarity and accessibility that struck me as far more useful and, therefore, generous. The poetry of everyday life, you could say, but in essay form.

To write a sentence, then a paragraph, then another, and to have someone else read those lines and immediately understand what I meant to express—I wanted to try to do that.

That year, 1998, was the height of the memoir boom, evidence of which streamed through the office on a daily basis, some of it compelling, much of it horrible. But even at its very best, when a woman was able to present herself with honesty and intelligence, her experience was inextricably bound to the people around her, as if her story didn't exist apart from theirs. It was different for men; they knew how to present themselves as singular agents, even heroes.

Maeve was the first woman I'd ever read who wrote about herself not in relation to someone else—whether lover, husband, parent, child. She simply walked around New York City alone, watching. Her point of view was as clear and contained as an ice cube.

Walking through Washington Square Park, she watches a couple on a bench fighting, just before dawn. From a hotel room many floors up, she watches an old woman dropping a letter out the window, one page at a time. On the A train, a man offers her his seat; she politely refuses and then spends the rest of the ride anxiously regretting her refusal—here, of course, she is watching herself.

That last one was my favorite. I'd always been daunted by New York City, cloaking my provinciality in smug disinterest, as if the small towns of my close acquaintance were world enough. Brennan's short scene on the subway was a chink in the great wall of my resistance, and when I peered through I saw that New York wasn't merely the dense, brutal megalith I'd feared, but also an unpredictable, infinite chain of human interactions, each a tiny drama that flared into being as quickly as it disappeared.

A longing to leave Boston welled up in me like a flood.

I wish I could say I brought the book home and read the whole thing in one night, without getting up even for a drink of water, and the next day bought a bus ticket to Penn Station. The truth is, it took a while.

———

Often after work R and I went running. Once, we saw a woman jogging along with her toddler in one of those rugged, all-terrain strollers—the embodiment of modern motherhood, multitasking exercise and child care, Mrs. Having It All. R smiled and pointed "Look, there's you someday." My stomach lurched. There was no way I was going to become that woman, but I didn't know how to say it.

What I wanted was too ridiculous to voice. What I wanted was to be Maeve Brennan—a woman I knew so little about that she wasn't even an actual person to me, but a disembodied mood. It would be several years before her biography was published, fleshing out the bones I rattled in my pockets, and it took me nearly another decade after that to find and have dinner with one of the last people she'd known. For now all I had were her books, which for the time being were more than enough to keep stoking my imagination.

Because my way of coupling was to merge completely, whenever I felt the need to be separate, if only for a day, I got nervous and suppressed it. While with R, I developed a new habit of simply slipping this uncomfortable desire into the citadel of Maeve's all-seeing, almost oracular tone, which created a mental space that felt safely contained and powerful all at once, practically glamorous. That The Long-Winded Lady is herself a fiction, in the way all writing about the self ultimately is, increased rather than diminished her appeal. Stepping into her point of view showed me how to look at the world around me more closely, and—crucially—to forget myself. From this vantage, the most ordinary interactions—conferring with the pharmacist, ignoring the old man barking obscenities from his lawn chair on the street corner, sharing a knowing look with the woman making my cappuccino—shone with significance and drama. I could almost pretend that I was a writer, too.

Quite a few of her essays featured her eating alone at a diner in lower Manhattan called the University Restaurant, and so I began to imagine myself.

In my mind's eye there I was, sitting in a red vinyl booth, alone, reading, taking a sip of coffee, carefully placing the cup back on its saucer, occasionally glancing out the window onto the sidewalk's everyday bedlam, a person who knows exactly what it means when someone says "Fourteenth and Broadway" or "Just take the 2/3 train; it'll be faster than a cab at this hour."

The fantasy was irresistible—and bewildering. As I'd done when I'd written poems, I held the image in my mind and walked around it, looking at it from every angle, interrogating. To be a woman sitting by herself in a crowded New York City restaurant, amid the bustle and clatter of other people's lives—what kind of a thing was that to want? What was I saying to myself?

That I wanted to be alone?

As if. Me, alone. Me, the conversation addict.

Talking was so central to my sense of self that I'd never even thought to question it, and now that I was, I saw that this brook sprang from a source so deep inside me that I couldn't even name it, and once the stream passed through my mouth and hit air, it vanished into vapor.

Did becoming a writer require being alone?

Which wasn't an option, because being alone meant not being with R, whom I loved, obviously.

I circled and circled.

Was it that I didn't want to be married?

But of course I wanted to be married. In college I'd decided I'd marry by thirty—that seemed enough time to learn a little bit

about the world before settling down. To choose to not do something so normal and expected would require a very good explanation, which I certainly didn't have.

Before, I'd looked at the adult women I knew—those older
than me, in their forties and fifties and beyond—to see who I
wanted to become. Now I consciously divided them into married
versus unmarried, and it was revelatory.

The first thing that struck me was how the single women of
my acquaintance were exceptionally alert to the people around
them, generous in their attention, ready to engage in conversation or share a joke. Having nobody to go home to at night had
always seemed a sad and lonesome fate; now I saw that being
forced to leave the house for human contact encourages a person
to live more fully in the world. In the best instances, the result
was an intricate lacework of friendships varying in intensity and
closeness that could be, it seemed, just as sustaining as a nuclear
family, and possibly more appealing.

I began to listen more closely to the variations in these
women's advice. Married women, especially those with children,
tended to assume a superior stance, as if their insights into
people and relationships came preapproved, even though single
women drew from a larger store of experiences and had often
seen more of the world, from which the wisdom I wanted to discover is derived.

Yet, for all their vitality and stores of empathy and insight,
none of these single women had actively chosen her state, or even
simply failed to meet "the one." Each had come to it through
some form of bad luck, whether death or divorce. Most were
on the lookout for love, only one or two swore they were done
with it, but all of them behaved as if their married selves had
been their true selves, and this present-day version a peculiar
aberration.

None seemed to enjoy what I imagined to be Maeve's quietly confident self-reliance. That this was sheer projection didn't exactly strike me at the time.

And if my faith in her, this woman I knew next to nothing about, sounds misdirected, a touch magical, that's because it was. When the present feels as endless as an impossibly long hallway between airport terminals, white and sterile and numb, we're particularly receptive to signs.

In the winter of 1999 I did two things: apply to two graduate schools in New York City, and write an essay about Filene's Basement, in the Maeve Brennan tradition—an urban flaneur's wanderings through a bustling retail emporium. In the doing, it became a memory of shopping there with my mother. After waiting for the managing editor to leave his office, I left the essay on his desk chair.

If he published the piece, I decided, I was a real writer. If he didn't, I had to figure out a new plan.

It was, of course, preposterous to put my entire fate in someone else's hands.

A week later, he left the essay on my desk chair, with the word *Yes* circled in red.

Not long after, I heard back from the schools I'd applied to: I'd been accepted to both, and New York University had offered me a fellowship. The instant I received the acceptance e-mail, I knew I wanted to move to New York City alone, but once again, I didn't know how to say it out loud. To even *think* of leaving my boyfriend on the cusp of thirty felt recklessly immature. I kept telling myself it was time to quit my spinster fantasies and grow up.

In August R and I packed the contents of our Somerville apartment into a U-Haul and drove to Brooklyn.

Recently I came across a study by the social psychologists Hazel Markus and Paula Nurius that illuminated my fascination with Maeve Brennan—and the necessity of increasing culture's store of heroines in general.

The thirty subjects had recently experienced a significant breakup or death of a loved one. After self-diagnosing where they ranked in the recovery process, the subjects were divided into two groups—"good recovery" and "poor recovery." Each group was given a list of attributes and instructed to choose the ones that best described their "now selves," as in, who they were in the present. The same list was given to a control group of thirty people who had not experienced a crisis.

The researchers were working in the critical domain of "self-knowledge," a technical term for the store of information you draw on to answer the question "Who am I?" This information bank is a collection of "self-schemas"—understandings about yourself that you've accumulated over time; e.g., "I'm a pretty good swimmer" or "I'm a terrible dancer" (which just about sums up me). In other words, we look to the past to describe who we are in the present.

Markus and Nurius believed that a third sphere had gone unexamined: the imagined future. They posited that along with our "past selves" and our "now selves" we all contain "possible selves"—our ideas about who we wish to someday be, as well as who we're afraid of becoming. These possible selves could simultaneously be the rich self, the thin self, the married self—and also the lonely self, the sick self, the homeless self. A junior lawyer in a firm, for instance, may hope to be made partner—the successful self—while at the same time worry she's about to be laid off, in which case she'd become the broke self, the depressed self, the self who can't make her car payments.

These possible selves are crucial, the researchers theorized, because along with self-schemas, they're what you draw on to shape your perception of yourself in the present. If the junior lawyer feels that a promotion is imminent, the gap will narrow between her now self and her possible self, and she'll be more confident, which probably helps her get the promotion.

What Markus and Nurius wanted to know is whether these possible selves not only influence how you feel about your "now self," but also function as incentives that actively motivate you to achieve your goals.

They'd assumed the "good recovery" group would feel better about themselves than those in the "poor recovery" group, but this was not the case. Instead, both crisis groups described their "now selves" in extremely negative terms: *lonely, underachiever, poor, weak, resentful.* Certainly, this is how I would have described myself those first several years after my mother had died, when I was living with R. Just as, before her death, I would have fallen into step with the noncrisis subjects, who chose much more positive words: *optimistic, secure, adjusted, loved, confident.*

Next the subjects were asked to describe their "possible selves." Looking to the future, the "poor recovery" respondents saw themselves as unpopular, a failure, likely to experience a breakdown or to die young—outcomes even more dire than those of their now selves. In contrast, "good recovery" respondents believed they could be powerful, independent, rich, creative, and so on. (As did the noncrisis respondents.) This was as expected.

Here was the surprise: the "good recovery" respondents felt their positive possible selves to be significantly *more viable* than those who hadn't experienced any tragedy at all.

The researchers theorized that the mere presence of possible selves is an important element of recovery and can even be liberating, offering hope that the miserable present is transitory. Likewise, negative possible selves can become imprisoning, thwarting the ability to make necessary changes.

Obviously, as someone who'd experienced a crisis in her early twenties, I strongly identified with the study. I'd long sensed that Maeve Brennan served a psychological purpose for me. By climbing into her point of view and trying it on for size, testing the fit and feel, mulling her decisions, eventually even buying the perfume she'd worn, I was cobbling together a template for my own future.

As a possible self, Maeve embodied my longings—for an independent self, a writer self, an elegant self. Her relative obscurity was crucial to my choosing her. A preordained heroine—some prepackaged version of Amelia Earhart or Frida Kahlo—meant to inspire with her larger-than-life accomplishments, would make me feel small by comparison. I'm no wilting lily, but nor am I a daredevil or an artist for the ages. As the great Margaret Fuller put it in 1845, in her *Woman in the Nineteenth Century,* the first major feminist book in America:

> Plants of great vigor will almost always struggle into blossom, despite impediments. But there should be encouragement, and a free genial atmosphere for those of more timid sort. . . . Some are like the little, delicate flowers which love to hide in the dripping mosses. . . . But others require an open field, a rich and loosened soil, or they never show their proper hues.

Surely, by the twenty-first century, women "ought not find themselves, by birth, in a place so narrow, that, in breaking bonds, they become outlaws," as Fuller wrote. I was just another person trying to figure out how to live, and I needed a boon companion to talk with, not an idol to adore.

It had never occurred to me that this private process might affect anyone but myself. So when I reached this final part of the study, I nodded in rueful recognition:

> Positive and negative possible selves . . . often make it difficult for an observer to fully understand another person's behavior. . . . Thus, difficulties in an interpersonal relationship may reflect the fact that one person's behavior is being guided by a possible self that the other person has no access to, or is unwilling to acknowledge.

It was paradoxical, actually: Though my pursuit of my "possible self" had brought both R and me to New York, I was in thrall to this vision in ways I didn't know how to articulate, and so I hid in plain sight, lying by omission, so to speak. My conscious self was trying to "do the right thing." Meanwhile, it's likely that R, who had never suffered a crisis, wasn't quite as captivated by his own "possible self."

More broadly, the study validated my inchoate aversion to prepackaged heroines. What I was actually responding to was how our culture's paucity of options results in a necessary overemphasis on the available few..

Hazel Markus, one of the authors of the psychological study, explained to me the relationship between possible selves and the cultures we live in. She was inspired to study self-schemas by the women's and identity movements of the late 1970s. "Black Power, Latinos, Chicanos—all of it was premised on the idea that you should claim and reimagine your category. I was very impressed by this concept that representational autonomy is important for women and minorities," she said.

Did this mean there's a verifiable gender component to who is most influenced by possible selves, I asked.

"I don't know of a good study that actually pins down men versus women," she said, "but in my own experience, I find that women are very focused on their possible selves, perhaps more so than men are, and feared selves have a hand in that." Men, she posited, tend to have more independent selves, and feel more immediately in charge of their lives, and therefore don't worry quite as much about the future.

She said there's an inarguable cultural discrepancy. Our Western emphasis on the individual makes us believe we are singularly responsible for and have control over the shape of our lives, she explained, whereas in the East there's a greater awareness that many factors—norms, obligations, expectations, other people, the situation, luck, circumstance—determine how our lives turn out, and if they turn out the way we want. "In those Eastern worlds, the idea of having a positive self is less important, because the individual isn't afforded as much efficacy," she said.

"Possible selves are particularly important right now in the West," she continued. "We need much better and many more models. We need movies where women are attractive and interesting and have great lives and may not be married."

She cautioned that conjuring possible selves on our own isn't enough—institutional support is also necessary. "Schools, workplaces, laws, norms, the media—they all need to make it clear that there are other ways to be a woman or a member of one minority group or another."

She paused, then added, "The West's focus on the positive makes the feared self particularly powerful. In Eastern cultures the negative is also part of life. You can't avoid it. Light and dark are braided together. It's important to have some failures. Having possible selves that didn't materialize is how you gain experience and mature and develop as a person."

Little did I know when I chose Maeve Brennan that she'd also guide me in this respect. The main reason I was able to glamorize her as a possible self is because I knew next to nothing about her life. Much later, when her biography was eventually published, she'd assume a new role for me: the feared self.

At any rate, I'd found her: the first of my five awakeners.

4

The Columnist

Neith Boyce, circa 1898

I'VE ALWAYS KNOWN THAT A BOOK WILL FIND YOU WHEN YOU NEED to be found; in New York I learned that so does history. In the doing, I met my second awakener.

R and I had only been in the city for several months, but already we lived in two separate realities. His was the daytime ghost town of our two-room apartment in Brooklyn Heights, and the social isolation of his freelance magazine editing. Mine was an

all-out, interborough carnival. The city was enormous and deaf-
ening and arranged to suit my pleasure—the trains were timely,
Katz's sauerkraut bin was bottomless—and I hopped on and off its
carousel, electric with possibility. This is what I'd come for, noise
and hustle and grit; I loved my new school for being unabashedly
un-collegiate.

Evenings, borne back by the subway, my neon fizzled; emerg-
ing from the station into the hushed gentility of our new neighborhood, my lights cut out completely.

By dumb luck we'd landed on one of the more desirable blocks
in Brooklyn, in a brownstone on a street actually called Cranberry, a quiet byway of worn slate sidewalks and tall, leafy trees
just off the Promenade, a long esplanade that overlooks the East
River and Manhattan skyline and glittering expanse of New York
Harbor, even the Statue of Liberty herself—and I hated it, all of
it. Living amid so much ready-made beauty felt inimical to my
striving; I was smothered by the sensation of having been handed
a prize I'd yet to earn.

Even worse was the neighborhood's eerie resemblance to New
England. Frail, elderly men in blue button-downs and khakis
were a fixed feature of my peripheral vision, heads nodding beneath their canvas boating hats, as if once again they'd gotten
lost on the way to the yacht, docked circa 1960 in a marina that
no longer existed. The quaint clapboard houses with their pretty,
painted shutters could have been airlifted from my hometown; the
haughty brownstones radiated the same smug complacency as the
historic brick town houses on Boston's Beacon Hill. When I ran
across a 1946 essay by Alfred Kazin, in which he describes the
brownstones of Brooklyn Heights as fortresses "that shut out the
street and shut in the people who live in them," with only their
weathered wooden front doors to "redeem them from pompous-
ness," I laughed out loud—until I reached the very next sentence,
and a chill ran up my spine: "But there is a touch about them, too,

that reminds you of the merchants' houses of Newburyport . . . where everything looks out to sea."

It was worse than I'd thought: I was back where I'd started.

R and I hadn't learned that it's possible to eat out cheaply and well in New York, so we continued as we had in Somerville, staying home to cook our meals and saving restaurants for special occasions, as if settling into quiet domesticity were possible, or even recommended, in this sleepless city. After dinner we'd sit on the sofa to read, one's feet in the other's lap, the traffic heading toward the Brooklyn Bridge like the din of some far-off party. Our routine was as sound as a well-rigged ship, the two of us drifting in the general direction of marriage without ever actually discussing it.

But walking through the city, I heard the firm, sure click of Maeve Brennan's heels on the pavement. When I cinched my coat against the cold, I imagined my passing shadow as hers. I wore her point of view like a pair of borrowed glasses, assessing everything I saw with her insatiable omniscience. I was most alive when alone, negotiating odd encounters on the subway, surging along the sidewalk with a million faceless others. It was an expansive sensation, evasive, addictive. Each morning I rushed from the apartment to find it, as if late for an appointment.

One afternoon, nosing through a used bookstore, I picked up a book by Vivian Gornick and found myself reading about her decision in the early 1970s to leave her husband and live by herself. She'd been exactly my age. She woke to their first morning apart infatuated with solitude. "The *idea* of love seemed an invasion," she wrote. "I had thoughts to think, a craft to learn, a self to discover. Solitude was a gift. A world was waiting to welcome me if I was willing to enter it alone."

The book vibrated in my hand, a telltale heart.

I'd never been alone in my life. As in, truly alone, made to rely solely on myself for a substantial stretch of time. Obviously I was independent; independence was my generation's birthright. Yet all through my comings and goings I'd been looked after, listened to, accompanied, coddled, whether by parents or boyfriends; essentially, I'd led the life of a child. It wasn't merely that my identity was constructed entirely out of my relationships with other people—my relationships *were* my identity. My relationships took the place of myself.

As I paid for the book and left the store, I wondered: Who was I on my own?

How could I possibly become an adult if I didn't know how to answer that?

More important: How could I possibly become an adult if I didn't know how to take care of myself?

It was a perfectly reasonable question, relevant to just about anyone. It had nothing to do with gender. And yet it had everything to do with gender. Because the question concealed an uncomfortable truth: as a woman, I wasn't *required* to take care of myself—ever. Here in the year 2000, the future itself, men were still expected to be breadwinners and providers. No matter how hot my ambitions burned, I always knew, deep down, that if I couldn't make it as a writer, and if I failed to find my way in the working world, I could create personal meaning and social validation through getting married and having children. I had an escape hatch; men didn't.

Only now did I see the implications of this double standard. To be genuinely independent, I had to be both emotionally and financially self-sufficient, truly so, prepared to not merely split bills with a boyfriend but weather any potential future disaster on my own.

In the 1970s, to leave an unsatisfying marriage, as Gornick had, or decide to forgo the institution altogether in pursuit of a meaningful career, was a significant political act, a battle in the larger war of reinventing interpersonal relationships and righting the balance between the sexes. A lot had changed in thirty years. My liberal milieu took for granted that women should go to college and have careers and be equal partners in marriage. The idea of divorce was sad, sure, but commonplace. Casual sex was ordinary.

But—and here's what surprised me—though marriage was no longer compulsory, the way it had been in the 1950s, we continued to organize our lives around it, unchallenged.

One evening in early fall R and I treated ourselves to dinner at the Middle Eastern café around the corner that let you bring your own wine. It was still warm enough to eat outside; we had the sidewalk seating area to ourselves. After the waiter uncorked our extra-large bottle of Syrah, we tilted back in our flimsy slatted chairs and started to talk, about our usual things—school, work, family, friends, what we were reading and thinking and feeling— and kept talking all through dinner—steaming pillows of pita hot off the griddle, mounds of tangy hummus, leg of lamb drizzled with mint-mayonnaise—and drinking, until finally our tongues were so loose that R just came out and said: "It's not always easy for someone like me to be with someone like you."

We'd finished our meal and were on to our second big square of warm, flaky baklava, dense with honey.

"You know, someone not sexual like you," he continued.

At first I didn't understand what he was saying. Not sexual? What was he talking about?

"I love sex!" I said.

I licked the honey off my fingers as if I was making a point, picked up the wine bottle, and divided what remained between our two glasses. As I did, his words sank in.

He was right. I wasn't a "not sexual" person, but I'd *become* one. I'd noticed that I was less interested in having sex than I used to be, but I thought that's just what happens after a few years. It was part of growing up, making compromises, settling down. I'd been trying to make my peace with it.

There was a rectangle of light on the sidewalk, as if the streetlamp had dropped a train ticket, and I looked at it and thought about my fixation on Maeve Brennan, the way I'd imbued her with something resembling liberation: she'd been my passport out of myself, and Boston, and now here I was, finally, on a warm fall night in Brooklyn, not alone after all but with a man I loved, drunk, no choice but to look the truth right in the face: The Long-Winded Lady was about as asexual as a person could get.

Rather than deal with my growing curiosity about life on my own, I'd furiously buttoned it into a trench coat, waterproof and cosseted, where it remained safely apart from me, something to moon over and fantasize about, like an unrequited lover. Rather than openly and honestly being in my relationship with R, I'd developed an unrequited relationship with my own repression.

What had been merely a constant, low-grade yearning for even a sliver of conversation with my mother spiked into a feverish need to talk to *anyone* here in this new city where I knew hardly a soul and R was my only close friend.

"God," I said. "You're right. What do we do?"

Here is what I did: In early December a man I'd interviewed for a freelance magazine assignment invited me to drinks, and at the end of the night he kissed me and I kissed him back. I had forgotten about the power of the unknown. I pulled away and told him I had a boyfriend and couldn't see him again. And then I lost my mind. I saw him again—on my lunch hour, before class, in the library stacks. And then I stopped. But everything was changed. For six weeks I waded through the wreckage, searching for the courage to tell R what we both already knew and couldn't bear to admit: we were over.

For Christmas, R went to see his family in Cambridge, and I went home to mine. Though our mother had been gone four years now, my brother and I insisted on continuing her Christmas-morning ritual. Whoever woke first woke the other, and together we'd stumble downstairs, pour steel-cut oats into a pot of boiling water, and mix up scones from a favorite recipe she'd found while visiting relatives in Ireland. Like her, I appreciate a bit of pomp. I'd excavate my parents' gold-rimmed wedding china, the good silver, and linen napkins. In the dining room my father would build a fire, and because we could do this now that we were three instead of four, we'd pull our chairs around the hearth and balance our bowls and plates on our knees, the silver and porcelain glinting festively as we ate.

As usual, I was given quite a few books. When I peeled off the red paper and discovered a brand-new hardcover called *American Moderns: Bohemian New York and the Creation of a New Century,* by the historian Christine Stansell, I nodded uncomprehendingly, a touch embarrassed; I hadn't even known there'd been a bohemia before the 1950s Beat Generation. Apparently a bunch of Victorian radicals—*if ever an oxymoron!* I remember thinking to myself—had beaten Kerouac & Co. to the punch.

I still have the book. Inside the front cover my father wrote in ballpoint pen: "To Kate . . . Who knows, they may one day write about you and the creation of this new century. All my love, Dad. Christmas 2000."

"Hah," I said. Coolness—"that perfect mastery (or numbness) of self that enables the 'hipster,' the cool cat, to listen to the loudest and most throbbing jazz without displaying the least sign of emotion"—has been a membership requirement for every American bohemia since *The New York Times* published that definition in 1950. Nobody would mistake me for cool. Just that month a classmate had turned to me and said, "Were you *actually* born yesterday? Is it possible for an adult human being to get as excited about things as you do?"

On the train back to New York City I decided to give the book a go. I'd taken the bus into Boston's South Station to meet up with R, and after we'd found a pair of empty seats, we settled in to read, each of us cocooned in our own amber beam from the overhead lights. At some point he fetched our favorite Amtrak feast—cans of Budweiser and microwaved hot dogs—though I didn't notice until he returned and asked me to pull down the tray tables. Then I forgot him altogether. As the train lumbered along that grubby stretch of Northeast Corridor, I dropped straight out of the present and into the past.

I've always loved novels in which the house is a character in its own right—the "sea-moistened" island summer house in Virginia Woolf's *To the Lighthouse,* where during the off-season "loveliness and stillness clasped hands in the bedroom"; the savaged, roofless, half-lived-in Blackwood mansion in Shirley Jackson's *We Have Always Lived in the Castle,* "turreted and open to the sky"; Tara, the palatial antebellum plantation house that outlasts love and war in Margaret Mitchell's *Gone with the Wind.* Stansell expands on that tradition: a history of a moment in time centered on a public space. Washington Square Park is so integral to the milieu she'd studied that it becomes the beating heart of the story she tells.

It just so happened that I'd been walking through that very park every day on my way to classes.

The site then, at the turn of that century, was in the process of becoming almost exactly what it looks like in this new one. In the 1870s the park was redesigned and improved—curved pathways wending beneath the towering maple and oak trees were carved into the grass; the big circular stone fountain at the center was relocated from Fifth Avenue and Fifty-Ninth Street. In 1895, what had been a plaster and wood Washington Square Arch was replaced by today's grand marble version. But every other specific was unfamiliar. This cognitive dissonance made one hundred years seem both a blink and an eon.

When my family first moved to Newburyport, and my parents scraped off the dingy, dated floral wallpaper put up by the previous owners, they uncovered another layer beneath, and then another. And so it was reading Stansell's book: she'd peeled off the globalized '90s and Gordon Gekko '80s and punk '70s and folk '60s and Beat '50s and bebop '40s—all the way down to the bare, unvarnished planks of the turn of the last century.

I got out of my seat to stretch my legs and buy us another round of beer. In college I'd majored in American Studies; the period Stansell explores wasn't completely foreign to me. But as I lurched down the aisle toward the snack car, I realized that I'd more or less ignored the birth of the modern era, an odd oversight that suggested to me I found it easier to identify with a pen-and-ink illustration of a Puritan sweeping her hearth in the year 1641 than I did actual photographs of the bustled, tea-sipping Victorian urbanites I'd come across in college textbooks.

A troubling thought: After forty years of historians writing women back into history, was I blocking them back out according to aesthetic laziness; e.g., it was easier to imagine a broom than a bustle?

Well, wouldn't you know it—these very women I'd breezily dismissed were the ones who would have the most to teach me.

The period of time was brief: about 1890 to 1920. The cast of characters—journalists and novelists, artists and activists, male and female—is tiny. Nearly all have been lost to history, or have names that only ring distantly, from the radical journalist Louise Bryant to her husband, the radical journalist John Reed. Many weren't even known outside Greenwich Village, which wasn't connected to the rest of the city by subway until 1918.

But for a short while, this small enclave was home to a thriving community of late-Victorian rebels who laid the groundwork for a new way of living. Free love, socialism, Freudianism, pacifism—they practiced all of it, with an almost ecstatic earnestness, even agitating for birth control. Their mission, in short, was to create a better future through a fully emancipated society.

Essential to this revolution were women's rights and sexual liberation. "Certainly never before, and probably not since, did a group of self-proclaimed innovators tie their ambitions so tightly to women," Stansell writes, "and not just a token handful but whole troops of women, waving the flag of sexual equality."

Talk was their greatest tool, and with it they forged an all-inclusive "conversational community" that united genders and classes. "Free speech was self-conscious, flashy, daring, ostentatiously honest and sexual," Stansell reports, skipping "from poetry to birth control to the situation of the garment workers . . . a pastiche of speech, a bricolage." This glorious explosion of words obliterated the "mannered conversation of the patrician drawing room" and the "barren commonplaces of the middle-class parlor."

The writers among this group reveled in "confidence, discovery, self-delight" and "liked expansiveness and embrace, not doubt and mockery; crossing over lines, not drawing them." Their brief, shining moment has gone down in history as "the innocent revolution," "the lyric years," "the joyous season."

These people were the anti-hipsters.

In the manner of many an iconic moment, one oft-told story to emerge from the period is about an episode that—in hindsight— actually signaled its demise.

It was a cold night in January 1917. Six self-proclaimed "Arch Conspirators" (most famously, Marcel Duchamp, who'd already scandalized the world with his *Nude Descending a Staircase* four years prior) broke into the Washington Square Arch, climbed its spiral staircase to the roof, and staged a mock revolution of the most courteous variety: after stringing up Chinese lanterns and red balloons they sat on a picnic blanket talking and sipping tea by candlelight until dawn. Two of the six insurgents were women, one of whom read aloud the group's declaration of independence: Greenwich Village was seceding from the Union and would henceforth be known as the "Free and Independent Republic of Washington Square." Then they shot off their toy cap guns.

My kind of bohemians!

After four years of enervation in the stodgy faux-metropolis of Boston, these charismatic radicals felt like century-old emissaries of my own emotional storm. To break with the past and invent a new future was a rebellion I wanted to get behind. Indeed, I hoped I was already making it happen.

I was particularly intrigued with a woman named Neith Boyce—again, I'm ashamed to admit, because she, like Maeve Brennan and Edna Millay, felt so familiar. Like me, she'd moved to New York City from Boston in her twenties. Like me, she wasn't radical, but she was clearly independent and strong. She'd been the sole female reporter at an influential (now defunct) city newspaper. She "harbored strong literary ambitions and was determined to launch a career that would spirit her away from the destiny of marriage and motherhood," Stansell wrote.

She sounded like someone I might like to know.

I squinted at the photo, but I couldn't tell much from what I saw: a shadowy profile of a young woman with pale skin and heavy-lidded eyes, dark hair pulled back in a loose knot.

Today, when I flip to page nineteen, where her entry is acknowledged by a faint pencil checkmark in the margin—a signal to myself to look her up when I got home—I marvel over how the doors to our futures can be as unassuming as they are unexpected.

Neith's place in recorded history is so slight that it took me a week to finally hear her voice (so to speak). A footnote had led me to the bottom of New York University's Bobst Library, where I threaded a spool of film into a microform machine and started to scroll through ancient issues of *Vogue*. Finally, there it was, May 5, 1898:

> I was born a bachelor, but of course several years elapsed . . . before my predestination to this career became obvious. Up to that time people acknowledged threatening indications by calling me queer, while elderly persons who wished to be disagreeable said that I was independent. . . . It hurt them to think that the unblemished escutcheon of the family should be invaded by the pen rampant and shirt-collar, saltier-wise, argent, of the bachelor girl.

It was the opening salvo of The Bachelor Girl, Neith's recurring column in praise of the single life.

The day it became evident that I was irretrievably committed to this alternative lifestyle was a solemn one in the family circle. I was about to leave that domestic haven, heaven only knew for what port. I was going to New York to earn my own bread and butter and to live alone.

In 1898 women still laced themselves into corsets so tightly it was believed they actually breathed differently than men—from the top of the chest, not the diaphragm. To go swimming, they wore elaborate and cumbersome "bathing costumes"—generally a knee-length flannel dress embellished with lace or embroidery and worn with bloomers, dark stockings, high lace-up slippers, and a cap; a beribboned burka by another name.

More relevant, marriage and motherhood were the entire point of a Victorian woman's existence. As I'd learned from Edith Wharton's novels, until a daughter of the upper class turned eighteen and was formally presented to society, she was kept at home among matrons who oversaw her training in the feminine arts (ballroom dancing, light conversation, pouring tea, etc.); her subsequent betrothal—which, ideally, took place before the year was out—and its attendant flurry of social activity (the engagement dinner and rounds of celebratory parties, all of it closely chronicled in the society pages) was the most exciting period of her life. Status confirmed, family wealth consolidated, she retreated into the domestic fold. ("I am becoming ardently matrimonial," Alice James, Henry James's sister, confided to a friend in the mid-1870s, "and if I could get any sort of man to be impassioned 'bout me, I should not let him escape.")

I couldn't decide which astounded me more: that one of these antique Victorians so blithely rejected marriage, or that her column saying as much appeared in a national fashion magazine not exactly known for championing the feminist cause.

My heart beat faster. I read on:

I never shall be an old maid, because I have elected to be a Girl Bachelor. And as to regretting this choice, you know the saying of the philosopher, "Whether you marry or not, you will regret it."

The philosopher she referred to was most likely Kierkegaard, who said something along those lines, as did Darwin around that time, listing the pros and cons of matrimony. That both were men is no coincidence; ambivalence over marriage wasn't a woman's prerogative.

And yet, as I came to learn, Neith wasn't ahead of her time—she was exactly of it, articulating the unspoken desires and sating the curiosities of a large portion of *Vogue*'s readership. The term *bachelor girl* was coined in 1895 to describe a specific breed of middle-class woman who chose to pursue the new educational and vocational opportunities opening up around her, which allowed her to live alone and support herself—so very unlike her sister the spinster, who was closely associated with the home, and the working-class women for whom work was an economic necessity. From roughly the 1870s to the 1910s, the marriage rate among educated women fell to 60 percent, 30 percent lower than the national average; clearly, for more than a few the single life was a deliberate choice.

That said, Neith was perhaps a touch too articulate for her editors (all of them women, I assume); in the next issue's table of contents the word *fiction* is appended to the title of her column. By the third installment of The Bachelor Girl it's gone again. All through the summer and into November she invited readers to ponder the true stories of a real-life happily unmarried woman.

Her point of view is straightforward: living the bachelor life isn't easy, and it's not for everyone, but if one cultivates a few key qualities and habits it can be the best game in town.

To start, a Bachelor Girl must, above all, be confident, as, "without self-confidence, no Napoleon nor even a war-editor or a woman reporter ever achieved success."

Clean clothes increase morale: "The linen collar—of the latest mode, be it understood, and fresh at least once a day—has tended to strengthen the backbone of the bachelor girl."

It doesn't hurt to have patience for small-minded sorts, as the Bachelor Girl's "point of view is rather a new one, and persons who are wedded to good old points of view, most respectable people in fact, hate the effort of adjusting themselves to uncertain new ones."

Her aim, after all, isn't merely to live an independent life but also to "convince the world that she is possible."

Given the "brain-energy" this mission requires, it's crucial to surround oneself with like-minded people. This means eliminating "non-essential social elements (otherwise bores)"—a radical suggestion at a time when the bulk of a woman's day was spent following the convention of paying calls—and getting "the most good from the greatest possible number of fellow-beings."

By definition, the Bachelor Girl has very little in common with her married peers, and she doesn't fool herself into thinking otherwise. This is why you'll "find bachelor girls largely flocking by themselves," all of whom "have some definite everyday occupation"—which is to say, they make their own way and aren't supported by a trust fund or a generous great-aunt. The Bachelor Girl is self-sufficient, economically and philosophically.

Threaded through Neith's practical guidance are anecdotes about her domestic misadventures. By the late 1800s, massive demand had sent urban rents skyrocketing, making boarding-houses and residential hotels, longtime fixtures of the American landscape,* the only affordable option for women who wanted to live on their own. As expected, Neith appreciates her boardinghouse for providing the independence she desires, but she can't stand the food, so she and a fellow girl bachelor, Olivia, get their own apartment. Soon enough, her roommate reveals herself to be a humorless penny-pincher, and so Neith returns to the boardinghouse.

"The thing that was responsible was a difference in our ideas of economy, or rather the fact that I had no idea of economy, whereas to Olivia it was a necessary condition of existence if not the foundation of the moral law," she explains. The bright side: "I was not a man and married to Olivia."

Whether by coincidence or design, at this point in the series fashion illustrations of bustled women in feathered hats run alongside the column, as if to remind readers that the writer is indeed female.

The experience with Olivia leaves Neith wary of "the cooperative feminine ménage," but eventually her longing for good food wins out, and she moves into a communal house with six other like-minded career women plus a housekeeper. Things start out well. Each night they gather for a civilized dinner at a nicely laid table. But they can't for the life of them keep a housemaid—the last quits claiming she's afraid of the "crazy ladies"—and anyway, at the end of a year, Neith is the only one who hasn't succumbed "to the prevalent matrimonial epidemic."

Decades before social psychologists published academic papers explaining that one's lifestyle choices are heavily influenced by one's social circle, Neith laid it out herself:

I realize the deadly character of the engagement germ, which consists in its contagious quality. I know that if one girl, in

---

* During the nineteenth century, an estimated 70 percent of the population boarded at some point in their lives.

a house where there are seven, becomes engaged, it is seven thousand chances to one that the other six will follow suit— provided, that is, that there are available suitors, and there generally are if one is not particular.

Beneath the brittle scrim of Neith's slightly antiquated diction is a certainty and clarity that took me completely by surprise— her pre-ideological perspective felt far more modern than the one my contemporaries and I assumed when we spoke about our own lives. She was funny without being mean, strong-minded but never didactic.

Finally, here it was, the conversation I'd been looking for.

I'd been content all this time to keep Maeve Brennan a fantasy. Her mysteriousness and omniscient point of view discouraged prying, and it seemed only right to respect her wishes. With Neith it was different. Her direct address to the reader made her feel more approachable, almost as if she were asking me to find her.

After a bit of digging I located Carol DeBoer-Langworthy, a professor at Brown University, who'd been researching Neith's biography for fifteen years.

She told me that Neith had been born, the second of five children, in Indiana in 1872 to a schoolteacher with literary ambitions and a Civil War hero turned book agent. That they decided to name their daughter after an ancient Egyptian deity who never married—well, it's hard not to get mystical about that.

In scholarly terms, the goddess Neith was an example of a "female parthenogenetic cosmogenesis"—a virgin mother who created herself out of her own being and gave birth to the universe, considered by theologians to be one of a handful of deities that gave rise to Christianity's Virgin Mary. Like her Greek counterpart Athena, she embodied both male and female powers, presiding over war, hunting, and weaving, and was always depicted alone. Her patron temple in the lost city Sais housed a midwifery school with female doctors and students, and she was said to reweave the world on her loom every day. Her symbol was a shield and two arrows, which in some eras was seen as a spindle (yet another commonality with the spinster), and she was usually depicted wearing a red crown; coincidentally, or not, Neith herself had her father's red-gold hair ("Titian blonde," as it was commonly referred to then and for some reason isn't anymore).

The family lived in a modest frame house that grew more boisterous with each baby—another three were born in fast succession—until 1880, the peak of the national diphtheria epidemic, when all four of her siblings died in one week.

Neith was eight years old, old enough to understand what was happening without understanding it at all. After a dark, difficult year, her parents packed up their house, shut the door on the past, and set out for California, which made good on its fabled promises. Henry helped launch *The Los Angeles Times* and *The Los Angeles Tribune,* and Mary founded an arts club that eventually became today's Rose Parade.

In 1891 the family moved again, this time to Boston, where they seem to have slipped easily into the East Coast media establishment; Mary was an editor at the progressive journal *ARENA,* and Henry worked as a publisher. Neith, however, loathed their new city upon arrival:

> In the dim gray atmosphere shapes of people all dressed in black wandered vaguely about. Life was diminished, all faces were sad or worried or just blank, the air was foggy and sooty, the buildings gray and grimy, the streets narrow and crowded with dingy forms.

More than a century after she lived there, that city had felt much the same to me.

Writing was Neith's greatest release and satisfaction, and though, like most women of her generation, she didn't go to college, she was fortunate enough to have politically progressive parents who strove to encourage her predilection. In Los Angeles she'd published little pieces in her father's newspapers. Now she wrote reviews and articles for *ARENA,* and when she was twenty a firm in which her father held a stake published her first book, a volume of nature poetry.

To Neith's enormous relief, when she was twenty-four the family relocated to Manhattan and quickly went their separate ways: following a brief stint together in one of the newly built apartment buildings in the East Twenties, the elder Boyces moved north to the suburb of Mount Vernon, and as soon as she found a job, Neith got her own place, downtown.

"Just the sight of the city, not yet prickling with skyscrapers nor buzzing with motors, was exhilarating," she remembered years later. New York City "was not closed in upon itself, it seemed in connection with the world, it seemed alive."

Work—by which I mean paid employment outside the home, in factories and offices and schools, rather than the ancient unpaid labors of child-care and housekeeping—is central to the evolution of all women in America, and fundamental to that of the single woman.

The first reason is practical and obvious: for centuries, the majority of women were barred from making money and simply couldn't afford to live comfortably (rather than on the margins, as prostitutes, beggars, or vagrants) on their own. Unless a woman was born into means, marriage was a financial and social necessity, her only chance to leave her family of origin and (hopefully) secure the economic standing of herself and her future children. As the historian Gerda Lerner observed, even the choice to remain single was a matter of electing one form of dependency over another: nuns relied on their male superiors; unmarried daughters on their male family members; prostitutes on the "protection" of male authorities. Propertied widows could lead relatively independent lives—but even that grim good fortune required marrying first. Well-paid work, then, and the ability to be self-supporting, gave a woman the option to push off marriage until she was older, or avoid it altogether.

The second reason is more intriguing: single women are perceived more positively when the economy needs them—meaning that macro-level financial forces have contributed mightily to their public reputation. It happens to have been a Newburyport native, businessman Francis Cabot Lowell, who (unwittingly) triggered the country's first significant wave of respected single women.

In the early 1800s, as water-powered machinery began to surpass traditional horsepower, Lowell thought to harness the fast-moving Merrimack River farther downstream, thirty-five miles southwest of Newburyport. In 1813, he established the Boston Manufacturing Company; in 1826, the company was incorporated with several others into America's first planned factory town, named in his honor, today known as the cradle of the Industrial Revolution.

The early factories of Lowell, Massachusetts, were staffed primarily by young women between the ages of fifteen and thirty who came by the thousands from the farms of New England to work the massive looms that turned raw cotton into cloth—neo-spinsters, if you will. They lived in cramped boardinghouses, their wages were only half those of the men, and the working conditions—their days started at five o'clock in the morning and lasted fourteen hours, for an average of seventy-three hours a week—were brutal. In an autobiographical account published in 1883, a woman who started her factory career at age ten wrote that "a great many of the better class of millgirls" were there to "secure the means of education for some *male* member of the family. To make a *gentleman* of a brother or a son." But for others, the chance for economic independence, not to mention a life away from their families, was a formidable lure. By 1840 there were eight thousand of them, 80 percent of the entire mill workforce.

Living and working together created a powerful sense of community. They proudly called themselves the "factory girls" and published the first American magazine managed and edited solely by women, *The Lowell Offering.* In his travel memoir *American Notes,* about his famous 1842 visit to America, Charles Dickens raved about the journal, describing it as "four hundred good solid pages, which I have read from beginning to end." (Indeed, a pair of Boston-based scholars argue he drew on several of its anonymously published stories to pen *A Christmas Carol,* which came out the following year—yet another instance of the single woman's invisible contributions.)

The "mill girls" (as they were also known) were politicized, as well. In 1834, eight hundred of them went on strike to protest wage cuts; in 1845, more than 1,500 banded together to protest deteriorating factory conditions, forming the Lowell Female Labor Reform Association, the first major union of working women in the United States.

By the late 1800s mill conditions had drastically worsened, but the Industrial Revolution that had given the factory girls their independence set into motion an ever-rising tide of products and publications that in turn created yet another wave of female wage earners: the thousands of young women who left their small towns and farms for New York City, drawn like iron filaments to a magnet, settling into crevices, finding jobs in factories and offices, living in communal boardinghouses and even their own apartments. This was the wave Neith rode.

In 1893, a Mrs. M. L. Rayne published an incredibly helpful guide called *What Can a Woman Do,* a survey of every possible employment option available to women. According to Rayne, in the 1840s there were only seven industries open to women in Massachusetts (including teaching, keeping boarders, and working in the cotton mills); by 1893 there were roughly 300,000 women in that state alone earning their own living in nearly three hundred occupations, from journalism, law, and medicine to engraving, cigar making, beekeeping, and retouching photographs.

Key to women's ascent was the typewriter. Invented in 1867 in Milwaukee, Wisconsin, the original model was decorated with floral decals and mounted on a treadle table, like a sewing machine; promoters proclaimed it perfect for a woman's "nimble fingers." In 1870, only 4 percent of stenographers and typists were women; within a decade their ranks had quadrupled; and by 1900, they were at almost 80 percent.

More crucially, as they had been in Lowell, women were a source of cheap labor. Due to institutionalized sexism, the unavoidable fact that this first round of female hires had little to no prior work experience, and "functional periodicity"—the widely held belief that menstruation was so debilitating that it prevented women from working full-time, therefore rendering them undeserving of full wages—employers found it very easy to justify paying women less than men. (In the late 1890s, in an ingenious effort to obtain equal pay for equal work, one of the new woman physicians, Stanford University's Dr. Clelia Duel Mosher, invented a series of abdominal breathing exercises to counteract menstrual pain, called "moshers.")

In her 1893 guide, Mrs. M. L. Rayne was forthright about this inequity—"Women, as a rule, received from twenty to thirty per centum less than men for the same or equivalent services," she wrote—but, hewing to a popular conservative line at the time, she urged her readers not to worry overmuch, arguing that a large percentage of men provided for a family of eight or ten, compared to "single women clerks who are working for themselves only." Besides, she reasoned, "the adjustment of false averages in wages, even in these cases, may be a wrong one, but it is one which time and justice will remedy." Unfortunately, her optimism was misplaced; after World War II this same argument was revived to keep women out of the workforce, and the wage gap still hasn't closed.

As the first women to feminize the workplace, these low-level clerical workers paved the way for higher-ranking female reporters and editors, who now seemed just a little less threatening. In 1885, when a young woman named Elizabeth Cochrane, incensed by a misogynist column in *The Pittsburgh Dispatch,* submitted an angry screed under the name "Lonely Orphan Girl," the paper published an ad asking the author to come forward, and they offered her a job. Before the decade was out Nellie Bly (she'd assumed a pen name) had moved to New York City and become one of the most famous newspaper reporters in the country. Her imitators were legion. In 1898, the year Neith published her *Vogue* column, an estimated four thousand women in New York City alone were working in journalism. (To this legion, Mrs. M. L. Rayne offered fair warning: "I urge women to be sure of their ability before they enter the flinty paths of journalism, where it is a sin to be ignorant, and where you are expected to be wise, witty, sensible, poetical, and versatile for very moderate pay," she wrote in a section of her book called The Lady Journalist.)

Obviously this flood of proudly self-sufficient workers couldn't be contained by the term *spinster*—and so a new one emerged: the New Woman. She was, by definition, independent, and often a suffragist, but not necessarily. Henry James initially popularized her moniker in the late 1870s and early 1880s with Isabel

Archer and Daisy Miller—fictional heroines who were ultimately punished for their independent spirit—but it was quickly reappropriated by its real-life paradigm and used respectfully by the public, men included. In a 1913 letter to a friend, the political writer Randolph Bourne described New Women as such:

> So thoroughly healthy and zestful. . . . They shock you constantly. . . . They have an amazing combination of wisdom and youthfulness, of humor and ability, and innocence and self-reliance. . . . They are of course all self-supporting and independent; and they enjoy the adventure of life; the full, reliant, audacious way in which they go about makes you wonder if the new woman isn't to be a very splendid sort of person.

Theoretically, the New Woman was free to be sexual, though in practice Victorian social censures and frank classism proved hard to surmount. One of the ways in which non-bohemian privileged women laid claim to the "respectability" that differentiated them from the immigrant and working classes was to present themselves as "passionless," a fiction that must have seemed particularly necessary to new members of a middle class uncertain about their social status. Too, I suspect it was difficult enough infiltrating a male-dominated labor market without bringing your sex life to work. This connection between class and sex continues today, of course: often a woman is driven less by "morality" than by not wanting to be considered a slut, and so she rounds down the number of men she's slept with, for instance, or even, in the case of a promiscuous childhood friend of mine, audaciously tells her fiancé that she's a virgin. In this way women continue to police themselves and other women.

Emancipation from the domestic prison was an inarguable good for everyone. But it came at a price. In a male-dominated workplace, a woman had not only sexism to contend with but the strange predicament of being regarded as a novelty, an immigrant in her own land, forcing her to find a way to reconcile her gender with her ambition. Some went ahead and brought sex to work, playing up their womanliness and incurring whatever favors might follow (exploiting her "erotic capital," as we'd put it now); others tried to adopt the ways and mannerisms of men. As we know, this negotiation continues today.

For those women who also had literary and intellectual ambitions, this reality was even more complicated. Like Neith, many were hired quite literally *for* their otherness. Newspaper publishers, fast on the scent of a growing demographic, sought to attract female readers by adding special new "women's pages" peddling fashion, décor, and cooking tips. As Mrs. M. L. Rayne put it, "Household departments, fashion letters, such as Jenny June furnishes to a dozen papers simultaneously; children's column, market articles, art criticisms, book reviews—these are nearly always the work of women."

On the one hand this was good news—more jobs and more authority. On the other hand, it shunted the majority of women to a "pink ghetto" that wasn't (and still isn't) taken seriously. Even a young and formidable Nellie Bly was demoted to this beat at *The Pittsburgh Dispatch* before sending herself to Mexico as a foreign correspondent.

Even more paradoxical was being a New Woman with her own first-person column—a plum gig with a catch. Her task, in essence, was to explain herself to a public that was still trying to understand who she was.

On the surface, this was a positive, even liberating exercise. The New Woman is rare in the world of neologisms for being descriptive and aspirational, rather than, as is the case with many stereotypes, limiting and derogatory. The term arose in tandem with a specific demographic in real time, providing those within its ranks an enlarged sense of self; the job of the columnist was to tantalize the rest with an expansive new role to fantasize about that wasn't Wife or Mother—or defined in terms of *not* being a wife or mother, as with "old maid." (And, thanks to the prevailing fashion for pen names, her true identity was often secret.) Writers such as Neith pioneered a radically new way of being female in public—without them, Maeve Brennan might never have become The Long-Winded Lady.

The catch? On an individual level, it's impossible to quantify the cost of mining your own life for sellable anecdotes, even—or especially—when your audience is large. But on a much grander scale, the New Woman was unwittingly building a sort of gilded cage: by putting her own life up for display, she was perpetuating the sexist tendency to equate women with "merely" personal matters, and even collaborating in her own objectification. Today, nearly every female writer I know has had to decide at some point whether or not she'll accept an assignment to write about her dating life, a conundrum that is almost never presented to men.

When it comes to job hunting, things aren't so terribly different now than they were a century ago: it was a family connection that introduced Neith Boyce to Josephine Redding, the first editor of *Vogue*. Founded only four years earlier as a weekly, *Vogue* catered expressly to the New Woman. Here is Redding describing types like Neith in an 1895 editorial:

> What women are concerned in is developing their own individuality, and hence they refuse to call any man master, be he husband or spiritual guide. Personal freedom is more precious to them than the protection of the best men. The women they envy are not those who are simply wives and mothers, but those

who by honest intelligent work have attained distinction in any line of effort, and whose creed has been self-reliance.

Not surprisingly, Mrs. Redding took a shine to Neith, who not only played the part but also looked it, always a convenient accident, and perhaps even especially so when the popular images of the New Woman perpetuated by the media—tall and fit, smartly turned out in her crisp cotton shirtwaist and ankle-grazing skirt, forever striding confidently along the sidewalk—was so appealing.

It took some doing to see that unfettered vision in the 1903 portrait Carol DeBoer-Langworthy had posted on her website. Standing against a gray background, Neith looks suspiciously like the stolid matrons she mocked. Her outfit—a black high-waisted skirt and matching embroidered jacket, black fur stole draped around her shoulders, black-gloved hands tucked into a black fur muff—is formal and contained. Her thick, wavy hair is smoothed neatly beneath a very respectable black hat.

But her large, drowsy eyes and curved lips give her face a sultry, intelligent expression that hints at a far less conventional woman. Ditch the furs, lose the hat, loosen the corset, and it's easy to see how she'd catch the eye of a forward-thinking editor. Almost immediately upon her arrival in New York she started contributing freelance articles and short stories to *Vogue*.

A freelance gig wasn't enough to live on, however, so Neith stayed with her parents and, though she was temperamentally reserved and not especially interested in socializing, astutely accepted Mrs. Redding's invitations to the dinner parties she hosted at her apartment—"networking," we'd say today.

It was during one such evening she met a man who helped her land a full-time job reporting for a daily newspaper called *The Commercial Advertiser*. With a new weekly salary, just enough to cover room and board, Neith was able to leave her parents' watch and moved farther downtown, into The Judson Apartments, a residential hotel on "Genius Row"—the southern edge of Washington Square Park—named for all the artists it harbored. (A few years later, Neith's contemporary Willa Cather would move into the boardinghouse next door, eventually known as The House of Genius, thanks in part to her presence.)

Without knowing it, I'd been walking past Neith's building on my way to class each day. Her actual living space no longer exists as it once did (today it houses the King Juan Carlos I of Spain Center at New York University), but I didn't need to actually see her place to imagine it: high ceilings, a few pieces of furniture—mahogany, I decided—including a wardrobe fitted with a full-length mirror so she could make sure her shirtwaist was smooth and buttoned correctly before she left for the office each morning. A place as clean and uncluttered as a finely made decision.

That Neith Boyce was the first real friend I'd made in New York might sound odd, but she gave me the conversation I'd been hungry for, and not a moment too soon. Since I couldn't exactly walk back through time and knock on her door, I did the next best thing, staying later and later at the Bobst Library each night, reading about her and the people she knew. I liked to go to the high-up floors and work at a table near the giant plate glass windows overlooking Washington Square Park.

There was something so surreal about . . . everything. This park that had outlasted so many people. All the many iterations of femininity it had seen. How even I, "a dutiful daughter," as Simone de Beauvoir once described her young self, was living a life so different from my mother's; when she was my age she was married, about to become pregnant with me. I was beginning to think that this habit of mind—constantly tracing myself back to my mother, to where she'd begun and left off—wasn't idiosyncratic, but something that many if not most women did, a feature of the female experience. *Did men do this, too?* I wondered. It still didn't seem possible that I lived with a man my mother had never met. What would she make of my strange desire to be on my own? Was the voice in my head telling me to quit my spinster fantasies and grow up already hers, or mine? Or was it the voice of something larger, the culture itself?

One afternoon in early January I spent several hours in the library basement finding and printing out the last installments of Neith's column. By the time I finished and walked outside, day had turned into evening; snow blanketed the park, erasing the cars, filtering the glare of the stoplights so they glowed like gas streetlamps. The arch glittered and shone. Nights like this it was even easier to pretend that Neith's park and mine really were one and the same. I felt my cell phone vibrate in my pocket. Cell phones seemed surreal. Ordinary civilians equipped with portable communications devices, like secret agents. My mother had never seen a cell phone or even had an e-mail address.

Z seemed surprised to hear my voice.

I'd met Z in the fall, during my first full flush of New York City. He was at least six foot six, and three times my width. A scar tore down the left side of his face. His knuckles were the size of walnuts. But when he stopped me on the subway platform to ask for directions, none of this registered. Someone had asked *me*—a person who didn't leave the house without her plastic-coated folding map, which she consulted while standing on street corners, in broad daylight—for directions. Grandly I escorted him up the escalator.

He had a rich, pleasant drawl. He was from Georgia, I learned. The bag in his hands held his boxing gloves. He was on his way to the gym. He was going to be the next Mike Tyson. Next month he was fighting at Madison Square Garden, and would I come watch?

Would I ever! I'd never known a boxer! I gave him my cell phone number and told him to call me with details.

Like a proud cat I brought my story home to R, just in case he needed reminding that New York City is leagues more exciting and interesting than Boston.

At first I liked it when Z called. He was funny and, unsurprisingly, contentious. He would needle me to attend his fights; dictate long, convoluted instructions about how to get there from Brooklyn Heights, involving multiple subway changes, a bus ride, and a long walk, all of which I would scrawl with good intentions on the back of receipts, and then he'd call me a week later to tease me for not showing up. We'd banter, I'd strike another bargain, and then I'd forget about him until he called again.

I didn't mean for him to become a secret. Somehow his phone calls arrived at odd, private moments, when I was deep in the library stacks, or waiting in line to buy a blueberry muffin for breakfast—moments that slip unspoken among a day's detritus. Unthinkingly, I stopped bringing the story back home to R.

A few weeks before Christmas Z had called to say he'd bought me a present. "I may have only met you that once," he'd said, "but I remember you perfectly, and this will *fit.*"

I'd never felt threatened by Z, but this was creepy. I reminded him, as I often did, that I had a boyfriend, who might not appreciate the gesture. Z sighed, exasperated. "Kate, I know that. This present is about me appreciating you for being my friend. It will fit perfectly." For a while, when I saw his number flashing on my cell phone, I didn't answer.

The holidays had come and gone, so when the phone vibrated this January evening, I forgot to screen it.

Z started in on the usual litany about his fights, as if nothing had changed. A chill went through me. Something about the call coming in the middle of my snowy park reverie made his voice seem an invasion. I so badly wanted him to end his monologue and hang up that at first I didn't understand what he was talking about; I just heard the shift in his tone . . . "And she was small, like you," he was saying. He was talking about his old girlfriend, back home in Georgia. "And so when I saw you on the subway, and you were nice, you reminded me of her. And she died, you know. She died last year. So when I saw you, small like her, all these feelings came back up. I just want you to be my friend, Kate," he went on. His voice was low and serious and rushed forward like a gathering mob. I didn't know how to stop him. "And so this is what I want. I want you to talk to me on the phone once a week, for just fifteen minutes, that's all, and I will give you three hundred and fifty dollars. I just want you to be friendly; you don't have to do anything. Just talk to me."

My heart slammed shut, as if he'd just unzipped his fly and exposed himself. I mumbled something about how I didn't want to do that, and immediately hung up. When he called right back, I didn't answer. (He never called again.) All the way home I burned with shame. Who was I to treat his naked loneliness like an affront? I'd been stringing him along, enjoying the illicit thrill of talking in secret to a strange man, safe in knowing I never had to see him in person. Obviously he was lonely; why else did I think he called me all the time, gamely ignoring my deflections?

For days I chastised myself. What had I possibly been thinking? It was one thing to play at being alone, another to actually be it. I was deluded, I decided, to think myself like Neith, "born a bachelor," even if I was armed with "individuality, pluck and a sense of humor." I had absolutely no instinct for self-preservation, and, worse, I wasn't merely naïve—I was willfully so. Even when all the signs pointed to danger, I professed not to see them. For what? An ego boost? I suspected it was even darker than that: I only had learned how to be good, so when I wanted to be bad, I had to pretend at it. If I let this disingenuous self loose on the world, I'd likely wreak destruction and get killed in a heartbeat.

Besides, I'd be so *lonely*; who wants that?

And yet . . . wasn't learning how to cope with loneliness integral to learning how to take care of myself? And become an adult?

Those were the emotional costs; what about the economic ones? Could I afford solitude? I'd gotten used to splitting expenses with R. Striking out on my own in one of the most expensive cities in the world while trying to break into a profession as notoriously low-paying and unstable as writing seemed possibly idiotic. (In fact, it was.)

Neith had done it all without a tremor. When her Uncle Elia had tried to scare her into marriage, she took him to the mat:

> You ask me if I look forward to being a lonely old maid of forty? I answer no for two reasons. First—because the principal joy of being independent is to take no thought for the morrow, much less a morrow a score of years removed. Second—and conclusively, I shall never be an old maid, because I have elected to be a Girl Bachelor.

I was twenty-eight. It was the year 2000. Nobody was making me marry anyone. But the pull toward it felt as strong as an undertow, the obvious next step in a mature and orderly existence. And when I thought about being alone at forty—the inconceivable far future—I froze.

When I'd spoken to Carol DeBoer-Langworthy, Neith Boyce's biographer, she'd generously offered to send me an advance copy of her annotated version of Neith's never-published memoir, which she was preparing for publication. I'd gone from having next to nothing at my disposal about this "forgotten" woman to hitting the jackpot. The memoir encompassed her *Vogue* era, unplugged, complete with details not fit for print.

The sheaf of typewritten pages made an unusual document. Neith worked on it off and on for more than thirty years, finally finishing it in her mid-sixties. Along the way she changed the voice from the first person to the third, and her name from Neith to Iras, so it reads more like a novel than a memoir. Yet it also has a labored, almost stilted, feel and isn't nearly as funny as her Bachelor Girl column.

Even so, being privy to these private reminiscences was a thrill. There's a lunch date with the wife of her newspaper editor: the "rather stout matron had a juicy steak and salad," while Neith could only afford coffee and a doughnut. "But she did not mind Spartan fare—the meals at the hotel were rather skimpy too— and did not mind that her room looked out on dingy backyards and tenement fire escapes festooned with flapping garments. It was all her own, and her complete independence was enough. How she enjoyed it!"

Unlike the stereotype of the frivolous urbanite of our own time, or even the high-born New Yorkers who made a game of "slumming" in hers, Neith is refreshingly self-aware. She "liked to feel herself a worker among workers," yet, "certainly she had better conditions than most: the priceless privilege of doing work she liked, a place of her own."

Indeed, Neith's primary romance is with the work that makes her single life both possible and worthwhile. "Just going out of the door in the morning, looking on the Square, waiting at the Bleecker Street station till the El train came screeching round the curve, riding with other wage-workers downtown, walking up the dirty worn steps to the office and the day's work—she liked it all."

The newsroom is a boys' club, where the men are so unaccustomed to the presence of women that they "dressed simply in pants and undershirt, with their suspenders hanging down." Initially her being there is an annoyance; she can hear them grumble, "Here comes the lady copyreader," when she approaches, but soon enough her diligence and professionalism win them over.

It intrigued me to see firsthand evidence that Neith's status as a single woman, far from being a detriment, expressly facilitated her career.

Unencumbered by the demands of a husband and children, she was free to devote all her time and energy to doing exactly what she wanted, which was to work as much as possible. The world opened up. "She was working hard, money was needed, and ideas for stories blossomed on every bush."

Neith's little room—"her niche in the great city, like a swallow's nest on a cornice"—was not unlike how I'd imagined it: spare, with two windows, two chairs, and a tea table. She befriended a pair of fellow boarders, both newspaperwomen, and after work they'd get together and talk about their jobs. Some nights a shy Welsh painter would drop by, and he and Neith would sit "talking and drinking tea till the small hours of the morning." Other evenings she'd visit the "miniature salons" hosted by women living alone in the narrow houses of the West Village, where coffee and cake was served, and "talk was about art."

True to form, she has a few scathing words to say about marriage. At her cousin May's wedding, she's shocked by the bride's radiant smile:

> Surely marriage was nothing to look so exuberant about, and coming down the aisle chatting and smiling to one another, as though they were dinner partners, seemed all wrong. Considering what marriage led to—children, bills, quarrels, the frightening forced association of two human beings—surely it was

nothing to be light-minded about. [Neith] thought there should be a touch of sackcloth and ashes about it.

I wasn't a woman who needed convincing that she wanted to be alone, but I did need help seeing clearly what that reality might look like, and evidence that there were indeed rewards to be gained if I was bold enough to pursue them—that, as Vivian Gornick had put it, "a world was waiting to welcome me if I was willing to enter it alone." Neith Boyce offered all the proof I needed.

On January 15, 2001 (so reports my steadfast journal), I finally found the courage to tell R we should maybe, possibly start thinking about breaking up. We were at home on the sofa. I didn't tell him that I'd cheated on him (several months later he'd find out by reading my journal). I sobbed as I spoke. Over the past three years he'd become my best friend. What was I doing? Beneath that was a more abstract fear: this might be my best shot at a good marriage and all that portended—security, children, grandchildren—and if I walked away now, I could live to regret it.

He was justifiably astonished, having had no idea what I'd been up to, but also, confusingly for both of us, comprehending. He knew me well enough to see that my craving to be on my own was real, even if he didn't want it for himself. It took us five painful months to extricate ourselves. In May he moved out. I was to leave the apartment in August, when the lease ended, and start my second year of graduate school.

Unlike Vivian Gornick, on that first morning alone I did not wake infatuated with solitude. Breakups are always painful, but at least in the past I wasn't also losing my home. I was such a wreck that within the week my brother came down from Newburyport to keep me company, even though he'd just fallen in love. He found a dreadful temp job—something having to do with data entry, a class-action lawsuit, and mesothelioma—and stayed all summer long.

In July a friend and I took the subway to the end of the line and lay on Far Rockaway Beach beneath an overcast sky. I came home with a sunburn so severe, I couldn't take off my bikini or bear the touch of clothing and so lay on the sofa in the same bathing suit for two days, crying about the stupid mess I'd made of my life. My brother took photos and wouldn't let me see the results, because, he said, I looked like a crime scene. Later, my friend and I joked that we'd ruined our décolletages, but I actually had: where before there were perhaps seven freckles, now there are possibly one thousand.

I had one more year left in school. My graduate assistantship had ended, but I'd found a part-time administrative job elsewhere in the university and, between that and freelance writing, was able to cobble together a meager living. None of my activities, though, proved an emotional distraction. I couldn't stop obsessing over what I'd done. I'd ruined a perfectly good relationship for no good reason. I was willingly making my life harder than it needed to be. I missed R, desperately, and wanted to call him all the time, and did, for a while, until finally I made myself understand that it was selfish and cruel to seek solace from the person I'd hurt.

That summer I saw only those few people who could handle my breaking into tears unprompted, and I carried on reading Neith Boyce's unpublished memoir. The unbound sheaf of papers was too cumbersome to bring on the subway, so I'd wait until I was home in the evening and bring the stack down to the Promenade and read on a bench. Sometimes I'd pour white wine into a Mason jar and sip from it as if it were water.

One of the more unpleasant aspects of living in New York City is how daily proximity to wealth and glamour can instill a desire for it where none existed before. Now that I was a grown woman, an impoverished student between semesters, so un-hinged that she needed to be ministered to by her little brother, my life seemed particularly bereft and pathetic, the likelihood of ever seeing my writing in a fancy magazine such as *Vogue,* never mind being invited to dinner by its famously frosty editor, slim to none.

So it was especially gratifying to find Neith griping about the "fashionable literary" evenings at Mrs. Redding's apartment, where gentility "was a uniform assumed like dinner coat or eve-ning dress," and "talk, like wine, was served in little shallow glasses, and you had to be careful of them; you mustn't be excited by an idea or an emotion, or you might spill your wine." She had no interest in idle chatter; "the last new book, the last new play evoked no opinions in her; she hadn't any." But, observing that the other guests find her "good-looking but Sphinx-like," rather than force herself to be agreeable, she simply sits quietly taking it all in, and only speaks when someone asks her a question.

One night, to my surprise, a letter slipped from the unbound pages.

It was one photocopied sheet, typewritten, from Neith to a mysterious "H," dated June 19, 1898, during the time she was publishing her column in *Vogue,* about yet another dinner at Mrs. Redding's apartment. At first I chortled to see Neith at her most irreverent yet:

> Do you know what Mrs. Redding reminds me of? I'll tell you if (as she says) you won't tell on me. Do you remember the little old red-nosed man who came into a restaurant where you and I were dining one night—with a basket full of alleged flowers made out of "garden truck"—beets, carrots, etc.? Well, I know it has not a kindly sound but she seems to me like that—a person who has outlived life (for the old man had seen better days!) and

spends what's left of it in whittling out queer superfluous little monstrosities that nobody wants.

After that, she retreats a touch, a little guilty:

> Never tell, will you? With all that I like her and I admire her grit and pluck and the way she makes the best of things—and I love her for always wearing a hat when she looks so much better with one and also I like to hear her views of life, matrimony, etc. She likes me because I'm an independent young woman but I'm sure if she knew that I had ever thought of joining the vast majority her interest in me would cease and determine.

I looked up at the couples strolling along the Promenade. "Joining the vast majority"?

During the winter of 1898, the man who'd gotten Neith Boyce her job at the newspaper introduced her to his brother, Hutchins Hapgood. A Chicago native and recent Harvard graduate roughly her same age, "Hutch" had just returned from a world tour with his college chum Leo Stein, brother of Gertrude, and had joined the staff as a reporter.

"This was a rather short, broad-shouldered young man," Neith reported in her memoir, "dressed in a light-colored tweed suit which seemed too big for him and made him look almost as broad as he was long, and it was wrinkled as though he had slept in it. . . . He had a ruddy-brown face and bright blue eyes, a look of physical vigor and fire."

Neith uses the word *fire* three more times in her one-paragraph description of her new suitor. That very night, Hutch began bring-

ing her along to the new immigrant theaters he was discovering
for the paper—German, Italian, Yiddish, Chinese. They'd start
each evening at one of downtown's many small "foreign" restaurants and talk about books and plays and writing.

She explains that their biggest disagreement was over what
she called "life." Hutch, son of a self-made millionaire, was

> lyric about it; he found something interesting and likeable in
> almost every person, his sympathies were unbounded, he was
> open to experience and shut himself off from nothing.

Neith, the sole survivor of five children, thought it "a skin game
in which the dice were stacked against you and you were bound
to lose." She quoted Swinburne, Swift, and Hardy. He shot back
with William Wordsworth and Margaret Fuller ("I accept the
universe"). By spring Hutch was trying to woo her by reading
aloud poetry by Heine, and she was telling him she was too afraid
to love or marry.

As you might expect, her arguments were numerous and well
considered. She worried that a woman might be easily swamped
by the demands of "physical" and family life (by which I presume
she meant sex, pregnancy, and child-care), particularly with a
man like Hutch, who did nothing by halves. When she finally
confided in Mrs. Redding, the editor told her point-blank that
marriage, to Hutch in particular, would destroy her career. "I
hope you won't marry that terribly virile young man," she said.

Mrs. Redding's objection must have weighed heavily on Neith;
more than anything, she worried about her ability to find the time
and energy to write. When Hutch argued that "living in an ivory
tower wasn't the way to produce good stuff," she retorted with the
examples of Jane Austen and Mary Eleanor Wilkins, "presumably
spinsters when they were doing their main work," and even Edith

Wharton, ten years her senior, who was married at the time, but "might be considered to have the brevet rank of spinster, since she had no children."

She was onto something. Austen never married, Wharton didn't fully come into her own as a writer until she'd divorced her husband, and Mary Eleanor Wilkins—a wildly successful fiction writer in her day, who, like Maine's never-married Sarah Orne Jewett before her, often chose spinsters as her subjects—did in fact produce her best work before she married at age fifty.

In an effort to better explain her complicated feelings to Hutch, Neith shared with him one of Wilkins's most famous stories, "A New England Nun," published in 1891. It opens with a woman named Louisa Ellis, who lives alone in a little country cottage, peacefully sewing in her sitting room. At teatime she sets out a spread so lovely, it's as if she's "a veritable guest to her own self"—a beautiful concept, and one that Wilkins expanded on to prove the courage of her character's self-respect: "Louisa used china every day—something which none of her neighbors did. They whispered about it among themselves."

Her betrothed, Joe Dagget, who's been away in Australia the past fourteen years making his fortune, has just returned to claim his bride; they'll be married in a week. His presence is disruptive, to say the least. When the couple sits down at the table, he idly rearranges her books; she puts them back neatly in place. When it's time to leave, he inadvertently knocks her sewing basket to the floor. For his part, "sitting there in her delicately sweet room, he felt as if surrounded by a hedge of lace."

While Joe was halfway across the globe, both Louisa's mother and brother had died, and she'd been very much alone, but she'd come to discover that solitude suited her:

Greatest happening of all—a subtle happening which both were too simple to understand—Louisa's feet had turned into

a path . . . so straight and unswerving that it could only meet a
check at her grave, and so narrow that there was no room for
any one at her side.

By chance, she finds an honorable way to wriggle free from her
commitment to Joe (I won't spoil the story by telling you how),
and though the parting itself is mournful, upon waking the next
morning, "she felt like a queen who, after fearing lest her domain be wrested away from her, sees it firmly insured in her
possession."

The story closes with Louisa sitting alone at the window, gazing "ahead through a long reach of future days strung together
like pearls in a rosary, every one like the others, and all smooth
and flawless and innocent, and her heart went up in thankful-
ness . . . prayerfully numbering her days, like an uncloistered
nun."

When Neith showed the story to Hutch, he gruffly implied
that she herself was something like Louisa, and "what happened
to old New England spinsters was that they went dotty."

But Neith was seriously moved by the story:

If a woman wanted to live in peace and quiet and keep her
house neat, without somebody tracking it up, and wanted to
make preserves and potpourri of rose leaves, and sit by her
window and sew a fine seam, why shouldn't she? There were
always enough who wanted to get married and carry on the
race. . . . If a woman liked to play with words and set them in
patterns and make pictures with them, and was taking care of
herself and bothering nobody, and enjoyed her life without a lot
of bawling children around, why shouldn't she?

Hutch shared an apartment with two friends at The Benedick,
a residence for unmarried men named after the protagonist of

Much Ado About Nothing, also on Washington Square Park (today it's a coed dorm). In the play, the young Lord Benedick carries on "a merry war" with the lovely, witty Beatrice, both of them proclaiming to despise marriage and each other—until their friends trick them into seeing otherwise; the final act is their wedding. By Hutch's time, *benedict* was used to describe a male newlywed, particularly one previously thought to be a confirmed bachelor. In the tradition of the best romantic comedies, both roommates "pronounced Hutch a perfect bachelor and said she [Neith] was ruining him." Even the eternal optimist himself was skeptical. In May 1898 he wrote to his mother:

> There is a girl in N.Y. who has been much more to me than any other girl I ever knew. We are not engaged and it is practically sure that we never shall be. She is a "new woman," ambitious and energetic, a hard worker, more or less disliked by all my friends that know her, and she has no idea of getting married, at any rate to me.

I double-checked the dates. May 1898 was the month Neith's first *Vogue* column appeared. She'd been seeing him the whole time? Was she actually Beatrice to his Benedick?

In the end, Neith's abstract fears proved no match for a man she described as "a warm spring breeze bursting into the room," not only "unreasonable, unexpected, surprising," but also "honorable, kindly," a man who "wanted to make every little dinner that they had together a festival." Her autobiography concludes in 1899, less than a year after her final Bachelor Girl column ran in *Vogue,* on the night she took her place among the "vast majority"—but on her own terms. The marriage to Hutch would be completely egalitarian, as well as "tentative" and not "till death did them part."

The wedding was held in New York on July 22, 1899, at eight o'clock in the evening. The hairdresser had ruined Neith's coiffure; when she left the house, her hair was still damp and heavy beneath her veil. She and her father drove to the church in silence.

Upon arriving, she took her father's arm to walk down the aisle, and "like lightning a scene from the long past flashed back upon her": that moment from childhood when he had led her into the parlor full of small white caskets holding the corpses of her siblings.

We like to pretend that only single people are lonely, and coupledom the cure. The belief dates back to Plato's myth about the first human beings, shaped like spheres, with four hands and legs apiece, and two faces, like something you'd see in a video game. "Whenever they set out to run fast," he wrote, "they thrust out all their eight limbs . . . and spun rapidly, the way gymnasts do cartwheels."

These beings were too powerful and ambitious for the gods to keep around, but too useful to destroy, so eventually Zeus decided to simply slice them in half. "At one stroke they will lose their strength and also become more profitable to us, owing to the increase in number," he explained.

Afterward Apollo helped him turn each strange half-being into a whole, stretching the skin over the body-long gash, giving each a navel, and molding the breasts "using some such tool as shoemakers have for smoothing wrinkles out of leather on the form." The result, Plato concluded, is that "each of us is always seeking the half that matches him," and when this happens, "the two are struck from their senses by love, by a sense of belonging to one another, and by desire, and they don't want to be separated from one another, not even for a moment."

It's doubtful, though. Science tells us that, as with happiness, our predisposition to loneliness is encoded in our genes. Others are born into isolating circumstances that inculcate a propensity for more isolation. And studies have proven that long periods of extreme, unrelenting loneliness actually alter a person's molecular makeup, weakening the immune system.

But every life includes at least some loneliness. Most people merely suffer it like a recurrent pain that can subside for months or years at a time and then blaze up when conditions are just right: moving to a new city where you don't know anyone; staying in a bad marriage; losing someone you love; even just running an errand, when out of nowhere you feel to the core how alone we all are in the world, and it takes everything you've got to not set your basket of groceries on the linoleum and walk out of the supermarket.

Learning that Neith had conjured a funeral while at her own wedding made me wonder if emotional trauma can also strike like a lightning bolt and change every cell in a body, turning a person into a before and after, where before there was garden-variety loneliness, and after is a chronic condition that can be overcome with applied effort but forever alters that person's point of view.

Neith's marriage both did and didn't fulfill the implications of her wedding-night flashback. By nearly any measure she was extremely successful, both as a wife and a writer: Between 1902 and 1910 she had four children—two girls and two boys—and published four books; on the publication of her second novel, *The Folly of Others,* a newspaper critic named her and Edith Wharton "the two most interesting young writers of 1904." In 1908 she helped Gertrude Stein publish her first book, *Three Lives*. In 1915 she banded together with Susan Glaspell and Eugene O'Neill to found the famous Provincetown Players* theater company, for which she wrote and produced her own plays. By 1923 she'd published three more novels, a memoir, and scores of short stories in major magazines. Her themes—among them the need for men and women alike to experience periods of sexual experimentation, and the struggle to retain autonomy in marriage—were progressive and germane at a time of great social upheaval and, as such, found a ready market. With her earnings she bought a farm outside Richmond, New Hampshire.

For all that, Neith didn't write or publish as much as she hoped. Had the couple not left such an extensive written record of their marriage—letters, diaries, obvious depictions in their plays and published books—it would be perfectly reasonable to attribute the roots of her dissatisfaction to the demands of domesticity. In 1911 Hutch's father bought the couple an enormous twenty-room house in Dobbs Ferry, a pastoral town just north of the city, and the family left the Village for good. For the next eleven years, Neith stayed home changing diapers while Hutch traveled around the country reporting for his book and newspaper articles, making a name for himself as an anarchist labor writer.

In truth, however, it was Neith's old *Vogue* editor, Mrs. Redding, who called the score when she warned her not to marry "that virile man." Neith was by no means miserable; she loved her children and her husband, but life with him wasn't easy. Perhaps not surprisingly, he became interested in a form of free love popular among bohemians at the time, called "varietism." Unlike standard-issue polyamory, in which one person shares her/himself

---

* The Provincetown Players get a lot of screen time in Warren Beatty's 1981 film about the period, *Reds*. Neith isn't mentioned at all, but in one scene an unnamed character says something along the lines of, "I know Hutch likes that play."

equally among several partners, varietists engage in multiple re-lationships in order to enhance the primary attachment—in other words, what today is called an open marriage, though at the time there was little precedent.

Make that a one-sided open marriage: Hutch kept the door open for himself, stepping out often, and obsessively urged Neith to, as well. She simply wasn't interested (in a letter to him she described varietism as "crude & unlovely—and besides, it takes all the zest out of sinning!"); she tended to stay home vacillating between genuine indifference and occasional jealousy. Those rare times she did attempt to test the waters, he, evidently, flipped out. In 1908, after she fell in love with his good friend and proposed a ménage à trois, Hutch, furious, grabbed her by the throat. Later that year she suffered a nervous breakdown.

In 1918 their first child, eighteen-year-old Boyce, died in the Spanish influenza pandemic, and in some ways Neith and Hutch never recovered. After publishing his sixth book in 1919, Hutch stopped book-writing for twenty years; in 1939 he published a wanly received memoir of his own cultural displacement, *A Victorian in the Modern World,* and he died five years later, in 1944, at seventy-five. As for Neith, in 1923 she published her last two books—a memoir about Boyce and a novel she'd been working on when he died—and then stopped writing altogether, other than sporadically working on her never-published memoir. In the 1930s she started drinking heavily. For the seven years after Hutch's death she lived with her daughter Beatrix, before dying in Provincetown in 1951, at seventy-nine.

———◀—————

In Carol DeBoer-Langworthy's opinion, the tragic irony of Neith Boyce's life is that her desire to not be trapped by marriage led her into one so untraditional that it became her primary subject, ultimately limiting her career. The scholar Ellen Kay Trimberger believes that both parties "feared the sexual merging of a standard, bourgeois marriage," and that, rather than oppress or drain Neith, Hutch's many infidelities were something of a mutual aphrodisiac.

Both seem very good insights to me, but I'd like to add one more: it wasn't Hutch who was too progressive for his time—that was Neith. Hutch was too conventional.

It took me a while to realize this. Back in 2000, Carol had given me a mimeographed copy of Hutch's out-of-print memoir, *A Story of a Lover,* a deeply personal account of the couple's marital difficulties in 1906–1908 (that famous "seven-year itch"); by then they had three children under the age of five. When the book was published in 1919, it was immediately ruled obscene and all copies were confiscated. A censor-worthy relationship debrief by a sensitive intellectual? Sign me up.

Boy, did I have it coming. Hutch's reflections are so myopically one-sided, so nauseatingly self-important, so righteously certain that his wounded feelings and sexual urges are, in fact, the exact center of the universe, that I began to understand why Neith was perfectly content for him to gad about exhausting other women. (Even the *New York Times* reviewer dismissed it as "the history of the love life of a self-conscious neurasthenic.") Halfway through I gave up.

When I picked it up again ten years later, however, I was able to recognize Hutch's self-centeredness for what it was: a chronic case of culturally sanctioned male entitlement.

The word *feminist* didn't come into popular use until 1913, but both Neith and Hutch believed in and worked for women's rights. Indeed, for them and their compatriots, feminism was integral to the larger project of human freedom in general. Their friend

Floyd Dell's essay "Feminism for Men," published in the popular radical journal *The Masses* in July 1914, is so good that I can't help quoting it at length. Here's how it opens:

> Feminism is going to make it possible for the first time for men to be free.
>
> At present the ordinary man has the choice between being a slave and being a scoundrel.
>
> For the ordinary man is prone to fall in love and marry and have children. . . . He wants to see them all taken care of, since they are unable to take care of themselves.
>
> Yet, if he has them to think about, he is not free. . . . The bravest things will not be done in the world until women do not have to look to men for support. . . . [But] men don't want the freedom that women are thrusting on them. They don't want a chance to be brave. . . . They want to give food and clothes and a little home with lace curtains to some woman.
>
> Men want the sense of power more than they want the sense of freedom. . . . They want someone dependent on them more than they want a comrade. As long as they can be lords in a thirty-dollar flat, they are willing enough to be slaves in the great world outside. . . .
>
> In short, they are afraid that they will cease to be sultans in little monogamic harems. But the world doesn't want sultans. It wants men who can call their souls their own. And that is what feminism is going to do for men—give them back their souls, so that they can risk them fearlessly in the adventure of life.

Hutch believed these sentiments and worked hard for them; intellectually, both he and Neith were radically ahead of their contemporaries, able to think and talk about class and gender relations and analyze their emotional lives at an exceptionally high level. But Victorianism was the air they breathed, and emotionally Hutch was too deeply a man of his time to be able to let go of his selfishness. For all his talk of equality, he was perfectly comfortable putting his career—and sexual proclivities—front and center while Neith stayed home taking care of their children, and then, when she claimed to be too tired for or simply not interested in pursuing her own sexual extracurricular activities, he pouted and sulked, as if, on top of everything else, he was owed this, as well.

For years I believed that because Neith's books had never made a mark, they mustn't be very good, that her *Vogue* column was the most important thing she'd ever published—as a cultural artifact, not literature—and that her life was, therefore, more instructive than her work. Which is to say, it took until very recently for me to get around to reading her books—and what I found there astounded me.

Neith Boyce's novels are not mere curios; they're fascinating examinations of love and marriage through the eyes of a New Woman. My favorite is her third, *The Bond,* published in 1908, about the marriage between Teresa, a sculptress, and Basil, a painter, that is obviously based on Neith's own.

Teresa is an independent woman in her twenties—after getting married, she even keeps her bachelor rooms (which sound suspiciously like Neith's) just in case she needs some time to herself. She's not a suffragist, though her Aunt Sophie—who is herself married but believes all women should be financially independent of their husbands—thinks Teresa's consciousness will eventually awaken. "With your intelligence, you are sure to come 'round to us sooner or later," she says one day. "There's nothing like marriage, too, to make one see clearly the real position of woman. When you do see it, Teresa, you will want to stand up for your sex."

The story travels the ups and downs of Teresa and Basil's relationship, along the way mapping out an argument for and

against marriage. Aunt Sophie is staunchly against the institution (she considers it, on principle, "a hideous state of bondage").
Basil is more moody and Hutch-like. During some gloomy rant he
pronounces monogamy a foolish idea that we all waste an enormous amount of time trying to live up to. "Sex ought to be divorced from emotion," he says. "They don't belong together. We've
sentimentalized the thing till we don't know where we stand." He
thinks women are to blame. "Women naturally sentimentalize
[sex], and we've let them set the tone for our whole society."

Teresa works out her own philosophy during a flirtation with a
handsome young man named Fairfax. He represents the idea that
marriage is an institution necessary to the health of society, and
for raising children, and that "mere personal relations" are a very
small part of it. She disagrees, arguing that one should marry
because common interests and social relations "help the original
relation—they're in the line of its natural growth." That original
relation, the "bond" of the book's title, is her central concern; she
even comes to think that she and Basil might have been happier if
they hadn't had children. Ultimately Teresa realizes that, though
she values her independence, the connection she shares with Basil
is bigger than anything else. "He might be unfaithful," she thinks
to herself,

> but she never could [be]. How strange was that bond, deeper
> than will, deeper than any sympathy of mind, taking no ac-
> count of the many things in him that she deeply disliked. . . .
> It was infinitely more than a physical bond, it was a passion of
> the soul. How strange and how terrible!

The bond's strangeness was what made it all worthwhile. Toward
the book's end, sitting outside beneath the moon, Teresa feels
"with deep pleasure the tumult of the night, and, with something
that was not pain, the tumult, the exciting uncertainty of life."

Marriage today has come a long way from Neith's time, but one aspect that hasn't changed at all is its fantasy of certainty. It's true that the per capita divorce rate has dropped from its all-time peak in 1981 of about 5.3 divorces per 1,000 people—but even so, today nearly half of all marriages end in divorce. It's amazing, really, how deftly we hold in our collective consciousness this disconnect between what we want marriage to be and how so many marriages actually turn out. Freedom is unbearable. We opt again and again for the sugarcoated confinement of matrimony, a promise that life will work out just the way we want it—without that promise, false as it may be, the institution's many encumbrances might be impossible to bear.

I have come to think that one of the main reasons Neith married Hutch is because she suspected that her innate introversion and desire for stability and order would eclipse and distort her fierce autonomy—that, left alone, she actually would, in a sense, become a "dotty spinster," insofar as that means turning away from the world instead of sating her curiosities by living in it; in her case, a romantic partner was an escape hatch back to reality. Too, there was the matter of her being a woman in an oppressively sexist society, and Hutch was not only a chronic extrovert, but also a man: he could open doors to places and people and ideas more readily than she could. For her, then, marriage was a way toward more questions, more uncertainty—whereas for Hutch it was a way of maintaining his traditional male privilege while supplementing it with extracurricular adventuring that he did on his own.

This willingness of Neith's to exist inside the ungraspable strikes me as the bravest stance of all.

———◅█▻———

In August 2001, nearly a year to the day after moving to New York, R came back to the apartment in Brooklyn, where I'd been living with my brother all summer, and we emptied it out, reclaiming what had originally been our own and divvying up our shared possessions—lots of coffee mugs, basically.

As in Neith's time, renting even a studio was beyond my means, but unlike her I didn't have the midway option of a boardinghouse, which struck me as particularly unfortunate, given my indifference to cooking. So, though the last thing I'd ever expected to be doing at twenty-nine was living again with a roommate, there I was, in a convertible one-bedroom just north of Murray Hill, a neighborhood of loud Irish bars frequented by the kinds of frat boys I'd made a point of not knowing in college. But it was within walking distance of school, and the treetops leaned so close to the building that in summer the windows were crowded with bright green leaves. My roommate took the living room for himself and gave me the official bedroom, which had space enough for a big writing desk against one wall, a friend's cast-off IKEA sofa against another, and a bed in between.

My first night there I stayed out at a party until four o'clock in the morning, and when I got off the 6 train at Twenty-Eighth Street an eerily empty yet still-open McDonald's beckoned like an urban mirage. Back on the sidewalk I threw away the bag, peeled off the warm paper wrapping, and bit into the most delicious Big Mac I'd ever eaten. I chomped and strolled as slowly as I could, prolonging the delectable realization that waiting for me at home was nothing but an empty bed into which I'd crawl naked and drunk and stinking of fast food, disgusting nobody but myself.

And so it was that I reverted to my pre-cohabitation housekeeping habits, cooking as infrequently as possible and basically cleaning nothing ever, until the sink was so full of dirty dishes I had no choice but to wash them, thinking contentedly to myself, *Yes. Just a few years like this. Then I'll fall in love again and really settle down.*

5

The Poet

Edna St. Vincent Millay, 1925

A WOMAN AND A MAN ARE SITTING ON A DAYBED IN HER SMALL,
spare apartment near Washington Square. It's late on a winter
night in the 1920s, the early years of Prohibition. Red coals smol-
der on an iron grate, and the orange flames of a gas streetlamp
flicker through the bare window. The quilt's silky garden of pink
and burgundy roses is barely discernible in the shadows.

Abruptly she stands and sets her glass of bootleg gin on the floor. Her long navy dress feels and looks heavy as a nun's habit; in the dark he can't see the way it nips her narrow waist. He wonders if there's a lamp.

She lifts her hands to her throat, and a frill of lace at each wrist frames a face flushed from talk and drink. All down her front is a row of velvet buttons, which she starts to undo.

Her fingers take an eternity. They are as smooth and pale as ivory. One, two, three; finally, her neck is free. Four, five, six; her tender, freckled décolletage can breathe again. Seven, eight, nine, ten, eleven; her dress drops to the floor. Her bare tiny body is cool and luminous in the firelight, copper hair a blaze of tousled curls.

This is the silent motion picture that sprang to mind, fully formed, when I read somewhere that seeing Edna St. Vincent Millay undressed for the first time was a sight from which no man could recover. Soft-focus erotica, early-twentieth-century style.

For weeks I replayed the scene. It was better than being there myself; this way I was both seducer and seduced.

In all my daydreaming about being alone I'd somehow overlooked that in this century being single means "dating," which means having sex with people you don't know very well, which, after years of confining my personal life to long-term relationships, felt alarmingly public, as blatantly on display as the giant half-clothed teenagers pouting from billboards in Times Square.

That anyone who wasn't a prepubescent boy or a turncoat monk could be so enraptured by the sight of a woman undressed—particularly of the small, petite variety—was a tantalizing thought. It even bolstered my ego. Before New York, I hadn't particularly noticed my smallness, but here in this city of tall, angular sylphs it was easy to feel like a short squat sack of flour, a fire hydrant, a tree stump, the clumsy fly that the long, ectomorphic praying mantis eats for lunch.

This is not to say that I was some Little Red Riding Hood about to brave the dark forest of womanhood—besides, I reject the definition of "sexual awakening" as a one-off thing, confined to a finite period in a person's life. By now, thirty years old, I'd had at least seven so-called awakenings: my first explorations with B in high school upstairs in my childhood bedroom; that time, right after B and I broke up, when C rowed us to the middle of the Merrimack River, dropped anchor, and rested my head on a vinyl seat cushion so I could see the black night full of stars as he lowered his head between my legs; the propulsive need to have sex anywhere, anytime, after finally losing my virginity to J my sophomore year of college, before I'd met W (I'd believed my mother when she said teenagers were too young to handle sexual intercourse, and I waited as long as I could), most memorably and often in the backseat of his Volvo station wagon; the headlong, unquenchable rapture of my early years in love with W; nights on the vacant tar roof of L's building in Oregon, dizzy with disbelief over the ingenious ministrations of his thumbs. Each time, I thought sex couldn't get any better, that I couldn't learn anything new, and then someone would come along—another C, this time in Boston, and the candlesticks crashing off the mantel as we careened across his living room and down the hall and into his bedroom—and then R, a whole different world of discovery, this time slow and sensual, and even the sad waning of desire, its own kind of awakening.

It was the duality of the Edna anecdote that entranced me. Surely her suitor was no innocent, but a grown man well versed in free love. He'd reacted, I decided, to the intoxicating contrast between Edna's darkly cloaked inaccessibility and sudden, willful nudity—the quintessence, it seemed, of her own sexuality and that of post-Victorian America itself.

Was something so subtle even possible here in this epoch of coed dorm rooms and group houses, androgynous baggy T-shirts and constant sharing of the bathroom? If I could bottle that blend of circumspection and carnal pleasure, could I break my habit of serial relationships and learn how to be a woman for whom sex and love is a crucial part of life, but not its summation?

When I searched my library, however, I couldn't find a single passage that sounded remotely like the scene that, I was forced to conclude, I'd presumably invented.

You'd be hard-pressed to find another writer in the history of American letters whose physical presence had as profound an impact on men and women alike as Edna St. Vincent Millay's. To know her was to be seduced. It is a rare account, written either during her lifetime or after, that doesn't include a close, even near-erotic description of her petite stark white body (she stood at five feet one inch), flaming red hair, mystifying gray-green eyes, and entrancingly sonorous voice. Picture Natalie Portman crossed with Julianne Moore, but not nearly as pretty as either, as Edna had the power to lure people into believing her gorgeous even though she wasn't, exactly.

In a world that continues to presume that women can either be beautiful or brainy, Edna holds the dubious distinction of being among the first to prove (in the public eye, that is) the two poles reconcilable. Born in 1892—twenty years after Neith, twenty-four years before Maeve—she was blessed with not only uncommon genius but also a fragile prettiness that proved a useful passport. By the time she was coming of age, the popular image of the strong, independent New Woman was being eclipsed by the girlish, superficial Flapper, and her own version of femininity—a radiant amalgamation of desirable and unthreatening—was the perfect midpoint. It was an advantage Edna was happy to use. In the spring of 1912, having just turned twenty, she put the finishing touches on her 214-line poem "Renascence" and submitted it to a prestigious poetry contest, *The Lyric Year*. When the editor, a man, responded with a letter praising her verse, she replied with a photograph of herself. He asked if he could keep it.

Let's just say Edna lost out on the top prize but emerged the true victor. Appearing alongside the winners in a commemorative anthology published that fall, her poem incited a public sensation that biographer Daniel Mark Epstein ranks on par with that of the publication of "The Waste Land" and "Howl": readers fought over the verdict in letters and newspaper columns; the winner deemed himself unworthy and, Epstein reports, "excused himself from the awards banquet."

This was a big deal for anyone, but perhaps especially for a young woman with a hardscrabble background such as hers. Edna's mother, Cora, left her husband in 1900, and filed for divorce a year later, less than two weeks before Edna's ninth birthday. Though broken marriages weren't unheard of by the turn of the century, they remained exceedingly uncommon; between 1870 and 1900 the annual number of divorces went from 11,000 to 55,751, which was still less than 1 percent of the population (compared to 1981, when the country topped out at 1,219,000 of them). The increase was incredibly significant, however, not only in terms of sheer numbers, but because wives empowered by changing property and child custody laws filed the majority of those suits; most women who sought divorce were either those with enough assets who wanted to protect themselves from financial ruin, or those fleeing abusive husbands.

Legal rights didn't translate to social acceptance, however. A woman who filed for divorce was often criticized for not putting aside her girlish dreams of happily ever after and accepting reality for what it is, even if reality meant violence. In those instances when circumstances were felt to have called for divorce—in the eyes of, for instance, temperance-influenced types who supported liberalizing divorce laws so that women would be protected from drunk husbands—the divorcée didn't get another dream, another way to really *want* to live. Being a wife and mother wasn't just plan A; it was the only plan. To live otherwise meant to live without a template, consigned to the margins, discouraged from seeking a new and different happiness.

Edna's father wasn't a bad or violent man, simply a very ineffective and unreliable one. After leaving him, Cora brought her three small girls down to Newburyport, where they bounced between the homes of Cora's siblings before returning to Maine in 1904, when the divorce was finalized. Cora was a fiercely intelligent and hardworking woman who made her living traveling along the coast selling her services as a practical nurse and weaving hairpieces, which required leaving her daughters alone at home in Camden for long stretches. The only house she could afford was in the poor section of town, at the foot of Mount Battie, where the itinerant millworkers lived. According to her biographer Nancy Milford, Edna wrote explicitly about these experiences only once, in a notebook where she describes herself and her sisters, Norma and Kathleen, "flinging themselves against the front door, to close it and bolt it" against the unfamiliar men lurking outside.

Though an excellent student, Edna had no money for college, so after she graduated with honors from Camden High School in 1909, she stayed home for several years writing poems and confiding her dissatisfactions to her journal. In 1911 she started to draft "Renascence," which uses the topography of that little coastal burg—the mountains and bay islands and apple trees—to dramatize one woman's spiritual oppression and mystical rebirth.

What came next is so good as to seem apocryphal. In August 1912, three months after she'd submitted "Renascence" to that *Lyric Year* contest—and three months before the editor's verdict—she attended the end-of-season staff party at Camden's Whitehall Inn, where her sister Norma worked as a waitress. There was dancing and a masquerade competition, and then everyone gathered around the piano to sing. Norma asked her sister to recite "Renascence."

Picture the poet, long, loosened tendrils of hair forming a bronze halo. The room is packed with friends and neighbors, everyone in high spirits, pressing cool glasses of punch against their brows or pulling up a chair to rest for a spell. As Edna's voice rises above the crowd, the excited chatter and clinking glasses hush into a long, unbroken silence, until nothing but her words can be heard in the still, warm night:

The world stands out on either side
No wider than the heart is wide;
Above the world is stretched the sky,—
No higher than the soul is high.

Among the spellbound onlookers was an erstwhile fairy godmother in the shape of a middle-aged woman named Caroline B. Dow. She was so impressed with Edna's talent and presence that she visited her and her mother the following day. As Edna recorded it in her diary: "Miss Dow (Caroline B.) called;—dean of New York Y.W.C.A. Training School. Wealthy friends in New York who might send me to Vassar." All Edna had to do was apply. In September 1913 she was enrolled in the freshman class—still wearing the glitter of a cause célèbre, thanks to the *Lyric Year* fracas.

Four years at an elite, all-women's college fostered Edna's formidable intellectual capacities and provided a testing ground for the romantic swashbuckling to come. She threw herself into campus cultural life, starring in plays, publishing poems, and cultivating her already magnetic personality into a persona that proved irresistible to a captive pool of young women ripe for seduction. (She was a notorious heartbreaker even then.)

In 1917 Edna's first book, *Renascence and Other Poems,* made her the muse and celebrity of Greenwich Village bohemia, and as contemporary fans of her poetry are well aware, she took so effortlessly to the neighborhood's sexual politics, she fast became its emissary. She didn't merely sleep with whomever she wanted, male or female, whenever she wanted, and on her own terms; she also recorded the twists and turns of this avid romanticizing in poems so pleasurable and fun to read that they revolutionized the poetic landscape itself.

In a sense, I'd known Edna nearly my entire life. The first book I ever hid beneath my mattress was her second poetry collection, *A Few Figs from Thistles.* That I swapped it out several years later for the iconic 1950s S&M novel, *Story of O,* and then Anaïs Nin's volume of 1940s erotica, *Little Birds,* doesn't mean what you might think.

I discovered Edna long before I discovered sex, on my parents' bookshelves, during that excruciating phase after I'd finally outgrown temper tantrums and the torture of being forcibly sent to my bedroom, and had instead taken to willingly stomping up there myself, slamming the door, and erupting into storms of tears over how I loved the boy who sat behind me in homeroom so unbearably much that I was going to die and nobody understood and never would and, etc.

When I was four, my father had taught me to read with a volume of classic English children's verse. Our favorite was Christina Rossetti's "Who Has Seen the Wind?" a simple rhyming poem that's almost onomatopoetic in how, with just a few light strokes, it conjures the power of an invisible force:

Who has seen the wind?
Neither I nor you:

But when the leaves hang trembling,
The wind is passing through.

Who has seen the wind?
Neither you nor I:
But when the trees bow down their heads,
The wind is passing by.

Once I'd committed that to memory, the poetry I was taught at school seemed as suffocating as a too-tight turtleneck.

Enter the shock of Edna Millay, circa seventh grade. Her lilting rhythms picked up where Rossetti's left off, catching in my mind like a pop song. It was the passion that grabbed me, or me it—moth to flame, mutually magnetic. Her eroticism lay not in any frank sexual imagery—there is none—but an unabashed intensity of feeling. It was as if, by some astounding witchcraft, she'd taken all the torments of my preteen self—inscrutable lusts and hungers and yearnings—pounded them into iron ribbons, and forged them into cunning little shapes, sparking with em dashes and exclamation points, that I could stand apart from and regard from all angles, gorgeous and manageable, like a smoldering sculpture.

It was this potency, combined with the novelty of seeing exposed the incipient currents of my internal life, that gave me such a fugitive thrill, and made the mere act of holding her book feel deliciously taboo. It wouldn't be long before,

The first rose on my rose-tree
Budded, bloomed, and shattered,

as she put it in an early poem. I had no idea what that meant when I first read it, and I can't even be sure now. But it calls to my mind the moment when, alone in her bedroom, or maybe the bathtub, a girl deciphers her own physical pleasure, and her emotional storms are given another outlet, at which point reading romantic poetry doesn't quite cut it anymore.

And yet somewhere between my actual adolescence and the new developmental category sociologists call "extended adolescence"—which is to say, starting in college—I succumbed to the critical fashion of dismissing her work as second-rate and left her behind.

By the time I moved to New York, eighty-three years after she had, the collegiate idea of what one should and should not read had completely taken hold, and I'd forgotten all about her.

And then sometime that year, 75½ Bedford Street, known as the narrowest house in the city, as well as where Edna Millay had lived in the 1920s, went on the market, inciting a flurry of news interest. One afternoon before class I walked over to see. It's an impossibly tiny brick building, 9 and a half feet wide and 3 stories tall, 999 square feet in all, a wisp of the brownstones it's squeezed between, with two wide casement windows dominating the façade.

If Edna were a building, she would be this one: compact, ingenious, charming, unabashedly baring its interior self. Even the red bricks recall her red hair. (In 2013 it was sold again, for $3.25 million, $3,253 per square foot.)

My delight in her house returned me to her work, and once there I was surprised to find the barnacled hulls and ribbons of eelgrass and thick blankets of fog of my youth. At eleven and twelve, I'd had no idea she'd lived in Newburyport and Camden, Maine, and wouldn't have cared if I did. Our shared New England—"dazzling mud and dingy snow," the unmistakable thunder of "water striking the shore"—were the boring details I'd skimmed across to get to the juicy parts.

But over the next few years, as I acclimated to life sans R and with the addition of a roommate, it comforted me to know she'd come from the same place I had. The only landscape to make my heart both lift and ache is the ocean, and realizing that it had been this way for Edna, too, and that we had both grown up perched on the rocky edge of the continent, gazing out at a vast, choppy vista with sounds and scents as distinct as any animal's, uncomprehendingly deep and cold and wide, yet there to be waded through, swum in, boated across—surely this instilled in us a taste for possibility. To think we'd left our small seaside towns for the same big city!

Even in the boho-friendly Manhattan of the 1910s and '20s, writing was a profession most easily undertaken by those with means. In a 1924 essay, *Poetry*'s editor, Harriet Monroe, ventured "that a certain living lady may perhaps be the greatest woman poet since Sappho." She was kidding, sort of. After narrowing history's roster of important woman poets to Emily Brontë, Elizabeth Barrett Browning, Christina Rossetti, and Emily Dickinson, Monroe argues that Edna stands apart for the way "she has courted life and shunned none of its adventures." The danger, she writes, "has been that life might lure her away from art," and continues:

> The complications of a hunted human soul in these stirring days— the struggle for breath, for food and lodging, the pot-boilers, the flirtations, the teasing petty trials and interruptions—how could the poet in her survive all these, and put out fresh flowers of beauty?

What Monroe understood about the importance of Edna Millay's influence is something that's easily dwarfed by the poet's reputation for sexual promiscuity: she was a self-made woman with an extraordinary work ethic who managed to live by her wits—a rare achievement for either gender.

And so I buoyed myself with her example: *If she could do it, so can I.*

In the spring of 2002 I finished my graduate program and started working from my bedroom/living room/office as a freelance writer. Because I'd started contributing to magazines and newspapers as a graduate student, the transition was seamless enough, save for the fact that reviewing books makes it very easy to never go outside.

Rising rents had pulverized Greenwich Village's communal promises long before I came around; it was a given that those with creative aspirations lived anywhere but downtown Manhattan, whether in Brooklyn, Queens, New Jersey, or at any number of MFA programs scattered across the country, if not in San Francisco or Silicon Valley, where the new breed of so-called creatives were wearing flip-flops and playing Frisbee in boardrooms. (Indeed, the phrase "Greenwich Village isn't what it used to be" was used as early as 1916.)

The challenge my generation of writers faced was more abstract than real estate. By the start of this century, the booming magazine and newspaper industries that brought Neith and Edna into the public sphere had peaked as high as they ever would; those of us who finished college in the mid- to late 1990s spell-checked our résumés just as the mountain began to crumble, when there were still jobs to be had and careers to be made—even if each staff position was the very last.

I picture us en masse, straddling two cliffs—one the trembling pinnacle of "print," the other the pinnacle-shaped fantasia of "digital"—and in between a bottomless pit of insecurity. Petty rivalries and jealousies are elementary to ego-based endeavors; add the higher cost of living, the unchecked professionalization of late-stage capitalism, and you get a Tuesday night "happy hour" of desperate careerists in pressed button-down shirts and blazers, sipping sponsored cocktails from little plastic cups and breaking you off mid-sentence because there's someone with a bigger byline, or an editor he's trying to impress, just over your shoulder, across the room. You don't mind, exactly. It's ten o'clock already, and you've got to wake up early the next morning to meet a deadline for an online magazine that barely pays, but at least it's something.

And so during the day I'd sit at my desk and speed-read and take notes; at night I'd circulate among dinner parties at the homes of graduate-school friends and coast the ever-rotating publicity wheel of book launches and readings, where everyone was a potential employer or, increasingly, a guy I'd gone on a date with.

I'd been surprised to discover that the retrograde practice of "dating" was standard protocol, even though its implicit rules (boys pay; girls don't go all the way) had nothing to do with new social and sexual norms.

In college we'd roamed in loose herds from dining hall to coffeehouse to dorm room. Only rarely did we splinter away to actual off-campus restaurants, in which case the couple would split the bill. I wouldn't have been offended if my boyfriend had offered to pay—it just would have felt unbelievably weird. Here in the city it was actually expected that a man would ask, the woman would accept, and the man would pay, no question.

Occasionally an invitation entailed a movie or museum exhibit, but most often it was dinner or drinks, or more likely drinks, then dinner, then more drinks, whole evenings afloat on a river of vodka, a bottle (or two) of wine—which, by the way, I did not object to in the slightest. Dates were a luxurious relief from the grind of my everyday. A bistro's theater of decorousness, with its snowy white napkins and courteous waiters, and afterward, the degenerate bliss of a dimly lit bar, the clink of ice against glass, the soft gasp of a popped cork, the airy sensation of stepping back out into a night blurred at the edges with boozy wonderfulness . . . oh, how I loved it.

For the first time I felt like an actual person who lives in the world and could carry on a conversation with another adult about something other than the minutiae of what I did that day and whose turn it was to get the groceries. Coupling, I realized, can encourage a fairly static way of being, with each partner exaggerating or repressing certain qualities in relation to the other's. Along with meeting new people I was discovering a new self.

In the beginning I insisted on paying my half on principle and out of habit, until I realized that doing so sent the wrong message, no matter what I said. Apparently paying for dinner was how a man signaled his motives, proving to me—and himself—that he considered this "more" than a hookup. By accepting his offer I was showing that I understood.

As intended, playing by the rules left little room for ambiguity. I'm not proud to admit that more than a few times I went ahead and had sex with someone out of an obligatory sense of quid pro quo, even a confused sense of etiquette. Sometimes it was just less awkward to go with it. Perversely, even these baldly compromised transactions intrigued me, simply for being something I hadn't experienced before.

Generally, after three dates one of three things took place: 1) he'd express his lack of interest with a silent fade-out that made me go insane with anxiety; 2) I'd express my lack of interest with an overlong and tortured "it's not you, it's me" e-mail; 3) we'd devolve into a sexual entanglement that either was or wasn't physically satisfying but invariably thrived on noncommunication. After a while it seemed that everyone I knew was tangled in several entanglements at a time, as if we were all becoming intertwined, like a giant rat king, our tails a knotted mass, our mouths gasping for air.

Eventually I met a man at a lecture, and something clicked. He was ten years older, an art history professor so opaque and emotionally unavailable he might as well have been married, though he wasn't. Where R had been open and soulful, his emotions rushing forth through his eyes, every part of him leaning in to invite and comfort, T was intensely private, and interested solely in seduction, the achievement of which made his face close like a vault. But he was brilliant and courtly and subtle, with strong hands and a powerful torso that put me in mind of the Minotaur. The first time I went to his apartment, we started to kiss the moment he opened the door, then backed into a wall and slid to the floor. After that there was no going back. Every week or two he'd take me out to dinner at some restaurant I never could have afforded, where we'd talk about all kinds of things—his mind was so different from mine; I loved our conversations—then bring me back to his place in a cab; in the morning, before he woke up, I'd slip out of his bed and into my clothes and walk the thirty or so blocks through the just-stirring city to my apartment, euphoric.

To not be someone's girlfriend, to have excellent sex on a semi-regular basis without any of the obligations and expectations of being in an exclusive relationship—I couldn't get enough of it. Days would pass without our speaking or e-mailing, an oasis of solitude, and then his name would pop up in my in-box, and my pulse would race as we set our next date. The day of, concentrating on work was impossible; the simple acts of bathing and getting dressed took on ritualistic importance. By the time I was walking to the subway to meet him my self had vanished. I was all body, only body; indeed, nothing in my adult life had distilled me so thoroughly to pure physicality—it was like the days of track meets in high school, how I could focus only on the half-mile race to come that afternoon, and then the sickening thrill of the starting line, the entire universe narrowed to my single lane, the loud bark of the gun, the exhilaration of sprinting with and then through and then past a pack of girls, rounding the final bend, pounding down the finishing stretch, empty of everything but muscle and sinew and breath.

Obviously, this couldn't last.

And yet it did. And as the weeks and then months spun past we stuck like a song on repeat, never growing closer, never breaking off, and I began to grow uneasy. What *was* this? I'd been looking for romance without commitment, and now that I had it, I fell down a rabbit hole of semantics, anxious to define and control the experience with a word.

Though we went on dates this wasn't "dating," which implies a mutually agreed upon sense of forward momentum, yet surely two people couldn't just "hook up" for this long, and, anyway, our dates had the high tenor of "assignations," a term I rejected on account of neither of us being married or otherwise committed, though it did make me realize that there's no masculine version of "mistress," seeing that "lover" is gender-neutral and for some reason has fallen out of use, which saddened me; I liked how the word suggests there might be others in the mix, cloaking its user in a mysterious indefinability, the exact opposite of those rigid designations "girlfriend" and "boyfriend" and "wife" and "husband," which carry the associative weight of specific expectations and behaviors, and make everyone involved seem boringly transparent, even though, of course, they're not.

After a while, some of my friends started to say that he was "using" me, but I rejected that, too, on account of being too pat, too self-help; I was an equal player in this scenario, and who's to say I wasn't "using" him, even if for reasons I couldn't understand? Either way, a relationship based exclusively on dinner and sex was beginning to feel perilously like a business deal, one step from prostitution. One night, after too much wine, I made the cab stop and clambered out, announcing, "You know, I'm not your concubine!" He pulled me back in.

I wasn't proud of our "situation," as I came to think of it, and it didn't make me remotely happy in any rational or traditional sense, and yet I loved it absolutely, for how free I felt, and alive. The novelty and unpredictability were addictive; I grew increasingly disembodied, or maybe only-bodied is more accurate, retreating ever further into a counterintuitive sexual solipsism—counterintuitive in that, practically speaking, my involvements were multiplying. In between our dates I went on other dates, with other men.

Only now are we beginning to understand how profoundly the decoupling of sex from marriage has shaped modern courtship and the family. By the time I entered the fray, what seemed more immediately pressing was the decoupling of sex from emotion. Compared with Edna's all-in, no-holds-barred philandering, mine felt oddly . . . prophylactic.

Granted, my proclivities skewed my findings. At last, I was sustaining a life more wild, and less bounded, than the one I'd known again and again through serial monogamy, but—paradoxically—in my quest to not be "tied down," rather than open the door to all comers, I'd unconsciously altered my very chemistry: where once I'd gone for emotionally available men, I was now irresistibly drawn to the noncommittal, who had no interest in making me their girlfriend.

With them I felt bracingly invisible, objectified, absent, as if I could be anyone I wanted, no matter that my reinventions were almost comically modest and legible only to myself; for someone like me, who'd always remained within her fixed identity, the smallest alteration was an adventure. The type of man who (un-suspectingly) helped make this happen certainly wasn't in short supply, and they seemed to pride themselves on this quality, as if evasiveness were evidence of manliness.

What bothered me was the assumption that because I was a woman in her early thirties, I must be "desperate" for marriage. At first this seemed only irritating; every romantic encounter arrived in the same cumbersome frame I had to repeatedly disman-tle. But after a while, the fixedness of this belief felt not merely claustrophobic and repetitive but downright pernicious. Figuring out how you feel about another person is a notoriously complicated business. The ubiquity of received attitudes about what men and women did and did not want seemed to relieve everyone of the responsibility to actually examine their desires, leading to some pretty bizarre behavior.

One stifling August, a man I'd been only casually involved with—we hadn't even had sex—asked me to meet him for a drink. He was a good-looking lawyer with a dry wit, and we had an odd, sweet relationship; every so often he'd take me out for a romantic dinner, hold my hand as he walked me home, kiss me good-bye at my doorstep, and more often than not, not come in. We obvi-ously enjoyed our time together, but something fundamental was missing.

On this particular evening he surprised me with a most Vic-torian proposal: if I married him, he could offer me the financial stability I'd obviously never find as a writer, along with a brown-stone in the West Village and a country house in Connecticut. He hadn't bought them yet, he explained; we could choose them together.

We were sitting at a little round café table that wobbled when I set down my drink. I was speechless. Where had this come from? Clearly I liked him, but what had made him think we had a future together?

Having no idea how to respond, I said, weakly, that I'd think about it and get back to him.

I relay this anecdote not to convince you of my desirability, or even to point to the obvious fact that, contrary to popular belief, plenty of men are looking for committed relationships, but to show how the script's omnipresence convinces otherwise very intelligent, sensitive people to ignore their own complexity. Obviously this man wasn't in love with me, but regarded me primarily as an idea, even a solution—providing me with a fascinating glimpse into the fun-house mirror of my generation's gender politics. When men complained that women were looking only for commitment or marriage, I now understood what it was like to be sitting across from someone who considered me interchangeable with anyone else willing to fulfill the job description.

It was all very confusing. Between my hamster wheel of dates and my confounding "situation," I was elated and miserable simultaneously, laughing in the morning, crying by afternoon. Mistakes and pitfalls and longing and lust and, above all, liberty—at long last I had what I'd asked for, even if I was operating with half the grace of Edna Millay, or a quarter of it, come to think of it, which I started to do, more and more, and the more I thought about it, the more I came to suspect that she'd gotten a lot more out of this romantic adventuring than I seemed to be, and not only because it was radical in her day and clichéd by mine.

Historians know very little about what *really* went on in nineteenth-century bedrooms, but crucial to public mores was the belief that women weren't sexual creatures. When the pioneering sexologist Katharine Bement Davis, a Victorian herself, conducted America's first significant survey of women's sexual practices, she found that fully one-quarter of the one thousand married women she polled (most born before 1890, just two years before Edna) claimed to be "repelled" by their initial sexual experience, and those who admitted enjoying it were ashamed of their "immoderate" passion—attitudes that, of course, were merely public censure turned inward.

The combined efforts of Neith and her fellow radicals, along with the tireless (and thankless) work of social reformers like Margaret Sanger and Victoria Woodhull, ensured that the bulk of the sexual repression and gender segregation they'd grown up with remained locked in the nineteenth century. By the 1910s, Freud's theories of the inner life began to percolate, men and women were mingling in public places, and even the taboo subject of prostitution had become "the chief topic of polite conversation," according to an opinion magazine that declared 1913 to be "Sex O'Clock in America." The following year, the term "date" (complete with quotation marks) appeared for the first time in a mainstream publication, lending this racy new pastime a veneer of social respectability. In 1916, the first birth control clinic opened for business, and in 1920 women finally got the vote. By the 1920s, culture had been flipped on its head: now experts were diagnosing women who didn't like sex as unhealthy, and arguing that a mutually satisfying sex life was vital to a good marriage.

The discourse *sounded* different, but in many ways all this talk maintained and even promoted standard ideologies and conventions. Marriage remained the default container of sex and romance, gender roles were still fixed (women may have "natural" desire, but it is latent and depends on men to take initiative), and though it was now acceptable for women to claim pleasure, this was largely a result of separating it from its associations with prostitution (or bohemia). The result was a specifically middle-class sexuality, which became the new normative; putting the sex back into marriage, so to speak, but also putting marriage back into sex—a marked contrast from Edna Millay's verses.

When Edna wrote—"And if I loved you Wednesday, / Well what is that to you? / I do not love you Thursday— / So much is true"—she wasn't playing around. She had so many lovers that she hardly took the time to differentiate them in her poems, much to the disgruntlement of her conquests, who'd hoped for at least a compensatory brush with immortality.

"I've been a wicked girl," she confides in "The Penitent," in which she tries to muster up guilt for some unnamed "little Sin," fails, and finally concludes, "if I can't be sorry, why, / I might as well be glad!"

Her untouchability wasn't a pose. She kept a close watch on her heart, tracking its every surge and plunge, until her deeply felt subjectivity was her most powerful creative instrument. She was fearless with it, tripping up and down the tonal scales to reflect the slightest fluctuation in her mood—defiant, wistful, exuberant, indifferent. And, as I was coming to learn myself, spending a significant stretch of time in and out of relationships is a moody business.

In 1923, when she was thirty-one, Edna won the Pulitzer Prize for Poetry and started traveling around the country giving readings to packed auditoriums. Nancy Milford recounts how, for her audiences, whatever line may have existed between her life and her art was completely obscured by these performances. Onstage she appeared an astonishing creature, a real live New Yorker and honest-to-God poetess who looked and played the part: loose velvet robes dwarfed her diminutive frame, making her resonant voice with its clipped consonants and plummy vowels seem all the more dramatic in comparison. By then she'd adopted the Flapper look and was bobbing her hair; after her visit to Coe College in Cedar Rapids, Iowa, the campus newspaper noted that the percentage of bobbed hairstyles among students shot up from 9 percent to 63 percent.

When we "invented" adolescence as a sociological and developmental category in the 1950s, we robbed it of dignity, turning teenagers into a faceless mob of deranged hormones. In fact, it's a noble and brave and terrible time, and to be able to speak to that angst is what makes rock stars our heroes—and that's the other line on Edna, of course, that she was her era's version of a rock star; before there was Beyoncé to compare her to, contemporary critics called on Courtney Love. But when people talk that way, they're talking about her popularity. I'd like it to be said that she was a rock star in the truest sense: she went to the barricades for teenagers.

The rising generation of women just beginning to flex their own personal agency needed exactly such a voice, and her use of familiar, traditional forms—she was partial to rhyming couplets and the sonnet—helped deliver her radical version of female independence to a readership newly ready to receive it.

But was I? By the early 2000s, the audacity Edna pioneered had calcified into convention; the city was home to a yoga-toned army skilled in the arts of indifference and blow jobs—neoflappers, or so they seemed to me—and already I doubted my ability to cultivate the insouciance casual sex seemed to require. Maybe I was drawn to noncommittal types because maintaining a fulfilling sexual relationship that didn't consume my existence was so inconceivable, there was no point in my even trying, so I made do with half measures.

And so I wondered: What was Edna's secret? Did her mastery over her heart mean she could slam it shut whenever she felt like it? Was the self-help phenomenon du jour, *Why Men Love Bitches,* actually onto something? Did a woman need to be manipulative and demanding to pilot the shoals of sex and love?

If she could do it, so can I.

Now the question became: How *had* she done it?

Were it not for Edmund Wilson, I might never have found the answer.

It's often said that the best piece of writing about Edna Millay is the essay Wilson wrote about her in 1952, two years after her death. As with Neith Boyce's novels, though, I kept putting off reading it, thinking the reminiscences of a spurned suitor (she'd rejected his marriage proposal when they were in their twenties) would lack objectivity. Too, men from that period can sound so plummy and fatuous when they talk about women, so I was preemptively annoyed. But when I finally sat down and read the essay, I realized I'd underestimated him, which was rather short-sighted of me, given his stature in American letters.

The essay appears in his collection about the 1920s and '30s, *The Shores of Light*. He borrowed the book's title from the last line of an unpublished poem he'd written about Edna in 1922, when he'd been reading Virgil's *Georgics* and had become entranced with the phrase, which sounds even lovelier in its original Latin: *In luminis oras.*

He'd first laid eyes on her in 1920, at a party in New York, when someone persuaded her to recite her poems (the art of recitation was clearly hers). As Wilson remembers:

> She was dressed in some bright batik, and her face lit up with a flush that seemed to burn also in the bronze reflections of her not yet bobbed reddish hair. She was one of those women whose features are not perfect and who in their moments of dimness may not seem even pretty, but who, excited by the blood or the spirit, become almost supernaturally beautiful. She was small, but her figure was full, though she did not appear plump. She had a lovely and very long throat that gave her the look of a muse, and her reading of her poetry was thrilling.

What had I been thinking? It's hard not to like a man who sees a woman's beauty in her spirit, not the perfection of her face.

At this point she was living with her sisters and mother at the rather down-at-heels end of West Nineteenth Street, very close to the Hudson River. Wilson, who was an editor at *Vanity Fair,* had the very good idea to cultivate her friendship by publishing her poems in the magazine. In the doing, he fell "irretrievably in love," which, he says, was "inevitable, a consequence of knowing her in those days."

He recounts the time he brought her to see Bernard Shaw's newest play, *Heartbreak House,* which had just opened in New York. It was the fall of 1920, the very beginning of their friendship, and as they watched the performance, Wilson was surprised to see how immediately and completely she became absorbed by the play—perhaps this was the first time the critic had witnessed this poet's capacity to loose herself from her own subjectivity.

Toward the end of Act II he became aware that Edna had grown very tense. The characters have gathered in the drawing room of an English country house after dinner, when one of them, the callous beauty Ariadne, begins to taunt Randall, her husband's brother, who is hopelessly besotted with her and has been for a very long time.

"I get my whole life messed up with people falling in love with me," Ariadne complains, then continues to insult and harass Randall until he's reduced to tears, at which point she stands over him and scoffs, "Crybaby!"

When the curtain went down, Edna turned to Wilson and said, "I hate women who do that, you know." He goes on to muse:

> She must have had, in the course of those crowded years, a good many Randalls on her hands, but her method of dealing with them was different from that of Bernard Shaw's aggres-

sive Ariadne. She was capable of being mockingly or sternly sharp with an admirer who proved a nuisance, but she did not like to torture people or to play them off against one another. With the dignity of her genius went, not, as is sometimes the case, a coldness or a hatefulness or a touchiness in intimate human relations, but an invincible magnanimity, and the effects of her transitory feminine malice would be cancelled by an impartiality which was amiably humorous or sympathetic.

Putting aside his sexist notion of "transitory feminine malice," this reads to me as an admirably nuanced description of a ruthlessly discerning woman who could also be kind—the two qualities needn't be antithetical.

By the end of 1920, when she was twenty-eight, thanks to the high rates paid by *Vanity Fair,* Edna had enough money to move into her own apartment for the first time, two rooms and a bath on West Twelfth Street, near Washington Square Park—which had the unintended outcome of making her even more accessible to her suitors. She didn't want to marry any of them, and yet, as she told Wilson in a moment of crisis, "I'll be thirty in a minute!"

(This cracked me up: thirty had been my "deadline," as well.)

As he puts it, rather grandly, "It was decided she should go abroad."

He had reason to be grand; *Vanity Fair* would fund her travels in Europe in exchange for—I did not see this coming—satirical essays. As in, America's most famous poet, already known for her uncommon brilliance, two years shy of winning a Pulitzer, wrote silly little humor pieces for a glossy magazine. The thought would never have occurred to me.

Understandably, the publisher begged her to use her own famous byline, but Edna, as ever keenly protective of her reputation, insisted on using a pen name, Nancy Boyd (her great-grandmother's). On January 4, 1921, she sailed for Paris.

In 1924 the twenty-two pieces "Nancy Boyd" published over the span of two years were published as a book, *Distressing Dialogues,* which, though now out of print, I easily found online. The preface is written and signed by Edna St. Vincent Millay, with a dateline from Tokyo:

> Miss Boyd has asked me to write a preface to these dialogues, with which, having followed them eagerly as they appeared from time to time in the pages of *Vanity Fair,* I was already familiar. I am no friend of prefaces, but if there must be one to this book, it should come from me, who was its author's earliest admirer. I take pleasure in recommending to the public these excellent small satires, from the pen of one in whose work I have a never-failing interest and delight.

The pieces veer from droll to outrageous and made me laugh out loud. One of the earliest, "The Implacable Aphrodite," from *Vanity Fair*'s March 1921 issue, reads like a thinly veiled fictionalization of yet another encounter with what Wilson called her "good many Randalls," if not Wilson himself.

The story opens with Mr. White, "a man of parts, but badly assembled," telling the "graceful sculptress," Miss Black, that she is the most interesting unmarried woman of his acquaintance. They are in her studio, where she is serving him tea.

She says, "Oh, yes?" (while "languidly flicking an ash from a cigarette-holder the approximate length of a fencing-foil").

"Oh, if you only knew what a relief you are, what a rest!—a woman who is not married, who has never been married, and who does not insist that I marry her," he says.

"I know. But I am sorry for them," she says, with genuine sympathy. "That I am different from these women is through no virtue of my own, but only because I am blessed with a talent which releases my spirit into other channels. Whether that talent be great or small is of no consequence. It is sufficient to ease my need."

While Miss Black silently muses on the topic, Mr. White notices for the first time "the clutter of statuary about the studio." Rather than compliment the artist on her work, he asks after the identity of the model, who is clearly quite attractive. Miss Black confesses that it is herself. He adjusts his tie.

She continues their conversation. "In fact, you are the only man in my acquaintance, unmarried or married, who does not importune me with undesirable attentions."

He starts to breathe heavily, listing her many, many charms.

Oblivious, she ingeniously concedes that she is "besieged by suitors" who ring her bell all the livelong day, dropping to their knees and giving her their hearts.

Her heart, she jokes, belongs to her tea, that "accomplice of spinsterhood." She laughs: "If it will help me to remain a spinster, then it is my staunchest ally!"

As she companionably slices a lemon (with a dagger) and wields her sugar tongs (made from the hind claws of a venomous lizard), she mentions that she's soon to set sail for Europe, for her art—and all hell breaks loose.

He stutters. He groans. He shouts. He scoffs. He mocks her "putty figures." He drops to his knees and proposes marriage. He accuses her: "You're enjoying this!"

"No, really," she says. "I assure you—I am frightfully distressed—I had no idea you felt like this—I—"

Growling, "he yanks open the door and leaps forth, slamming it behind him."

Left alone, she pours herself a cup of cold tea and runs her fingers through her hair.

"Oh, dear, I *wish* I were not so restless!"

I've enjoyed so many of Edna's books over the course of my

life, but not until I read these tossed-off pieces—and one gets the sense, reading them, that they came to her very easily—did I feel I was getting a glimpse of the everyday self behind the poet's persona. "The Implacable Aphrodite" sits at the midway point between the saucy, game-playing version of urban love she sold through her early poems, and the deep, soulful passion of her later sonnets, revealing a woman who took herself seriously but was always up for a lark, and whose respect for herself extended to others.

Edna Millay wasn't merely an exemplar of "free love" in her own time; the long reach of her presumed prowess extends to this new millennium. In 2009, the cultural critic Cristina Nehring published a spirited defense of reckless romance, *A Vindication of Love,* featuring Edna as an ideal we'd all be wise to live up to.

Nehring's overarching argument—that contemporary love is a gutless affair, drained of lust and transgression by an over-age of political correctness—is, as I found, depressingly relevant. As is her excellent point that, after her death, Edna's literary achievement was eclipsed by a puritanical and sexist backlash to her sexual adventuring; her poetry, Nehring writes, "so recently regarded as masterful and wry—was dismissed as lightweight and frivolous—as inconsequential as its pretty, primping, sexually overactive author." Ah—so this is why after adoring Edna in middle and high school I'd jilted her in college.

But was Edna really a "queen bee," who, "by keeping her boys on alert . . . kept the decibel of her relationships at a crescendo," as Nehring claims? And is such behavior actually something to aspire toward? She describes the poet's life as "fiery and wasteful, gorgeous, dangerous, brief," as if her famous "First Fig,"

My candle burns at both ends;
It will not last the night;
But ah, my foes, and oh, my friends—
It gives a lovely light!

were her actual, lifelong credo, rather than an artifact of her youth.

Obviously Edna broke hearts. As Nancy Milford recounts, her more literary-inclined victims—John Peale Bishop, Floyd Dell, Edmund Wilson—were prolific with their dismay. "They wrote to her about their desperate hurt and anger," she writes, "they waylaid her on the street. To a man they felt that her leaving them meant far more about her inability to be faithful than it did about their need to secure her exclusively for themselves." Milford goes on:

> They talked about her chagrin, even when it was clearly their own; they talked about her promiscuity and her puzzling magnanimity. They failed to acknowledge the pull she felt between the excitement and energy of her sexual life, where she was a sort of brigand who relished the chase, and the difficult, sweet pleasures of her work.

Edna was no saint, but nor was she a "fiery and wasteful" person—she was a very scrupulous one bravely making her way, with great integrity, across an earthquake as it cracked beneath her feet.

Edna's generation came of age in a world poles apart from the one previous. As her own mother speculated in her diary in 1922, the year Edna turned thirty, "I wonder if the real difference between us is that the added generation has given her a courage I never had, to be honest, even with myself."

But at least one habit survived this outpouring of transparency: infidelity. Every so-called civilized culture safeguards against extramarital sex in some manner, leaving its citizens to contrive—and collude in—unspoken runarounds. In the case of Victorian America, pleasure-seekers relied on two fixes: flat-out secrecy, where only the conspiring adulterers knew the truth, which of course heightened the thrill; and an unspoken "boys will be boys" agreement to look the other way when a man stepped out on his wife, as long as he was an otherwise meticulous observer of convention. (There was also the opinion of Neith's husband, who explained at one of chatelaine Mabel Dodge's popular literary salons that "men are the victims" in the battle between the sexes, because, lacking the vitality of the working classes, and of women, they are forced to resort to infidelity. "The problem," he said, "is how to get the heat without the lie.") As the historian Peter Gay puts it in his masterful, multivolume study of the period, "What contemporary moralists were all too quick to call 'hypocrisy' was actually a way of carving out space for the passions—within reason."

Crucial to Edna's autonomy was honesty. By all accounts she didn't go in for sneaking around, preferring to focus on one lover at a time, even if just for one night. To the recipient, her refusal to pretend to feel something she didn't, or to behave the way they might have wanted or expected, surely felt coldhearted. In fact it was the opposite: remaining responsive to her own passions required an exceptional level of emotional vulnerability.

In a world that still takes for granted that "respectable" people either repress their emotions or flat-out lie about them, her insistent truthfulness was just as radical as her sexual adventuring, possibly even more so. After all, what was called "free love" then is merely a lot like the "casual sex" of our day, and, even now, at a time when marriage is optional, people continue to cheat on their partners, married or not.

Running like a current beneath all those allegedly sexless

nineteenth-century marriages (if not actually propping them up) had been an intensity and freedom of expression around same-sex friendship that we postmoderns can hardly begin to imagine. Men held hands or linked arms as they walked down the street; soldiers embraced one another to give comfort or solace. Adolescent girls cultivated passionate attachments that served as trial runs for the "real" relationship they'd someday have with a husband, writing love letters sodden with endearments, snuggling and sleeping in the same bed, often engaging in heavy petting, a practice regarded as so harmless that people rarely thought to mention it, leaving historians to puzzle out who was technically a lesbian and who wasn't—which, as the century wound up, and our fixation on slotting people into categories of sexual preference took hold, became increasingly important. It's as if, rather than make a grand prison break from the myth of female sexlessness, where a woman was either an angel or a whore, we simply replaced one set of classifications with another, locking our emotional selves into two new but equally rigid categories: homosexual or heterosexual. And, of course, only one of these two categories was acceptable.

"Oh, you mean I am a homosexual! Of course I am, and heterosexual, too, but what's that got to do with my headache?" Edna ostensibly quipped to a doctor.

A deep regard for the ungovernable had always been central to her character. From the start she intuited that what's interesting about our day-to-day existence resides beyond the boundaries we use to hem it in; indeed, that those boundaries don't merely manage our unruly wants but can choke them off until each of us is a law-abiding, cold-blooded carapace, or a liar. As she became an adult, whether by intention or instinct, she simply neglected to put her desires on a shelf, and she kept living as she always had, which is to say fully, and without deference to convention. This embrace of possibility, and willingness to improvise rather than "nail down" a life, discomfits and disrupts now as much as it did then.

Valorizing the very mythology that posthumously tarnished Edna Millay's literary reputation serves another kind of twenty-first-century pedagogy, one that says women should be chasing the sexual revolution's "zipless fuck," as Erica Jong so memorably put it in 1973, and "have sex like a man" as Samantha argued twenty-five years later in the pilot episode of *Sex and the City*—i.e., selfishly, callously, without emotional investment.

For contemporary women to take from Edna the lesson that sexual liberation means manipulating people to your own advantage, and leaving your heart at home, is to miss the point entirely. Transport Edna to our own era, and she's a lot like the rest of us—a woman who wanted to enjoy her youth as long as she could, and not settle for boring married sex, not right away, at least—with one crucial difference: How many of us today are able to unlace our contemporary corsetry of received attitudes?

Edna wasn't the didactic type, but had she been, I suspect she'd have told us that if there is a point to all of this, it's to take life very, very seriously, and to love whomever you want, as abundantly as you can. Her legacy wasn't recklessness, but a fierce individualism that even now evades our grasp.

So it comes as some surprise that Edna's salad days as an unfettered urbanite were relatively short: six years in all (including the nearly two spent abroad). In January 1923, a month before her thirty-first birthday, she sailed back to America; in April she took up with Eugen Jan Boissevain, a Dutch importer twelve years her senior who'd become part of the Greenwich Village scene; later that month her Pulitzer Prize was announced; by May the new couple was living together; on July 18 they married in a small backyard ceremony. The following afternoon, five New York newspapers announced the news, three on the front page, one with the headline "Famous Love Lyricist Belies Her Own Philosophy by Marrying"—surely capturing the sentiments of more than a few disappointed fans.

But not this fan, or not too much, at least. I can't claim to know why she married, but by now I can hazard a very good guess. Eugen was by all accounts a wonderful, big-hearted man, a self-described feminist who was an enthusiastic helpmate to his legendary wife and contentedly took on all the domestic chores so that she could write. Their open marriage ensured that she could continue to indulge her most enduring muse, her heart, without resorting to secrecy; indeed, her acclaimed 1931 sonnet collection, *Fatal Interview,* was inspired by her long-term love affair with a much-younger poet, George Dillon, which Eugen encouraged; for a while they even lived together as a ménage à trois.

Which is to say that in marrying, Edna did what she knew to be best for herself and her work: she created a new family. As Wilson went to great pains to explain, Edna's "overmastering passion" was her poetry. The life of the mind, he wrote, ferried her away from her "rather cramped" girlhood, and throughout her life remained "the great reality that made everything else unimportant"—everything, he says, except her mother and her sisters.

For nearly the entire time she lived in Greenwich Village Edna shared an apartment with at least one of her sisters, often both, plus their mother, and when the women were apart they constantly wrote uninhibited, confessional letters full of in-jokes and pet names. She helped to support them even when she was just starting out, and she was incredibly generous the wealthier she became. The four women were not without their rivalries and grudges—what close relationships are? Later in life, Edna even grew estranged from Kathleen. But central to her sense of self was this cocoon of unquestioned loyalty and affection; wherever she went in the world, it was her anchor and protection.

Being single can be, and often is, exhausting, even for those of us who aren't composing a life quite so publicly, or dramatically. Edna's romantic exploits in Europe were thrilling, but not having the actual, physical haven of her family to return to at night took its toll. A love affair with a married journalist ended badly. Toward the end of her first year abroad she was left with only fifty-three dollars, in six different currencies, and was in debt to a variety of friends. She got pregnant, forced a miscarriage, and nearly married a "pseudo-aristocrat . . . suave [and] oily," as a friend described him. When Wilson visited Edna in Paris, she told him that she "wanted to settle down to a new life: she was tired of breaking hearts and spreading havoc." When she returned to America, both her sisters were married and living with their husbands, and her mother was back living with her own sisters in New England.

All this time, Edna had been free to risk her heart, and be the impassioned single woman she was, because she was so secure in the love of her mother and siblings. Winning the Pulitzer Prize was not only a great honor, but also a lesson, if not something of a warning: in order to retain the love of her public, she had to keep on dipping and dipping into this well of passion that fueled her work.

A blueprint of Steepletop,* the seven-hundred-acre blueberry farm Edna and Eugen bought in Austerlitz, New York, could double as a template for their life together. Equal parts work space, sanctuary, and pleasure dome, its only concession to compromise is the location. Edna had wanted to buy property on the Maine

---

* Edna and Eugen named the estate after the delicate pink flowering steeple-bush, a native shrub that grew profusely on the property. After Edna died, she was laid in a coffin holding a steeplebush blossom.

coast, but Eugen convinced her that her career required proximity to Manhattan, a dilemma they neatly resolved by importing to Steepletop ground cover and white pine trees from Maine to mingle with the native blueberry bushes. In the midst of this transplanted terrain they built a tiny cabin at the end of a stone path, where she wrote four to five hours a day, six days a week.

The house itself—today it's open to the public—is big, at thirteen rooms, but it exudes a homey New England modesty, tasteful but never showy, as familiar to me as my own youth. Upstairs they each had their own private wing. Edna's was a writer's dream (this writer's, at least): a bedroom with a fireplace overlooking the kitchen gardens Eugen faithfully tended; an enormous white-tiled bathroom (the first tiled bath in the county); a workroom—this is the heart of the house—with a long table for spreading out papers when it was time to ready her books for publication; a cozy library with an armchair for reading and a little nook for naps.

Just as crucial to their mutual well-being as shared solitude was the company of their friends. Downstairs, the couple entertained in a wood-paneled dining room painted burgundy and cream (their Limoges dinner service looks like Edna if she were a set of china: pale pink rosebuds on an ivory ground, edges rimmed with gold). The living room has plenty of comfortable upholstered seating (as well as two pianos—one was Edna's, the other for visitors).

And then, outside again, tennis courts and a string of "pleasure gardens" each with its own distinct personality, and divided into "fully dressed" versus "fully undressed": the outdoor bar leads to a wall of irises shielding a spring-fed swimming pool and a hedge-rimmed square of grass—to gain entry one had to be nude. All around are a profusion of rose bushes and flowers.

Detractors complain about Edna's late work, which includes a lot of admittedly mediocre political poetry. Some go so far as to blame this decline on her marriage. The true culprit may have

been a 1936 car accident, which left her with severe nerve dam-
age, chronic pain, and, ultimately, a morphine addiction. In spite
of this, she and Eugen appear to have had a mostly satisfying
twenty-six years living alone together, contentedly without children. They spent most of the year at Steepletop and eventually
summers on their own tiny Ragged Island in Casco Bay, Maine,
working, gardening, swimming, seeing friends, and, after the
stock-market crash of 1929, becoming fascinated by racehorses,
even buying and breeding several of their own, until Eugen died
in 1949, and Edna the year following. Throughout, she wrote and
she wrote and she wrote. In this way, she never stopped being
herself.

6

The Essayist: Part II

Maeve Brennan, mid-1960s

A RECENT STUDY BY A LIFE INSURANCE COMPANY FOUND THAT nearly half of all American women fear becoming bag ladies—not only never-married women, who ranked highest, at 56 percent, but the divorced (54 percent), widowed (47 percent), and even those who are still married (43 percent).

I'd never been prey to this particular fear, sampling instead from any number of other horrible ways to wind up. You could be raped and murdered. You could *be* a murderer. You could be in a horrific plane crash and die among screaming, puking strangers (my own personal nightmare).

Yet, after only a year of trying to make it on my own as a freelance book reviewer, I became convinced that I was one misstep away from "living on the streets," as I'd put it to myself. I'd found plenty of work—*The Boston Globe* gave me my own memoir-review column, and I was able to get assignments from other newspapers and magazines (including *Vogue*; at last, distant colleagues with Neith Boyce)—but, most of it was very low-paying, and lacking the genius, confidence, psychological stamina, and live-in family support of someone like Edna Millay, I could hardly hold myself together. My income was so erratic that most days, by late afternoon, I'd become so consumed by anxiety, I had to stop whatever I was doing and make myself lie on the sofa, as if putting a toddler down for a nap. That I added to this earned anxiety one so irrational it ranks as frivolous—unlike many people who actually are a hair's breadth from living on the streets, I am lucky to have a close relationship with my father, who would have let me move home if worse came to worst—seems proof, in retrospect, that I used the fear as a goad: if I allowed myself to think I had a cushion, I might not keep moving forward.

Socializing was difficult enough in such a state, dating out of the question. My situation with T, once a thrilling escape from normalcy, became a painful, recurrent reminder of my loneliness; I broke it off, explaining I needed to find something "more." I began to understand the appeal of marriage: mutual support, splitting bills.

With mixed emotions—crushing failure very slightly alleviated by relief—in fall 2003 I took a job as a culture editor at a small (now defunct) daily newspaper. Housed in a nineteenth-century white-brick-and-cast-iron building on a chaotic corner of lower Manhattan, the office was like a sci-fi, all-era adaptation of

New Grub Street, George Gissing's 1891 novel of literary London. While enduring 1880s working conditions (the cooling, heating, and plumbing systems were constantly breaking down—in winter, my office attire entailed never removing my red wool coat and black vintage fur hat) amid the 2000s soundtrack of trilling cell phones and ceaseless staccato of fingers on laptops, I played a glorified girl Friday circa 1940—editing jazz, architecture, and book reviews—while my overlords, two men my age, colluded in their own fantasy of 1960s-style cigar-and-martini meetings to which I was never invited. Rather than give up my hard-won relationships with other, more collegial editors and surrender myself entirely to this joke of an operation, I continued to write freelance book reviews in the mornings, before work, and on the weekends. Most nights kept me at the office until eight or nine o'clock.

----◀▥▥──

Surrounded by newspapers, I acquired a taste for reading obituaries, which is how I learned about the life and death of the pioneering feminist scholar Carolyn Heilbrun, in early October of that year.

The following weekend I bought a paperback of her seminal study *Writing a Woman's Life,* first published in 1988. By the time I'd finished reading, I'd underlined nearly the entire thing, beginning with the first sentence, where she states there are four ways to write a woman's life: autobiography, fiction, biography, or, "the woman may write her own life in advance of living it, unconsciously, and without recognizing or naming the process."

Is this what I've been doing, I tentatively, hopefully wondered— *writing my own life, unwittingly, in advance of living it?*

Such is the odd fate, even now, of the feminist project: progress is so fitful, and went unrecorded for so long, that an idea doesn't have to be new to be eye-opening.

But it was her observation that we know so little about "the unmarried woman who, consciously or not, has avoided marriage with an assiduousness little remarked but no less powerful for being, often, unknown to herself," that made me see with blazing clarity why the voices of Maeve Brennan and Neith Boyce and Edna Millay called out across the decades. Along with filling in for my mother as intimate interlocutors, they were showing me how to think beyond the marriage plot. The conversations I had with them created the pages that were my life.

The force of my revelation confused me. It was the year 2003! I shouldn't have needed help thinking beyond the idea of marriage. Besides, by now, nearly two years out of my relationship with R, I had several good women friends in New York (a breakup, I'd discovered, was new-friend catnip), and we constantly talked to each other about our intimate lives. The Internet was a pulsating archive of diaries (a.k.a. blogs).

And yet, nowhere did I hear, or take part in, serious conversations about the lives of unmarried women. Instead, whatever candor had erupted in the 1960s had been sucked into a black hole of constant chatter about dating, sex, marriage, children. The notion of not marrying was apparently so outlandish that it was consigned to fiction, whether chick-lit or television, as if the very thought of single women was so threatening we had no choice but to trivialize it.

Until that changed, we were doomed, as Heilbrun observed, to live out our lives "among the suitors, without a story to be told, wondering whether or when to marry."

My demanding schedule abetted, rather than impeded, my romantic life. Now that I wasn't an anxious wreck, I started dating a lot—possibly too much, I decided one day, when I looked at my faux-leather-bound calendar and realized I went on dates more often than I saw my friends, not because I wanted to particularly, but because almost everyone I knew had moved to Brooklyn, and at the end of the workday it was just easier to grab a drink with some guy I'd met at a book party than travel to Carroll Gardens and back.

My roommate and I were nearing the end of our lease, and now that I had a full-time salary, I could finally afford to live on my own. I decided I'd return to Brooklyn—though not Brooklyn Heights. Since R and I had broken up, I'd only returned to the neighborhood once, for a party, and the moment I stepped off the subway, my heart seized. It was so pretty there, and quiet. Had I been a total fool to leave the kindest man I'd ever known? Should we have discussed the option of an open marriage—a better version of Neith and Hutch's, something closer to Edna and Eugen's? From that point on I'd avoided Brooklyn Heights entirely.

For a month or two I spent my free time scrolling through the cobalt listings of Craigslist until my eyes stung; at lunch I'd subway out to the farthest reaches of Brooklyn, lured by those old real-estate canards "cozy studio" (a basement with no windows) and "THIS IS IT!! Suny [*sic*] 1BDR!! Will go fast!!" (the attic of a six-floor walk-up fifteen blocks from the subway). In July, I succumbed to hiring a realtor, an exorbitant expense I wasn't even sure I could afford (in New York, the commission fee starts at one month's rent).

On our first day, after we'd speed-viewed seven apartments, she turned her car onto a street of handsome brownstones, just around the corner from where R and I used to go for French toast on Saturday mornings.

"Um, it's in Brooklyn Heights," I said. I'd already explained that this was the only neighborhood I wasn't interested in.

She raised her eyebrows as if to say, "What can you do?"

She parked before one of the grander specimens, fronted by an unusually wide stoop leading to a massive arched door topped with an elaborate lintel, like a mantel, as if we weren't entering a building, but a giant's fireplace. Once inside, she unlocked another enormous door, then another, until we stood at the base of a cavernous foyer dominated by a staircase leisurely winding up and up and up.

As we climbed, the thick maroon carpet swallowed our footsteps, so that her words sounded close and intimate. She was explaining that the building had originated as a single-family home in the mid-1800s and in the 1970s been converted into apartments, but I could hardly hear what she said, I was so distracted by the details: the white-painted wood scrollwork inscribing each landing with a long row of waves; the ornate arches embellishing every single doorway; the graceful swoop of the polished wood banister accentuating the staircase. (I later heard that in the 1980s the building had been full of homosexual bachelors and known as "The Flower House.") On the third floor, I followed her down a dark, narrow hallway toward a tall brown door. When she unlocked it, we stepped into a soap bubble afloat in the Brooklyn sky: one big room and a separate eat-in kitchen; eleven-foot ceilings; thick, handsome moldings; and gigantic, towering windows covering three walls, through which the weather was its own miraculous event, enormous and panoramic.

It was the spinster wish—as a space, if not yet my life.

Pleasurable solitude incarnate.

My knees actually, literally went weak; I wilted sideways and, before she could notice, stopped myself with a hand against the doorjamb.

I both saw and didn't see the imperfections: chipped, cracked paint; scuffed wood floors; kitchen appliances older than all four of my (long deceased) grandparents; no dishwasher, of course, and

I'd have to bring my laundry out to a Laundromat, but none of this mattered, obviously.

"The trundle bed comes with the place," she said, gesturing toward a single bed on the other side of the room.

I walked over and yanked on a handle, and a second, slightly narrower bed slid out beneath the first, like a jewelry-box drawer. The sun spilled through the empty frame, sketching a map of spindly shadows while the future unfurled: breezes gusting through the open windows as I curled up reading for hours; friends having a place to spend the night that wasn't my lumpy IKEA sofa; bringing a man home and—*screech*—becoming an urban legend: the single woman who sleeps in a weird single bed for children.

"Actually," I said, "I'd like to have it removed. How much is the rent?"

"Well," she said, "it's a little over your price range . . ."

My heart sank. I told her I'd have to think on it.

"Better hurry up," she said. "This place will go fast."

That night I couldn't sleep. In the morning I made a deal with myself: if the realtor could talk the landlord down one hundred dollars, which would be just one hundred dollars more than the very top of my price range, I would figure out a way to make it happen.

The landlord said yes.

A few weeks later, after dinner with a man I'd gone on a few dates with, I boldly invited him upstairs, "my first overnight guest," I added as inducement.

The foyer is an event in itself: when you stand on the ground floor and tilt your head back, you see eternity for a moment, and then, at the very top, set into the roof, a stained glass window of many colors. The overall effect is of a barely maintained grandeur.

Tonight, though, the foyer had a very strong odor.

"I guess it's the sort of building where you can smell what everyone's cooked for dinner," I lied, suddenly remembering that it had smelled like this, though less so, that morning, and then slightly less than that the day before. By now I suspected it was no longer just cooking smells, and possibly not even a dead mouse stuck in the wall, but perhaps a dead cat.

It had nothing to do with me, but I was slightly mortified.

Fortunately my apartment was odor-free. We had a very good night.

The next morning, after he'd gotten up and dressed and hitched his backpack onto his shoulders and turned the doorknob on the front door, he came crashing back into the bedroom, where I stood in my nightgown, confused.

When you're a single person of a certain age, stories from the dating trenches are your calling card. He's a jerk, you're a jerk—it doesn't matter. All that counts is there's a beginning, a middle, an end, and something embarrassing happens. Nobody doesn't like a dating story. There they are, your dinner companions, seated around the table, attentive faces ageless in the candlelight, the single among them nodding their heads in solidarity, the coupled relieved to not be you, or secretly envious, depending. You pause for a moment, take a sip from your wineglass, continue.

"And then he said, 'That is not a *cooking* smell. Someone in this building has DIED. What we are smelling is a ROTTING CORPSE.'"

"Oh, no!" they squeal in horrified delight.

"So I called the police to report the, um, problem, and they said they were already on it—they'd actually retrieved the body earlier that morning, before we'd woken up. Later, the super told me it was an old man I'd never met who lived in the apartment directly below mine. When the cleanup crew came to remove his corpse, the spine had lifted right up and out, like a feather, and the rest stayed on the bed in a thick, soupy puddle."

"Gross." "Please, I am eating." "Bet that dude you were dating never came back."

He did, actually.

In the days to come the odor of rot grew stronger, corpulent, sneaking like a plague of cockroaches through every conceivable crack, and lasted for weeks. I honestly couldn't tell which was worse: the agony of not knowing what that terrible stench had been, or the agony of knowing.

He was a smart guy, that guy I was dating, but we broke up eventually.

Him and another, and then another.

And then another! And on it went.

On a warm spring day in 2004 I sat at my desk ripping open yellow padded mailers, stuffing them into a recycling bin, and stacking the books they'd held into a pile. One advantage of my newspaper job was having access to the catalogs publishers send out to people in the industry announcing their forthcoming books—which is how I learned that at long last a biography of Maeve Brennan was in the works.

All through my dalliances with Neith and Edna I'd never lost sight of her. She'd become something like the amalgamation of all the women in my family: a vision of my future self who'd actually lived in the past; who was only eight years younger than my maternal grandmother, Margaret Healey O'Keefe, herself a first-generation Irish-American, who outlived Maeve by a year; a chimerical ever-presence I felt deeply connected to yet could muse about without the painful longing I felt for my mother. The thought that someone else might review the book made me sick with anxiety; immediately I secured an assignment with *Vogue.*

Whenever I'd met someone who seemed remotely interested

in literary history, or was even tangentially connected to *The New Yorker*, I'd ask if they'd ever heard of her. When the answer was yes, I'd invariably hear the same two rumors: she'd dressed beautifully (her editor, the writer William Maxwell, said that to be around her was to see style being invented), and she'd wound up a bag lady on the streets of New York.

I happily believed the first rumor and, because of this, refused to accept the second. Judging by her essays and short stories, I felt safe in considering Maeve to be one of the most healthily independent people I'd ever encountered. Everything she wrote issued from the same deep, pure well of integrity. She was funny, open-minded, empathetic, never egotistical, sophisticated without being pretentious. It was impossible that someone so exceptional could ever be defeated. Now that someone had written her biography, I could finally get the whole story.

That I believed I could assess a person's mental competence by the carapace of art that surrounds and more often than not obfuscates her is, sadly, just another instance of my willful naïveté, and my ignorance of the gulf between the person and the page.

The Irish scholar Angela Bourke had discovered Maeve around the same time I had, to even greater astonishment: Bourke's home in central Dublin was only two miles from Ranelagh, where Maeve had lived as a child. Over the course of seven years she found and interviewed seemingly anyone alive who had ever crossed paths with her subject—family, friends, colleagues, even an army officer who'd once flirted with Maeve over drinks in the lobby of the Algonquin Hotel—and came to the conclusion that, even though she'd lived in relative obscurity as a writer, her "courageous life as a woman alone in metropolitan America makes her an icon of the twentieth century even if she is not as well known as Marilyn Monroe, Billie Holiday, or Colette."

Like Neith Boyce and Edna Millay before her, Maeve had come to New York City in her twenties to become a writer, and though she was of a different generation—she was twenty-five years younger than Edna, who was twenty years younger than Neith—the conditions under which all three sought their independence were more similar than not.

While the years between 1890 and 1920 had been the single woman's most glorious moment yet, the two decades following were up for debate. After the vote was achieved in 1920, the sense of purpose—whether political or personal—that had galvanized and united freethinkers such as Neith and Edna petered out, and the flapper swanned into the public eye. Like *spinster* before it, the term had crossed over from England, where it emerged in the 1890s to describe both a prostitute and teenage girl; by the early 1920s it encompassed an entire emergent category of young women living lives unlike those of their mothers—in the eyes of an alarmed public, they might as well have been prostitutes.

Flappers were easily mistaken as New Women masquerading in a different silhouette: while stiff, restrictive corsets had created and accentuated their mothers' feminine curves, flappers wore new, more supple undergarments that smoothed the female figure, from elbow to knee, into the slim, straight stalk of a flat-chested boy's. Like their predecessors, the flappers challenged traditional gender roles and broke with convention, though in the eyes of many of the suffragists who had worked long and hard to engineer the emancipation of women, their methods of rebellion—smoking and drinking in public, bobbing their hair, wearing short, revealing dresses—seemed like so much empty posturing.

The flapper vanished with the Great Depression, as did anything smacking of frivolity and hedonism, at which point, for the first time in forty years, the single woman's status dropped. Now that heterosexual sex was considered integral to mental health, unmarried women were increasingly represented as lonely, celibate spinsters. Meanwhile, the labor market became a battlefield.

With so many people out of work, jobs became the privilege of men with families to feed—as if many single women weren't also supporting their parents, siblings, and families. (Wives fared even worse: by 1932, married women were prohibited by law from working in twenty-six states.) In 1939 the liberal journalist Norman Cousins reported that roughly ten million people were unemployed, while ten million married and single women held jobs. His solution: "Simply fire the women, who shouldn't be working anyway, and hire the men. Presto! No unemployment. No relief rolls. No depression." With the onset of World War II, when we started needing more bodies in the workplace again, single women enjoyed a short, sweet revival (before being devoured altogether by the 1950s). When Maeve Brennan arrived in New York City, several years into the war, the magazine industry was thriving, and single women were in a good place—for the time being, at least.

Aside from embarking on her career at a fortuitous moment in history, Maeve shared two other important advantages with Neith and Edna. The first was her parents: she, too, was born into a family that encouraged its most ambitious daughter to flourish. Her mother and father, Una and Robert, were political agitators who'd fought hard for Ireland's national emancipation movement, to which gender equality was integral. Robert served as Irish Under-Secretary for Foreign Affairs and director of publicity for the Republican Forces during the Irish Civil War, and in 1930 helped to found *The Irish Press,* which he managed until 1933, when he was appointed secretary of the Irish Legation and moved the family to Washington, DC. In 1942, when Maeve was twenty-five, after graduating from American University and working as a librarian, she moved by herself to New York, to the consternation of her parents; five years later they and her younger brother returned to Ireland. Her sisters, Emer and Deirdre, who'd both married in 1940, stayed in Washington. (All three were named after early queens of Ireland.)

The second advantage was the support of a powerful woman. Presumably through family connections, Maeve landed an interview with Carmel Snow, the Irish-born editor-in-chief of *Harper's Bazaar,* and was hired as a fashion copywriter. Soon enough, she had her own apartment: "one enormous room at the top of a beautiful house," as she later described it, just a few blocks north of Washington Square Park, off Fifth Avenue. The fireplace didn't work, and the stairs were dirty. But it had a wall of casement windows that overlooked the city and framed a "huge and always changing sweep of sky."

Aesthetics were paramount to Maeve. Bourke meticulously describes how once Maeve arrived in New York, she developed her own style. She grew her dark curly brown hair long and pulled it back in a high, tight bun, darkened her lashes with thick mascara and her lips with crimson lipstick, and was rarely seen without high heels, seamed stockings, and a red rose or carnation in her lapel. She's been described in reminiscences and letters as a "pixie," a "fairy princess," a "changeling," and inspired comparisons to her predecessor, Dorothy Parker, and Truman Capote's fictional Holly Golightly (she even smoked her cigarettes through a long, slender quellazaire). "Part of the enduring fascination of her writing," Bourke argues, "is the consciousness it reveals behind the laminations of that mid-twentieth-century image of femininity."

(My own arrival to the city coincided with the dawn of outrageously expensive "luxury" denim; R used to say that the moment I bought my first pair of $150 skintight, dark blue, cotton-spandex, low-waisted, boot-cut Diesel jeans—if not a personal style statement, at least a step toward one—he knew I was never going back to Boston.)

Maeve's living spaces were just as important as her appearance. She called it a gift for ambiance—by which she meant the ability to create a whole environment. Every single place she rented had a fireplace (whether it worked seemed not to matter), but not necessarily a kitchen. Once, after she'd moved into an apartment she liked, the landlord removed the magnificent gilt mirror that had drawn her there to begin with—"the one thing that might have held me to the place," she later wrote—so she moved out and back downtown, into two high-ceilinged rooms without a kitchen (but with, of course, a fireplace). When she joined the staff of *The New Yorker,* she had the walls of her tiny office painted white, the ceiling Wedgwood blue, and she brought in a little flock of potted plants.

After reading that Maeve finished off a pack of Camels a day (her colleague Philip Hamburger would surreptitiously leave them on the corner of her desk the night before), I didn't take up smoking, but the news that her perfume wafted entrancingly along the office corridors did inspire me to pitch a story on "signature scents," that glossy women's magazine slam dunk, so I could order a free sample of her favored Cuir de Russie (French for "Russian leather") from Chanel.

The day the box arrived—the publicist had generously sent me a full 6.8-ounce rectangular bottle—I almost trembled to open it. I was about to *smell* Maeve Brennan. Coco Chanel (herself a lifelong single woman) revolutionized the fragrance industry in the early 1920s by being the first to use heavy doses of aldehyde—a chemical compound that makes a perfume sparkle and last longer, as well as better conceal heavy odors, which must have been particularly appealing to all the women who'd suddenly taken up smoking. When I unscrewed the black top and spritzed my wrist, a thick, sumptuous fragrance filled the air, unlike anything I'd smelled before; I'm wearing it right now and I still find it difficult to describe. The promotional materials said "wild cavalcades, wafts of blond tobacco, and the smell of boots tanned by birch bark, which the Russian soldiers would wear" (according to Chanel's biographer Justine Picardie, Cuir de Russie "bottled

the essence of her romance" with the Grand Duke Dmitri Pav-
lovich of Russia). What reaches my nose is the enticing aura of a
more stolid, not-yet-synthetic age, back before "fast fashion" and
the Internet, when furniture came in heavy, matching sets, and
clothes weren't woven through with spandex, and our environments were resolutely material, replete with their various aromas
and textures.

Maeve started to write one of her best short stories, "A Young
Girl Can Spoil Her Chances," in the mid-1940s, when she worked
at *Harper's Bazaar* (it wasn't published for another twenty years).
As Bourke explains, the title was the sort of thing Maeve would
have heard growing up in Ireland, "a backlash of Victorian righ-
teousness that cautioned young women against competing with
men, much less outshining them, and warned of the dangers of
too much education"—an attitude that, of course, would contami-
nate America after the war. "It is easy to imagine an Irish woman's voice suggesting complacently that Maeve had 'spoiled her
chances,'" Bourke writes. "Easy, too, to understand the fury this
would have provoked in Maeve—for its irrelevance to the life she
had chosen as much as for its lack of sympathy."

The story itself—about an unhappily married woman's anger
toward her passive-aggressive bully of a mother—is a sort of
dramatic manifesto, expressed via narrative rather than rheto-
ric, against the inarticulate suffocations and invisible cruelties
of domestic life, which Maeve was very consciously not choosing
for herself. New York, Bourke points out, "did not require her to
cook, or sew, or even hand canapés around, and did not particularly expect her to marry."

Instead, she embraced the freedoms of a single woman, falling in and out of love, going to the offices of *Harper's Bazaar*
every day, and out any night of the week she felt like it—not, I
should note, with her co-workers. Though women socialized together during the day—shopping, going out for lunch—it was still

unheard of at night. After work, a date with a man was often a woman's only ticket out of the house.

One of the first friends Maeve made when she arrived in New York was Brendan Gill, a *New Yorker* writer who introduced her to his colleagues Joseph Mitchell, Philip Hamburger, and the cartoonist Charles Addams, all of whom were more than happy to be her escort. Maeve never wrote directly about her romantic life, but Hamburger told Bourke that she was briefly involved with Addams (whether before or after his marriage to a woman who purportedly resembled Morticia Addams, matriarch of the cartoonist's fictional *Addams Family,* he didn't say), and that he suspected she'd had an affair with the married Gill, as well.

If there were a line on the census for mistresses, would we see an all-time peak during the 1940s? The conditions were uncommonly conducive. As during the American Revolutionary and Civil War periods, World War II greatly reduced the pool of eligible men. But the mid-century single woman's experience was radically distinct from that of those who came before her.

The history of adultery is as long as the history of marriage. Well into the twentieth century, a single woman had to be uncommonly self-actualized, highly sexually frustrated, extremely desperate, or very much in love to be a married man's mistress and risk losing the social respect conferred by her presumed celibacy. By the time Maeve was an adult, the consensus that sex was integral to a woman's mental and emotional health must have made it easier for a single woman to rationalize her way into a relationship with a married man as being better than nothing at all. In this way, the mid-century woman wasn't much different from us.

Also like us, she had the option of working and living alone in big, anonymous cities—all the better for clandestine liaisons.

But unlike us, she operated without the personal expectation of equality brought about by the women's movement of the late 1960s and early 1970s, and in this way she had more in common with her Victorian predecessors. The balance of power between a married man and his mistress fit comfortably into familiar gender norms: nine times out of ten he not only had the emotional ballast and social sanction of a family, but he also made far more money. Too, because divorce was still anathema, and most people stayed in unhappy marriages, the age-old convention of men straying while wives looked the other way (whether consciously or not) remained.

It's easy to see how Maeve would have navigated this terrain. As a brilliant woman fiercely protective of her autonomy, she likely found the standard marriage-minded man and his conventional expectations rather boring, if not suffocating. When she joined the staff of *The New Yorker* in 1949, she was suddenly in very close proximity with quite a few appealing men, the majority of whom were married. Well, if they wanted to step out on their wives, that was their decision, wasn't it? Looked at this way, it's no wonder that professional single women were soon contending with a whole new stigma—that of the rapacious femme fatale, stealer of other women's husbands—that persists today.

The realization sent a chill right through me. The primary reason I've chosen to never be "the other woman" is my strong sense of sisterhood. It appalls me to think of betraying one of my own kind. But it stands to reason that women weren't feeling particularly sisterly during the 1940s and '50s. Back when we were confined to the home, we at least had the companionship of one another. As we started easing our way out—first to the textile mills, where we worked together all day and shared living quarters after hours; later, on the factory floors and in communal boardinghouses—we often forged a useful and consoling camaraderie. If not for this solidarity, the political actions taken by reformers from Jane Hull to Margaret Sanger, even the widespread culture of charity work that brought together working and upper-class women, might not have been so effective.

In comparison, urban professional life at mid-century was shockingly atomized for women. Long accustomed to regarding one another as romantic rivals, now we were also competing with one another for career advancement. Boardinghouses were largely obsolete, the marriage rate was spiking, and the age of marriage was lowering, meaning most women lived with their parents until sequestering off into a couple and disappearing into a house. This lack of time and space for communal experiences with other women, which was created *and* compounded by a society that did not prioritize such relationships, and placed marriage above all, ensured that "independence" was often a very lonely experience.

The famous Barbizon Hotel for Women was a gorgeously gothic backdrop for this toxic atmosphere. Built in 1927, it wasn't the first "women only" residence to cater to the working girl—the Martha Washington opened for business in 1903, the Trowmart Inn in 1906—but by the mid-1940s it was the most glamorous bachelorette address in town.

A 23-story, 700-room, pinkish-coral brick building on the corner of Sixty-Third Street and Lexington Avenue, the Barbizon lured ingénues from all over the country with glossy brochures promising a life of glittering good times. Essentially, an elite all-white sorority, dormitory, charm school, and convent rolled into one, it accepted applicants based on their looks, demeanor, and three letters of recommendation, and once there held them to "ladylike" standards (no male visitors without supervision; mandatory afternoon teas). Between the 1940s and the 1960s, everyone from Grace Kelly to Sylvia Plath to Joan Crawford was a "Barbizon Girl."

In 1957, recent alumnus Gael Greene exposed the sad realities of the place that Plath had already hinted at in *The Bell Jar* with a series of articles for *The New York Post*. Beneath the mystique, Greene reported, the Barbizon was little more than a holding pen for a lot of anxious women waiting to find husbands so their lives could begin. Drawn to the city by "something indefinable— something to do, a rent-paying job, romance, the alchemy that will transform an ordinary girl into an extraordinary woman," a Barbizon Girl had only a few short years to launch herself; if a resident hadn't moved out by twenty-five, she was pitied and feared by incomers.

No wonder Maeve, ever the lone wolf, chose different quarters. (Also, the minuscule, Spartan rooms were not up to her standards.)

In 1954, to everybody's surprise, Maeve agreed to marry St. Clair McKelway, a charismatic, irresponsible, hard-drinking, thrice-married writer at the magazine. She was thirty-seven; he was forty-nine. Their wedding was what she called a "very fancy" reception at Café Nicholson, a Parisian-style Midtown restaurant popular among fashionable artistic types (it closed in 2000). Their friend *New Yorker* writer Roger Angell compared the couple to "two children out on a dangerous walk: both so dangerous and so charming."

Soon after marrying, they moved to Snedens Landing, a somewhat tony community of artists and writers a fifty-minute drive north of the city (Betty Friedan was a neighbor). Maeve wrote less and less. Bourke speculates that McKelway's ebullient personality and their active social life as a couple left her much less in control of her time than she was used to. It didn't take long before his drinking got to be too much, and in 1959, when Maeve was forty-two, the couple amicably divorced.

According to all accounts, after the divorce, things went south for Maeve. Though she immediately started writing again, better than ever before, and found a homey stability in a friend's Hamptons summer cottage during the off-seasons, by the late 1960s she was moving constantly among rented apartments and hotel rooms and soon started widening her circle to include writer's colonies in New Hampshire and Cape Cod. Everywhere she went she brought at least five cats, and sometimes twelve. She continued to write but remained under the popular radar—beloved by readers who followed her work but unknown by the general public.

Around 1965 she wrote a letter to William Maxwell that included the following evocative passage:

> I will send you a note later about the specific difference between those writers who possess the natural confidence that is their birthright, and those fewer writers who are driven by the unnatural courage that comes from no alternative. It is something like this—some walk on a tightrope, and some continue on the tightrope, or continue to walk, even after they find out it is <u>not there</u>.

In 1969, when Maeve was fifty-two, her first two books came out: *In and Out of Never-Never Land,* twenty-two of her short stories from *The New Yorker,* and *The Long-Winded Lady,* her forty-seven collected columns, published for the first time under her own name. In a review of the latter for *The Atlantic,* titled "Talk of a Sad Town," John Updike recalled his own days as a cub *New Yorker* reporter in the 1950s, when he wasn't exactly "avid to extract from the Eisenhowered, sullen if not yet apocalyptic metropolis of those years the enchantment of Baghdad-on-the-Subway celebrated by O. Henry, by Scott Fitzgerald and Edna Millay," and applauded "Miss Brennan" for putting "New York back into *The New Yorker.*"

The author herself, however, was not faring as well. In his

review, Updike had noted her eccentric fondness for, "dismally enough," the West Forties, "those half-demolished blocks of small hotels and cellar restaurants and old coin shops between Fifth and Eighth Avenue." By now she was a full-time denizen of that blighted area, "living in a series of apartments and hotel rooms, pursued by creditors," Bourke writes. At this point Maeve wore her hair in a beehive, the dyed-red tower growing ever higher, her lipstick more sloppy. Her once-captivating enthusiasms had become unpredictable, overpowering obsessions. Bourke describes how at one point Maeve discovered Billie Holiday and bought every single one of her records, "which she played over and over again, for hours at a time, even in the office, on a portable phonograph," veteran editor Gardner Botsford told her.

I paused at this detail. Billie Holiday was born in Philadelphia in 1915, only two years before Maeve; by the 1940s, when Maeve moved to New York, Holiday was one of the most famous jazz singers in America, a legend in her own time—before dying at age forty-four of liver and heart failure. Both women had married briefly, unhappily. But I knew it was specious of me to compare them as single women; the political, social, and economic forces that shape the African-American single experience is an entire book unto itself. Bourke links the two women as creative souls who made themselves vulnerable in pursuit of the insights their arts express.

Maeve eloquently articulates that sense of communion in a Long-Winded Lady column published in November 1967. She's alone in a friend's apartment in the Village, sitting through a rainstorm on a green velvet sofa, listening to a cocktail party across the hall. She switches on the phonograph without changing the record she'd been listening to that morning:

The music strengthens, and moves about, catching the pictures, the books, and the discolored white marble mantelpiece as firelight might have done. Now the place is no longer a cave but a room with walls that listen in peace. I hear the music and I watch the voice. I can see it. It is a voice to follow with your mind's eye. *"La Brave, c'est elle."* There is no other. Billie Holiday is singing.

In the years following the publication of Maeve Brennan's books, anyone at *The New Yorker* outside of William Maxwell and Gardner Botsford—the only people close enough to know how continuously hard she was working—must have thought Maeve's best was behind her. And then, on March 18, 1972, she published the story that changed her life. Alice Munro called it one of her favorite short stories of all time. In Angela Bourke's words, it's a "swan song, or her kamikaze flight . . . and a suicidal assault on her own family."

Taking up twenty-seven pages of *The New Yorker,* "The Springs of Affection" chronicles three generations of two families in Ireland. It's told from the perspective of the never-married, eighty-seven-year-old Min Bagot, and opens with the death of her twin brother, Martin, whom she's been lovingly tending to in his final months. His wife, Delia, who'd "appeared out of the blue and fascinated Martin, the born bachelor, into marrying her" a half century before, died six years earlier, and now Min is the last sibling standing, which she finds fitting:

> She was the only one of the lot of them who hadn't gone off and got married. She had never wanted to assert herself like that, never needed to. She had wondered at their lack of shame as they exhibited themselves. . . . They didn't seem to care what anybody thought of them when they got caught up in that excitement, like animals. It was disgusting, and they seemed to know it, the way they pretended their only concern was with the new clothes they'd have and the flowers they'd grow in

their very own gardens. And now it was over for them, and they might just as well have controlled themselves, for all the good they had of it.

Min's bitterness is rank and palpable, "a study in spite, a monster of heartlessness," as Bourke describes. In the story Min ruminates over how, once upon a time, "she had believed she could fly sky-high, with her brains for wings," but life didn't work out that way, and rather than recognize that she'd been "done out of my right," everyone preferred to see her as a failure, saying, "She got too big for her boots, and Pride must have a fall." There was nothing she could do about it. "It is impossible to prove you are not a disappointed old maid," she thinks to herself. "A farmer's daughter is all she was, even if she had attended the Loreto convent and owned certificates to show what a good education she had."

The story itself is fiction—and yet the landscape and characters, houses and rooms, are all pulled directly from real life, meaning Maeve's relatives experienced the brutal shock of seeing themselves transformed through another's unforgiving eyes. Everyone knew that Min was none other than Maeve's beloved spinster aunt, the eighty-five-year-old Nan Brennan, and everyone agreed that she didn't deserve such vicious treatment. After the story appeared, Aunt Nan wrote on the back of a snapshot of Maeve, "Greatly changed for the worse, 1972."

And "so began a time that Maeve's New York friends cannot remember without pain," Bourke writes. She grew paranoid, started spending her nights at the office, nursed a sick pigeon she'd found on the street. When she received her paycheck, she'd cash it and stand on the corner of Forty-Fourth Street and Fifth Avenue, handing out bills to whoever took them. Her friends despaired, doing everything they could to help, and *The New Yorker* opened a bank account in her name, making regular deposits (she remained on staff until about 1980), but again and again she pushed away those who helped her. It's impossible to know what was happening: either the self-imposed estrangement from her family was taking its toll, her mental health was growing increasingly unstable, or some combination of both was unfolding.

In July 1973, when she was fifty-six, though she'd told everyone that her family was no longer speaking with her, Maeve flew home to Ireland, where she stayed for a little while at her sister's house in Dublin. In 1975, after Maxwell located her brother, Robert Patrick, to say she wasn't well, she left New York and moved in with his family in Peoria, Illinois. Within the year, without telling anyone, she returned to the city.

Maeve's Long-Winded Lady appears only twice more in the magazine. In September 1976 she recounts waking from a pleasant daydream of lying alone on the beach in East Hampton, where she'd once lived, to the realization that she is, in fact, on her bed in New York City, "and the cool ocean breeze is being provided by the blessed air conditioner." The daydream was nothing but "a mild attack of homesickness," she decides. "The reason it was a mild attack instead of a fierce one is that there are a number of places I am homesick for. East Hampton is only one of them."

Five years pass without a peep, and then The Long-Winded Lady appears for the last time on January 5, 1981. She thought she had a few observations to share, she explains, but then she got up to make some coffee, and when she came back they had vanished. It's a good thing anyhow, she tells us, as:

> They were a stilted crowd, and rather disagreeable, as though they had found themselves at a party that was not quite what they'd expected and where their clothes were all wrong. They all wore elaborate taffeta ball gowns that seemed to belong to the eighteenth century, and each ball gown was a different shade of green.

Come to think of it, she decides, they weren't observations after all, but complaints, and as such have gone to the complaints department, which she avoids at all costs, on account of there being "too many mirrors in there for my liking." After recounting a childhood memory of celebrating New Year's Eve in Dublin, she concludes with her very last published words:

> I must tell you now that I am praying to Almighty God for blessings on your house, with extra blessings to go with you whenever you leave the house, so that wherever you are you will be safe.
>
> Blessings on your house. Happy New Year.

Later that year a recently hired *New Yorker* staffer named Mary Hawthorne stepped off the elevator one morning and found a small woman sitting in the chair outside the receptionist's cubicle, staring at the floor. As Hawthorne recounted in a later essay, the stranger's gray hair was unwashed, and she wore a big black jacket and long black skirt. The woman sat there until evening and returned the next day, and "all the while, she continued her expressionless musing, never raising her eyes." It was Maeve, of course. Hawthorne had never heard of her before. She never saw her again.

After that, the track goes dark.

Sometime around 1990, a World War II veteran turned photo collector named Charley Justice who happened to be a fan of Maeve's writing was rummaging through a used bookstore and came across a blue box of her papers: her teenage diary, galley proofs for her *New Yorker* stories, letters to her sister and niece, and at the bottom, carbon copies of an autobiography of the Irish Revolution written by her father, published in Ireland in 1950, titled *Allegiance*.

Charley bought the box for five dollars and called his good

friend Richard Rupp, at the time a professor of English at Appa-
lachian State University. Rupp had never heard of *Allegiance* and
thought it incredibly good, worthy of reissuing; in his efforts to do
so he tracked down Maeve at Lawrence Nursing Care Center in
Arverne, New York, found her brother's name in a Miami phone
directory at the Library of Congress, and mailed a letter to her
niece, Yvonne Jerrold (using an address off one of the envelopes
he'd found in the box), alerting her family to her whereabouts.

In 1992, Jerrold received a package in the mail: a photograph
of Maeve grinning at the camera and a letter claiming, in a frail,
shaky hand, "I write every day in *The Irish Press* and get paid. . . .
I am married to John Kyoss. That is not how it is spelled & I have
a lot of children, boys and girls."

The Irish Press was the newspaper her father had founded.
Angela Bourke speculates that "Kyoss" could be "Jyoss." "Perhaps
at the end of her days," she writes, "Maeve's fantasy husband was
James Joyce."

On November 1, 1993, before her niece could visit her, Maeve
died suddenly of heart failure.

It was almost too horrible to be true. Maeve actually had
ended up a bag lady on the streets of New York. A fate feared by
so many single women, it's become a cliché.

What did it mean that this was the woman I'd aspired to be?

7

The Novelist

Edith Wharton, early 1900s

IN A SOCIETY ORGANIZED AROUND A STABLE FAMILY UNIT, THE
choice to live alone is, by default, unconventional. At one end
of the spectrum are those who are truly alone. The recluse or
hermit—the secular person who shuns human society in all
forms—tends to be regarded as eccentric, usually with disdain.
The loner is romanticized as a rebel, as long as he's a he (James

Bond, the Lone Ranger, the Marlboro Man) and doesn't reveal himself to be a psychopath.

At the other end of the spectrum is the "gregarious recluse," as the writer Annie Dillard calls herself. When an interviewer asked if this made her an introvert or an extrovert, she said it was a toss-up. I've always considered myself to be similar. I'm no recluse, but, like an introvert, I need a lot of time alone to reflect and recharge, and I am easily drained by being around others, but at the same time, like an extrovert, I'm energized by parties and conversation.

At the midpoint is what I think of as "social aloners," those who live alone amid like-minded people. Nuns and monks are a timeless example; for centuries, joining a convent was the only respectable way for a single woman to live apart from her family, whether she was genuinely devout or simply pragmatic, preferring vows of comfortable poverty and chastity to the miserable drudgery of a peasant marriage. The most glamorized version is the artist or bohemian who's drawn to a geographical area at a certain moment in time, such as Greenwich Village in the 1890s.

Some of these social aloners consciously prioritize their autonomy above all else. Growing up in Philadelphia in the mid-1800s, Mary Cassatt was so determined to become a professional artist that she decided early on, in spite of being born into a wealthy family, that she would never marry and would be self-supporting. In 1866, when she was twenty-two, she moved to Paris and struggled for years, until finding a home in the late 1870s among the then-radical Impressionists, then finally hitting her stride in the late 1880s with the deeply felt explorations of mothers and children that made her one of the most celebrated painters of her time.

Others pursue what I think of as "turbulent aloneness" by maintaining a volatile romantic attachment to another person (or persons) that enables seesawing between periods of intense isolation and connection. Frida Kahlo married Diego Rivera in 1929 when she was twenty-two, divorced him in 1939, and remarried him in 1940; the tumult created by her many affairs (and his) served her art well, as did their choice to live in separate houses.

I began dreaming about the idea of separate living spaces in 2000, when I read Brooke Kroeger's biography of Fannie Hurst, the highest-paid short-story writer of the first half of the twentieth century, and the first to publically pioneer this arrangement. In May 1920 (the year Edna turned twenty-eight, and Neith forty-eight; Maeve was a mere babe), *The New York Times* broke the story that the famous author, heretofore considered single, was not only married and had been for five years, to the pianist Jacques Danielson, but that she and her husband lived in separate studio apartments in the same building on West Sixty-Ninth Street. The article opens:

FANNIE HURST WED; HID SECRET 5 YEARS

Sailed Into Matrimony with Pianist "in a Bark of Their Own Designing,"

LIVE APART, THEIR OWN WAY

Meet By Appointment—It's a New Method Which Rejects "Antediluvian Custom."

In the story Hurst explains that she considers nine out of ten marriages to be "sordid endurance tests overgrown with the fungi of familiarity and contempt," and that by living separately from her husband she is able to keep her most sacred relationship a "high-sheen damask" rather than a "breakfast cloth, stale with soft-boiled egg stains."

The press piled on with sanctimonious editorials and outraged letters to the editor, inciting her chivalrous mate to publish a charmingly sensible defense of their living situation. To the charge of wastefulness, Danielson countered that "there are worse economic crimes being committed day after day in the average home of joint and domestic felicity." Indeed, "free from the strain of a marriage that has narrowed down the woman's scope so that creature comforts come to assume unduly large proportions, we find ourselves, with our multitude of outside interests undiminished, content to live on scales that I confess are below the powers of our respective incomes."

Finally, he punctured "the popular interpretation" that their life together was "one long rendezvous with alien interests." Hurst, he posited, likely spent more time at home than the average woman. She was there working at her desk six hours a day, and had friends over for dinner three to four times a week. "We are both workers and must devote long evenings to study and reading and practice," he added, "so all in all, I hardly thing [*sic*] we can be classified as a pair that has thrown off the responsibilities of the usual marriage ties in order that we may play promiscuously. Rather, as it has worked itself out, we have thrown off the rusty shackles of some of the outworn matrimonial impositions, in order that we may have more liberty to live up to more of the responsibilities of our lives and our work." For a while, among those who could afford it, a "Fannie Hurst marriage" was much in vogue.

Today, there's a sociological term for their domestic arrangement, called "Living Apart Together," or LAT. Hard numbers are impossible to come by, given that the Census Bureau doesn't yet count this demographic, but surveys indicate that in the United States between 6 percent and 9 percent of the population has a partner who lives elsewhere, and throughout northern Europe it's a solid 10 percent, a quarter of all those not married or cohabiting.

As with all categories, the lines between them are blurred. Throughout her life, even though she spent most of it abroad, Mary Cassatt maintained extremely close ties with her family;

in 1874, when she took up permanent residence in France, her sister, Lydia, also never married, came to live with her and stayed until her death in 1882. Simone de Beauvoir and Jean-Paul Sartre shared a lifelong open relationship, yet unlike Neith and Hutch, Edna and Eugen, and Frida and Diego, they never married (or had children) and always lived apart. The never-married abstract expressionist Agnes Martin left New York City for Taos, New Mexico, in 1967, when she was fifty-five, built an adobe home, and lived alone until her late eighties, when she relocated to a one-bedroom apartment in a retirement community, where she died, at ninety-two. Though a recluse, she was religiously devoted to art, and by virtue of participating in an expressive form, even if she wasn't in direct communication with her peers, she shared characteristics of the bohemian.

Society's favorite version of the single woman is the Grande Dame (French for "great lady"). She is post-menopausal, and therefore sexually unthreatening, as well as wealthy and accomplished, though not necessarily professionally. The thrice-married, widowed Brooke Astor made the grade by single-handedly overseeing a massive family fortune with the political savvy, if not the credentials, of a stateswoman. Despite her advanced years, this made her the exact inverse of a Hag or Crone (*crone* derives from *carogne,* Old North French for "carrion"), those almost onomatopoetic denigrations of older women, which sound so much harsher to the ear than the male versions: Geezer, Old Dog, War-Horse. The grande dame may live alone, but unlike the hag she's not an outcast; her superior status relies on her relation to a moneyed elite. For instance, fashion designer Vivienne Westwood is a grande dame, while the pioneering primatologist Jane Goodall is not (or is, perhaps, only in chimpanzee circles). Were a grande dame a building, she would be the opulent Park Plaza Hotel but not the equally imposing, serious-minded Library of Congress.

Being single is like being an artist, not because creating a functional single life is an art form, but because it requires the same close attention to one's singular needs, as well as the will and focus to fulfill them. Just as the artist arranges her life around her creativity, sacrificing conventional comforts and even social acceptance, sleeping and eating according to her own rhythms, so that her talent thrives above all else, nurtured the way a child might be, so a single person has to think hard to decipher what makes her happiest and most fulfilled. Studies show that a woman who lives alone is more likely to have an active social life, and maintain family bonds, than her married peers, not simply because she has extra time on her hands, but because those very bonds are what sustain her.

If it sounds as if I know what I'm talking about—well, it took me quite a while to get here.

In the fall of 2004 I switched from the newspaper's culture desk to lifestyle features, and I came to love being a newspaper editor. Assigning stories, working closely with writers, finding the just-right photograph or artwork, devising headlines and photo captions—it was all invigoratingly hectic and absorbing, and every day taught me something new about the city.

The old longing to write continued to nag, though to write about what, exactly, I still didn't know. Finally living alone, in an apartment I loved, was changing me, making me greedy to have absolutely everything be the way I wanted it to be. R and I had lived well together, but ultimately the security we'd created was false and became smothering. In comparison, sharing an apartment with a roommate had at first felt refreshingly temporary, and then, eventually, unnervingly so, as if it were a way station to some indefinable, always-distant destination rather than an actual home. Within the four walls of my own little studio I could create the present on my own terms, which had the surprising effect of making the future seem closer at hand, as if it weren't at the end of some impossibly long hallway, after all, but as near as tomorrow. Maybe I could stay forever (as long as the landlord didn't hike up the rent or sell the building).

But longing to do something is, of course, a far remove from doing. ("Longing, we say, because desire is full of endless distances," wrote the poet Robert Hass.) The hard-won knowledge that I couldn't live alone—in New York City, at least—off writing freelance essays and book reviews made my astonishingly low salary and mediocre benefits package gleam like the proverbial golden handcuffs—a cheap, plastic kind, with the gold paint flaking off. I suspected that had I been conversant in things more people want to read about—politics, science, fashion, pop culture—my way forward might have been more direct; on its own, my only specific intellectual interest—dead forgotten female writers—was laughably uncommercial.

One afternoon, during my daily tearing of the yellow padded envelopes, out popped a book that looked like a prewrapped gift: hot-pink polka dots on a white background, a ribbon of script declaring *Entertaining Is Fun!* I flipped it over and saw that it was a reissue of a 1941 how-to manual by someone I'd never heard of before, an interior decorator named Dorothy Draper.

The effect this information had on me was strange and immediate. I'd always considered interior decorators a variety of snake-oil salespeople, preying on the vacant imaginations of status-obsessed socialites. Not that I'd ever met a socialite—or a decorator. Yet out of nowhere, and for no reason I could discern, this silly little guide to throwing parties suddenly seemed a key to something large and important.

I decided to research Draper and write an article about her for the newspaper, and as I did, an escape route began to emerge. Dead forgotten female writers and dead forgotten interior decora-

tors actually had something in common—both were women trying to forge professional identities under conditions that weren't
hospitable to their gender, and in the doing they shaped the way
we live today. Perhaps these two so-called beats could add up to a
new professional life?

When the editor of the Home & Garden section of *The New
York Times* called the day my Draper article appeared to say
that he liked it, I figured freelancing for him about this newfound
interest was as good a reason as any to quit my job. For the next
six months I saved as much money as I could, and in May 2005
I gave my two weeks' notice, dragged my desk from my bedroom
into the less-sunny and therefore less-hot kitchen, and invested
in an air conditioner. Setting up a full-time freelance life is not
unlike launching a small startup company without seed money or
funding.

It was a promising start. Along with writing home-related
features for *The New York Times,* I continued with my *Globe*
memoir-review column, and I pitched an undergraduate course on
arts criticism to my old employers at New York University. My
boyfriend—he of the infamous night of the corpse—a journalist,
helped me see that my affection for dead forgotten female writers
was indeed worth writing about, and I applied for a fellowship at
an artists' colony. I'd describe how Maeve, Neith, and Edna had
influenced my own thinking about the single life. I called it "The
Dead Spinster Project."

In June, my childhood best friend, Willy (short for Willamain),
mentioned that a college friend of hers was helping launch a
home-decorating magazine at Condé Nast, and she offered to put
me in touch. I figured, why not? I'd never read a decorating magazine or considered working for a women's glossy—I'd hoped that,

a century after Neith, I could bypass the pink ghetto—but surely
their freelance rate was better than anything I'd made yet, and
now that I was alive to the way a house or apartment looked, the
idea of exploring interiors intrigued me.

I can't remember what I wore to that first interview, but by
the fourth (and what my wallet hoped would be the last), with
the editor-in-chief, I'd run out of nice clothes. The morning of,
I sprinted to my favorite vintage store and returned clutching a
black cotton dress from the 1950s that looked exactly like what
I imagined Maeve might wear: fitted bodice, short cap sleeves,
wide square neck, full skirt of razor-sharp accordion pleats falling
to the knee. At this point the job under discussion was no longer
freelance writer but senior editor, and I was pretty sure I didn't
want it, but everyone in my life had convinced me that you don't
turn down a job until it's offered.

Over the course of the interview process I'd come to discover
that for someone who'd never read a decorating magazine, I
had very strong opinions. The term "home décor" was awful—
co-opting a French noun in no way elevates or disguises the inherent prissiness of seriously contemplating throw pillows and
paint colors. Could there be anything less essential? The conspicuous consumption that fueled the industry was flat-out in-
defensible. To dedicate my waking hours to such an enterprise
would be the metaphysical equivalent of tending to a window box
of silk petunias instead of running through a field of wildflowers.
It denigrated, even mocked, everything I valued.

My own approach to "décor" was to drag home an Edwardian
wardrobe listing against a trash can like a dusty squire in need of
another drink, or to fall headlong on Craigslist for a green velvet
horsehair sofa and stalk it for weeks before talking the owner
into a price I could afford, plus free delivery if possible, and then
arrange my new treasures however I liked. Somehow it worked. I
still take such satisfaction in scavenging that even now I silently

resent my first-ever brand-new furniture purchase—a handsome eggplant linen sofa I found on radical markdown at a high-end store—for not chipping in and pulling its weight.

Now that I was thinking about it, I realized I'd been this way my entire life. As a girl, a favorite pastime was rearranging my bedroom. In sixth grade I saved up my allowance to repaint it "Art Deco" (actually South Beach by way of *Miami Vice,* though I didn't know the difference): hot-pink walls, turquoise trim, and pink plastic flamingoes flanking the window. Throughout my peripatetic twenties I'd faithfully dragged my ever-expanding collection of flea-market antiques from one apartment to the next, no matter how ridiculously cumbersome, as loyal to them as pets. I suppose they were my pets.

These were idle pleasures, though, not central to my sense of self or my ambitions as a writer, and I worried that making a full-time job out of a frivolous hobby would encourage people to take me less seriously. By "people" I meant potential future editors, particularly men. It's no secret that the fashion and design glossies are run almost exclusively by women, and struggle for respect in the publishing world.

And yet . . . as the interview process wore on, it was already becoming clear to me that I couldn't live forever on freelance writing alone. I'd been earning so little since finishing college that along the way I'd made the executive decision to pretend that my massive student-loan debt simply didn't exist; I'd ignore it until the robocalls grew too unbearable, then plead to pay only the most minimum amount, which I'd dutifully manage for a while, until I didn't have any money again, and I'd retreat back into denial. The calls were starting up. (And, yes, a million years later I am still paying them off.)

Soon enough, I knew, I'd be looking again for editorial work, which pays better than writing. I was glad I'd acquired this vocational skill; it meant I'd always have another way to be self-supporting. I wondered if Neith would have stayed single if she'd been able to make more money. Surely Maeve's *New Yorker* salary was what enabled her to afford living alone for so long, and even leave her unsatisfying marriage. Every life entails compromises; perhaps one of mine was that, in exchange for the luxury of living alone in New York City, I couldn't write full-time about those things that mattered most to me—a high bar, anyhow—but I could split the difference and be an editor-writer. It's certainly a common arrangement, and not a bad one, as far as compromises go. When I filled out the application, on the line for "salary requirement" I recklessly doubled what I'd been paid at the newspaper.

The weather was uncommonly mild that July, so I was spared a stifling subway ride en route to the interview, but even so my cheap shoes rubbed at my heels, and by the time I hit the midday chaos of Times Square I was already walking with a slight limp. In an effort to elevate myself from more than just another bookish girl without any fashion sense, I'd accessorized the black 1950s dress with Willy's 1970s acid-yellow pumps and a circa 2000s butter-yellow bag—"vintage with a modern twist," in fashion magazine parlance. As I approached the Condé Nast building, a trio of impossibly tall, impeccably dressed women spun through the revolving glass door and swanned off to lunch. I looked down at my clashing yellows and felt embarrassed for myself.

The editor-in-chief had me wait in the lobby for a full hour before she was ready to see me, but when I walked into her enormous sun-filled office, she looked me over from behind her huge white desk and said, with ironic approval, "Hot."

When the managing editor called to offer me the job, the salary was one-third more than the one I'd stated on the application.

I accepted the offer and started work the following week.

----◄█▶----

My transition from Grub Street to luxury journalism was not a smooth one. It's one thing to know, intellectually, that consumer magazines thrive on the insecurities of their readerships, another to actually be manipulating those insecurities, which, it turns out, fanned my own. I'd never been around so many perfectly groomed women at once—I imagined this must be what sororities are like. Manicures, blowouts, high heels, cleavage, white teeth bared, diamond rings sparkling. I felt so out of place, and alienated from myself, that I began to retreat from the journalist boyfriend, who accused me of not being ready for the sort of intimacy he wanted. Before long we, too, broke up.

I was alone again, but this time differently so; cleared of the static of a fraught relationship I was able to hear more clearly my own thoughts, and wouldn't you know it but Maeve, Neith, and Edna were up there chattering away, just waiting for me to join them. Downstairs, my fingers tapped industriously on the keyboard, writing photo captions about divans and the "rage for greige"; upstairs, my secret coven leaned over a card table spiking the teacups with whiskey and carrying on lively debates. Maeve didn't get what all the fuss over sex was about. Sure, she said, she was no prude, but the men seemed to like it a lot better than she did. Neith argued that this was purely a historical-moment problem: practicing free love had made the men really good in bed; however, by Maeve's time, they'd all forgotten about the clitoris. Edna was skeptical: perhaps you prefer women?

That fall my application to the artists' colony was accepted. Because I still hadn't found an actual, real-life conversation I liked about being single, I began to think that this hodgepodge bull session going on in my head might be all there was, and that maybe, if I wanted to read a book about it, I should try writing it myself. It seemed the right moment. By now I hadn't been in a steady relationship for four years, and I'd been mulling over the topic for eight—I was a bona fide spinster!

That Christmas I extended my vacation with all the "personal days" I'd been saving up, put my research materials into boxes, and packed them into a rental car. The morning I left for New Hampshire, the sky was as gray as concrete, the wet trees as black as streetlamps—until I turned onto the dirt road leading to the colony, and, close up, they reintroduced themselves as a hundred shades of rural: sage, mushroom, pussy willow, dove ("Memories growing, ring on ring / A series of weddings," Plath once wrote about winter trees).

When I parked the car and stepped out, I smelled smoke from a wood fire and heard the crunch of ice beneath my feet. This, I thought to myself, is what it means to be alone: this spectacularly acute aliveness to every color and scent and sound, the knowing that there is nothing between you and the vibrant, pulsating universe except this coat, these boots—which, you just as instantly realize, are exactly all you need.

I'd been given my own little cabin deep in the snowy woods. The next morning I sat down at my desk, looked proudly at my neat stacks of books—a prospector surveying her plot, feverish with the promise of gold—turned on my laptop, and spent the next two weeks crying, or trying not to.

I'd had no idea that writing about being single and living alone would be so difficult. In fact, I discovered, I had absolutely no idea what I was talking about. In my fantasy life, the one I shared with these dead women, I was confident and optimistic; in my actual, lived life, I was hopelessly unsure about my choices and often felt painfully lonely.

By now, at age thirty-three, comparing myself to my mother had become an increasingly unnerving habit. Every year I'd do the math, calculating where I was in relation to where she'd been, and then, on the prediction that I'd also die when she had, figure out how many years I had left.

What, I wondered, was I doing with all this freedom? Cycling

through relationships without any clear idea of what I was looking for, or even what I wanted. Working too much at a job I didn't
like, which contributed nothing meaningful to the world.

I was out of balance with my cohort, as well, as if I'd reverse-
engineered the proper order of things: while they'd run around
and experimented through their twenties and were now settling
down, I was headed in the opposite direction, a boat drifting into
the eye of the storm as the rest motored closer to shore.

That summer, the month he turned twenty-nine, my brother
had proposed to his girlfriend, the one he'd met four years earlier, just before coming to stay with me in Brooklyn. Nearly
everyone from high school and most of my friends from college
were married, or soon to be, and as for ex-boyfriends: W married in 2005; R met his soon-to-be wife in 2006 (today both
couples have two children). Even the close friends I'd made in
New York were "joining the vast majority," as Neith had put it.
All of us wanted to believe this wouldn't change anything. But
it did, invariably, in ways small and large. It's a rare friendship that transcends the circumstances that forged it, and being
single together in the city, no matter how powerful a bond when
it's happening, can prove pretty weak glue. Alliances had been
redrawn, resources shifted and reconsolidated; new envies replaced the old.

Whereas before we were all broke together, now they had
husbands splitting the rent and bills, and I couldn't shake my
awareness of this difference. A treacherous, unspoken sense of
inequality set in, which only six months into my new magazine job
had radically reversed: I'd become the one who could afford nice
restaurants while they had to channel their disposable incomes
toward a shared household, and I felt their unspoken judgment
just as before they'd felt mine.

One newly married friend lashed out at me for never inviting her to parties. I tried to explain: Didn't she see I was going

because someone else had invited me? And that if I didn't go, I'd be home alone, whereas she had someone to keep her company? When a dear friend said, "You know, I may be married now, but I'm still just like you! I can still do whatever I want!" I blanched. She'd been on her own so recently herself. Didn't she remember that being single is more than just following your whims—that it also means having nobody to help you make difficult decisions, or comfort you at the end of a bad week?

For entire days I sat in my cabin staring at the fireplace, disgusted with myself. Since moving to New York I'd been working nonstop, trying to earn a pocket of quiet and repose within which I could finally, actually, be a "real" writer—and now here I was, squandering that very chance.

When you're coupled, and especially if you're parents, time is a precious commodity, or a contested territory under constant renegotiation. To get more of it, you beg or borrow or outright redraw the border when the other isn't looking, and savor your briefly expanded plot of land as best you can—an all-girls weekend with your college roommates; an afternoon hike up a local mountain; even those delicious few minutes at the salon, when you surrender your head to the sink for your hair to be washed. One of the top editors at the magazine, married with children, claimed her greatest luxury was being alone on an airplane without Internet or cell service—the only time she had to herself.

When you're single, you are often buried in time, your mouth and eyes and ears stuffed with it. You hate it, rail against it, do whatever you can to get rid of it—work too much, drink too much, sleep around, make unsuitable friends, create an imaginary future filched from the lives of dead forgotten female writers, as if the economics and politics of their day weren't so entirely different from mine, as if a person can have a wish about what her life could be that's divorced entirely from context.

I didn't have any answers. All I had were questions, each of which I was still too inside of to be able to think about with any clarity.

This, I thought, *is what it means to be alone:* You are solid, intact, and then, without warning, a hinge unlatches, the chimney flue swings open, the infinite freezing black night rushes in, and there is nothing to do but grope in the cold to set things right again.

My failure was total. As soon as I got back to New York, I gave up the project, and writing in general, and tried to embrace my role as an editor at a home-décor magazine.

Sometimes I wonder if in childhood a fairy or folktale stamps our psyche and becomes an unconscious template. If so, I have two: "Beauty and the Beast" is surely the root of my preference for men whose looks sneak up and take you by surprise; and Marlo Thomas and Alan Alda's retelling of "Atalanta," as heard on Gloria Steinem and Co.'s *Free to Be . . . You and Me* album, about the princess who refuses to marry unless her suitor can best her in a footrace, is self-explanatory.

Maeve's favorite was Hans Christian Andersen's "The Little Mermaid"; in her biography, Angela Bourke draws a parallel between the predicament of the mermaid—who has to choose between "staying where she is loved and safe, and losing everything, including her voice, in order to see and know a larger world"—and Maeve's own.*

Neith refers in *The Bond* to the story of Bluebeard, which

---

*   Seen through the prism of Friedan's "feminine mystique," the original exchange between the mermaid and the witch is chilling: "But if you take away my voice," said the little mermaid, "what is left for me?" "Your beautiful form, your graceful walk, and your expressive eyes: surely with these you can enchain a man's heart. . . . Put out your little tongue that I may cut it off."

seems fitting; she herself was an uncommonly curious woman married to a man who, for all his good intentions, did his best to rein her in.

Edna drew from fairy tales and classical mythology so frequently that I hesitate to posthumously pin her with only one, but I've come to think that the story of Daphne and Apollo was hers—as in, she was the nymph. Her 1918 poem "Daphne" opens with, "Why do you follow me?— / Any moment I can be / Nothing but a laurel-tree / Any moment of the chase / I can leave you in my place / A pink bough for your embrace." Which sounds an awful lot like her 1917 poem "Witch-Wife," which opens with, "She is neither pink nor pale, / And she never will be all mine," and closes on, "But she was not made for any man, / And she never will be all mine." Edna was herself quite pink.

In her memoir, *A Backward Glance,* Edith Wharton—one of America's most celebrated grande dames—claims that, when she was a girl, everything from the tales of Mother Goose to those of Charles Perrault left her "inattentive and indifferent," while "the domestic dramas of the Olympians roused all my creative energy." This did not surprise me in the least. Whereas I as a child had tried to *worship* the Greek gods, she actually felt "at home" with them, as she put it, seeing in their behavior that of "the ladies and gentlemen who came to dine."

This difference in perspective more or less sums up why I'd never considered Wharton a candidate for my secret coven.

As far as I was concerned, she herself had sprung from the head of Zeus, a formidable, world-famous novelist from the moment of birth—someone to revere, not gossip with over whiskey-spiked tea. In a city teeming with lost eras, hers is as immutable as geology. If you'd told me that she'd willed into being the granite lions guarding the New York Public Library, or the constellations wheeling across the ceilings of Grand Central Station, I'd have believed you. Maeve led me to New York, but it was reading Wharton's novels in college that properly introduced me to it, and because of that I've always been grateful to her, possibly sycophantic.

That I couldn't personally identify with Wharton's gilded world had no bearing on my reverence—or so I thought. It's rumored that her father's side of the family inspired the idiom "Keeping up with the Joneses." Their own nuclear unit wasn't the wealthiest of their extended clan—as she explains in her memoir, the depreciation of American currency after the Civil War forced her parents to economize by renting out their town and country houses to profiteers—but they certainly belonged in her era's version of the one percent: the family of five (Wharton had two older brothers) spent their self-sought "homelessness" traveling through Europe, staying at grand hotels and friends' country estates. Though never formally schooled, little Wharton returned to Manhattan with a head full of classical music and art and was soon conversant in French, Italian, and German. At eighteen, she had five poems published in a single issue of *The Atlantic Monthly*—not that anyone cared, especially. Her old-money milieu groomed its women to be purely ornamental and actively discouraged any evidence to the contrary. The point of her existence was to marry.

Which she did, in 1885, just in the nick of time—twenty-three was four years too old for her set—seemingly without protest or second thoughts. Yet another reason I'd never pegged her as one of my own.

In fact, after rereading *The House of Mirth* (a rite of passage for any unmarried, bookish, urban neophyte), I began to think Wharton actually had it out for single women. I didn't like Lily Bart the first time around (along with my Henrietta Stackpole complex, I instantly distrust exceptionally beautiful heroines who trade on their looks), but now that I was single, too, I felt more sisterly toward this lost soul. I'd have thought Wharton above punishing someone for wanting what she herself had simply been born into. Also, the ending is a disgrace, not to mention un-feminist (talk about scare tactics!).

But while I was at the magazine, a new biography of Wharton came out and I learned that she had not, in fact, sprung fully formed from Zeus's head. She didn't publish her first book until she was thirty-five years old, and it wasn't a novel, but a home-decorating manual. It took another eight years after that for her to become a bestselling author.

Surely you can imagine my surprise upon learning that America's grande dame had launched her writing career as an expert on draperies and sconces. Her station had influenced my reverence after all—in a fillip of reverse bigotry, I'd mistaken wealth for invulnerability, and I'd forgotten that she, too, was an actual person.

"It took 'Pussy' Jones a painfully long time to turn into the writer Edith Wharton," observes her biographer Hermione Lee.

And so I'd found my fourth awakener. Soon enough I was calling her Edith.

Right before leaving for the artists' colony, I'd met a man at a friend's holiday party. D is extremely tall, with a very slight stoop to his shoulders, uncommonly large, navy-blue eyes, and the most disarming sincerity I'd ever encountered. We'd chatted briefly in the kitchen, and later, before he left, he walked over to me and said, "I would very much like to take you to dinner. May I have your contact information?"

Accustomed as I was to the standard vague mumble, usually via e-mail—"Hey, we should hang out sometime"—I was surprised and charmed by this direct approach.

While I was at the artists' colony he'd left me a voice mail message wishing me a happy New Year. Coming as it did amid my meltdown, I received it ambivalently, but once I was back in New York, ready to be a whole, new, un-miserable, non-writing me, I accepted his invitation.

On our second date, at a French bistro in Tribeca, we couldn't stop laughing—over what, I have no idea. He is very, very funny, and eccentric, a visual person and also an actual visionary (he invents new ways to use preexisting technologies). Talking with him was almost a cross-cultural exchange. I couldn't get enough of how he kept saying things I couldn't comprehend.

At one point he announced, "I'm a provider. All I do is work—I want to work so the woman I marry can do whatever she wants."

I laughed. "Really? Why do men continue to think they have to be the breadwinner?"

"I don't know," he said. "It's just how I am."

From someone else the announcement would have felt boringly male-chauvinistic, but from this obviously gentle and chronically sincere person it seemed okay.

Later that night he asked, "Have you ever considered dating a man who plays video games?"

I hadn't, but now I did.

Not since R had I been so at ease with another person. Our separate fascinations dovetailed into a curiosity cabinet that we filled on epic walks through the city, poking through Japanese toy stores and old archival print shops and the last remaining outdoor flea markets. He brought his camera everywhere and maintained massive digital files of seemingly everything he'd ever seen or done. Like me, he has an archivist's soul.

Too, I liked that he's ambitious and scrappy (he was launching a technology startup from his living room). At this point I was working full-time at the magazine, continuing with a new *Globe* column, and teaching the arts-criticism class at New York University—a genuinely workaholic schedule. I was up each night until one o'clock and awake again at six the next morning, but he didn't mind. When I was so exhausted I couldn't decide what to eat for dinner, he'd suggest we have breakfast instead, and we'd go to a diner for pancakes.

My friends liked him. My family did, too. It felt nice to be taken care of. And he was so good at it, a born caretaker. One weekend, when I was breaking down over all the work I had to get done, he actually scooped me up like a child and walked in circles around his living room, saying over and over, "One day you were little Katie Bolick in a little town, and then you came to the biggest city in America, and now look at yourself! It's all worked out!" It was so ridiculous and sweet that I couldn't help laughing through my tears.

The man Edith married, Teddy Wharton, said to be the best-looking graduate of Harvard Class of 1873, was from a distinguished Boston family. He was hardly her intellectual equal—he'd made it through college on deep pockets and bonhomie—but he was convivial good company, and he shared her love for travel. He's gone down in the Wharton annals as a royal waste of her time, but at the outset she was genuinely smitten, writing to her governess (and lifelong friend) a few weeks before the wedding, "It seems almost incredible that a man can be so devoted, so generous, so sweet-tempered & unselfish . . . he is one of the people whose charm makes itself felt at once."

Teddy didn't have to work, either—his mother gave him an allowance—so the couple spent their early years traveling between family summer houses and then wintering in New York City and Europe. Nearly a decade passed after her first publication in *The Atlantic Monthly* before she published again—between 1889 and 1891 she sold a story and a few poems to *Scribner's Magazine*—and then she fell silent.

She was busy, for sure, traveling and entertaining. Being a society wife was a full-time occupation. She got sick a lot, too, and complained often of fatigue. But what surprised me is how much she struggled with self-confidence. As she confessed in a letter to her editor at *Scribner's*: "I seem to have fallen into a period of groping, & perhaps, after publishing . . . I might see better what direction I ought to take and acquire more assurance (the quality I feel I most lack). . . . I have lost confidence in myself at present."

When I'd first arrived in New York, I'd been shocked to discover that *The Atlantic Monthly* wasn't a demographic anomaly— the publishing industry is overwhelmingly white, upper middle class, and Ivy League. For a while, I envied the entitlement these people carried so unthinkingly, as if they were simply owed writing assignments and staff positions and didn't have to earn them. I was convinced, as I worked my multiple jobs and scraped to get by, that, unlike me, all those people on easy street were completely free of insecurities.

By now I know better. It's even possible that those of us who move to New York City from the provinces have a somewhat easier time becoming adults than those who grew up here. Natives are blessed with countless enviable advantages, but what they don't have is the swift, firm yank of geographic relocation. Instead, if they are so inclined, they must manufacture their extraction from who they once were by other means, which is invariably much slower and differently painful.

My father likes to say that for change to take place, a person needs "a push and a pull." Edith had the push (innate talent and drive), no pull (financial necessity or external encouragement), and plenty of reasons not to write: her family's anti-intellectualism; a paternalistic culture that didn't expect women to work, and if they did, rarely took them seriously; the implicit expectation among elites that success is a given, and failure unheard of—and failure is, of course, integral to risk, without which writing is impossible.

In 1893 Edith took her first tiny step forward: she and Teddy finally bought their own house, in Newport, Rhode Island, the fashionable resort where her family and social circles summered, and she discovered a talent for decorating—at last, a creative outlet that didn't raise eyebrows.

With that, the dam broke. Not content to merely do up her own home, over the next few years she collaborated with a new friend, the architect Ogden Codman Jr., and together they wrote a how-to guide, *The Decoration of Houses*, published in 1897.* The book sold out immediately and quickly became one of the most influential decorating guides of the era; its ideas about how our homes should look and feel set a template for "good taste" that is venerated to this day. Technically it's an instruction book for the one percent. But really it's a sweeping, deeply informed history of European and American architecture, written with great authority and humor so dry it's almost imperceptible, as well as, if you look closely enough, a primer on the parallels between sociology, psychology, and architecture. "It seems easier to most people to arrange a room like some one else's than to analyze and express their own needs," reads one such gem. Another:

> [But] it must never be forgotten that every one is unconsciously tyrannized over by the wants of . . . dead and gone predecessors, who have an inconvenient way of thrusting their different habits and tastes across the current of later existences. The unsatisfactory relations of some people with their rooms are often to be explained this way.

---

* According to the *Merriam-Webster's Collegiate Dictionary*, the first known use of the word *décor*—from the French verb *décorer*, derived from the Latin noun *decor*, meaning "beauty, elegance, charm, grace, ornament"—also appeared in 1897; the term does not appear in her book.

Might not the same be said about our ideas regarding marriage and family?

We expect our great writers and painters, our shambling intellects and wild-haired Einsteins, to be so beholden to the life of the mind that they hardly notice the chairs on which they sit. That Edith masterfully described chairs—and sofas and rugs and hats and dresses—in her fiction I'd somehow taken for granted, as if she was simply very good at this particular literary device. To discover that her appreciation for surfaces went far deeper than that, and was indeed intellectual and personal, even an expression of something essential to her being, unlocked my own appreciation not only for these very same, so-called superficialities, but for myself.

In 1901 Edith went a step further, converting her architectural principles into bricks and mortar, and designed and oversaw the construction of her own country house. Set on 130 acres of rolling greensward in Western Massachusetts, The Mount, as she called it (after a home of her great-grandfather's), is, like the woman herself, a welter of contradictions masterfully contained.

Anyone can visit today. You enter the property along a dirt road that wends for a half mile past the greenhouse and stable and through thick, shady stands of evergreens, before dipping slightly and culminating in a walled courtyard abutting the back of a white stucco-and-wood mansion modeled on a seventeenth-century English manor (she'd hoped for stone or brick but couldn't afford it). The front of the house faces the opposite direction, looking out onto Laurel Lake and the mountains beyond, as if its maker, so wrapped up with broader vistas, didn't even think to try to impress you, her visitor.

Instead, you discover, she wished to nourish and entertain—

herself and others. I've never been to a house so grand that, once you're inside, feels so intimate. The spacious entry hall, dining room, drawing room, and library are big without being cavernous, and they are convivially interconnected with copious doors. Wandering through and between them, you feel Edith's presence not in a ghostly, hair-raising sort of way, but in the particularity of the layout and details, and how they allow you to physically experience the inner workings of a unique mind.

In Edith's opinion, the standard American nineteenth-century conception of what a house should be—essentially, a safe haven, a refuge from the world beyond—was a morbid holdover from feudal times, when castles and forts were designed with the sole intent of protecting their inhabitants from barbarous intruders. She far preferred the ancient Roman ideal of civic sociability, when people did their living not shut away indoors, but on the street and at the baths and forum (for men, that is; women stayed home with the children).

The estate is a rejection not only of conventional standards, but also of the "flat frivolity" of her upbringing, particularly her nearly two decades of dutifully playing society wife. Unlike the massive mansions of Newport, intended for show and big, garish parties, The Mount is designed for seclusion, work, and quality time with close friends and colleagues (most famously, Henry James). For the first time in her life, Edith was free to spend her time as she wished. All through the summer and fall, "small parties of congenial friends succeeded each other," as she wrote in her memoir, without putting a dent in her own productivity.

A rejection is significantly different from outright rebellion, however; as she wrote about décor in *The Decoration of Houses,* "Originality lies not in discarding the necessary laws of thought, but in using them to express new intellectual conceptions." Edith didn't want to leave her past in the dust, instead to retain the best parts and refashion them into her own version of the good life, what she called the "complex art of civilized living"—an elegant balance of work, leisure, and socializing. To this end, the estate is something of a proto-live-work space writ large, with each room serving a highly specific function.

The executive suite, so to speak, was Edith's wing on the second floor: an antechamber opening onto two high-ceilinged rooms with four big windows apiece and a bathroom between. Sunlight floods the east-facing bedroom in the morning, and in the afternoon filters gently into the west-facing boudoir. Otherwise, the two spaces are as different as night and day.

The room to the left, the boudoir, was her "public" space, where she conducted housekeeping business with her staff, wrote letters, and received her closest friends. The walls are a saturated blue-green, not unlike the famous Tiffany's box, and richly ornamented with elaborate decorative moldings and inset panels depicting large vases of roses. The massive fireplace is made of an unusual red-and-white marble; matching ruffled toile curtains hang to the floor. Outside, tall, closely set evergreens brush the windowpanes. The overall effect is one of seclusion and contemplation, a comfortable haven for quiet conversation or for administering quotidian details.

In comparison, the bedroom is a monk's cell (Teddy had his own). Her most intimate space, where only her maids and beloved dogs were allowed, it's the innermost room mentioned in one of her most frequently quoted passages, in which she compares a woman's nature to "a great house":

There is the hall, through which everyone passes in going in and out; the drawing-room, where one receives formal visits; the sitting-room, where the members of the family come and go as they list; but beyond that, far beyond, are other rooms, the handles of whose doors perhaps are never turned; no one knows the way to them, no one knows whither they lead; and in the innermost room, the holy of holies, the soul sits alone and waits for a footstep that never comes.

The innermost rooms common to most women of her class were decorated to encourage idle repose; Edith planned hers for maximum productivity, as efficient as a modern-day office. The walls were kept bare, and the ceiling is plain. The fireplace is an inconspicuous gray marble. The windows are hung with simple white curtains that don't obstruct the view, making the landscape itself the only decoration (anticipating by half a century the "views as wallpaper" in Philip Johnson's iconic Glass House). On a clear day, the room feels like a container of air suspended on miles of silence.

Edith did her writing in bed, "after bath and before breakfast," as she once told a friend. On a typical morning she'd wake with the sun, prop herself up against her pillows—she liked goose down, and a delicate linen sheeting—lean her writing board across her knees, and work steadily until noon, filling sheaves of foolscap with her neatly looped cursive, letting each page drop to the floor as soon as she'd finished. Afterward, while she lunched with houseguests outside on the terrace, her secretary would gather the mess of fallen papers and type them into order.

Other than Edith's servants, few ever witnessed this tableau, but descriptions of it were passed from one friend to the next until it became part of her lore. Like the large pocket sewn onto the front of Emily Dickinson's sole remaining dress, stocked with envelope scraps and a pencil should inspiration strike, or Mark Twain's flamboyant white suit, the image encapsulates what we imagine to be Edith's very essence: her queenly stature, steely discipline, silverware and bone china glinting in the sun—a gimlet-eyed critic embedded (literally!) in the belly of the beast.

Afternoons held a group excursion of some stripe: long walks, gardening, horseback riding, touring in her motorcar through the countryside. After a sumptuous dinner, she and her guests would retire to the library and give readings (Walt Whitman was a favorite choice; she and James both considered him "the greatest of American poets") or stargaze from the terrace.

And so the template was set. The period of 1902 to 1911 was the most transformative of Edith's entire life. She published six novels, three short-story collections, three works of nonfiction, and one volume of poetry. She freed herself from what had become an unhappy marriage (officially divorcing in 1913). She experienced passionate love for the first time, during (and after) a brief affair with an American journalist named Morton Fullerton. Most important, perhaps, she forged the work and social habits that allowed her to live alone, very happily, until she died at seventy-five.

As she wrote in her memoir, by 1905, the year she published *The House of Mirth,* an immediate bestseller and the novel that made her famous, "At last I had groped my way through to my vocation. . . . The Land of Letters was henceforth to be my country, and I gloried in my new citizenship. . . . The incredible had happened! . . . My recognition as a writer had transformed my life."

By dreaming The Mount into being, she'd set the stage for her own singularity.

It's almost too good to be true: while urging America to cut loose from tradition, Edith herself had "broken through the chains which had held me so long in a kind of torpor," as she described in her memoir. Picture Bruce Banner as a Victorian lady morphing into the Incredible Hulk, her exploding figure reducing her corset and hat and parasol to mere shreds, whole matching bedroom and dining sets falling away like shattered china.

Except, this Victorian lady didn't become a green-skinned monster. She remained a lady, a larger, stronger, and more formidable version of the one she'd been. This was the irony of Edith's great escape: she broke free of convention while remaining in place. In the doing she redefined her relationship to the home and, along with it, ours.

And so it dawned on me: taste, like appetite, is something we're born with. Both are subject to and even shaped by culture. Interior decorators—the good ones, at least—are people who have an exceptionally high sensitivity to their environments, as well as an intuitive ability to manipulate color and spatial relations.

At the magazine, a lot of my time was spent looking very closely at the rooms of a house, decoding why one room felt dramatic, say, and another calming, and translating these visual equations into words. It was surprisingly fun to discover the ways in which interior decorating conforms to its own innate laws, like science. Oh, not rocket science—but a genuine system that, when properly understood and applied, has the ability to shape our moods and how we think.

Some of the variables were blessedly obvious: A pair of matching lamps establishes a pleasing sense of symmetry. Pale colors make a room feel larger; dark colors create a close, cozy feel. More intriguing were concepts such as scale. I learned that if you want to combine many different patterns in one room, just keep them all in the same palette, and the result won't feel chaotic. Or, a tight, close floral print is nice in small doses, but she who wallpapers an entire room in tiny roses with matching curtains and bedclothes invites eyestrain and headaches.

In her autobiography, Elsie de Wolfe—a contemporary and fan of Edith's, as well as the woman credited with inventing the profession of interior decorating—recalls the day she came home from school to discover that her parents had redone the drawing room. Like Neith, she refers to herself in the regal third person:

> She ran [in] . . . and looked at the walls, which had been papered in a design of gray palm-leaves and splotches of bright red and green on a background of dull tan.
>
> Something terrible that cut like a knife came up inside her. She threw herself on the floor, kicking with stiffened legs, as she beat her hands on the carpet. . . . She cried out, over and over: "It's so ugly! It's so ugly."

Whether you interpret that passage as the tantrum of a spoiled child or early evidence of the legendary interior decorator to come depends perhaps on your own hardwiring. For me it was like looking in the mirror.

I'd been carrying around a similar memory for as long as I could remember, and one I simply didn't know what to do with; there was nothing *memorable* about it—no point, no drama. I'd written it down several years before, when R's mother had invited me to a daylong writing workshop in the Berkshires (not far from Edith's house, though I didn't know it at the time), and we'd been instructed to "free write," which I hate doing, so I'd petulantly grabbed the first thing that came to mind, a stubborn, pointless memory:

> I am seven years old, and I have just come home from school. I set my books on the stair and wander into my favorite room, as I do every day—and scream.
>
> The walls have changed. When I left for school that morning the living room was its usual deep, dusky orange; now it's a tart cranberry.

The orange-ness of those walls was the spirit of that room, the point of it. At night, after dinner, I would sprawl with my schoolbooks on the rug before the fireplace, my parents stationed reading in their armchairs, and watch the orange flames cast onto the orange walls flickers of scorched, shadowy apricot, and sink into this all-embrace of heat, parents, bedtime, rug. There was no better pleasure than letting my head rest on my papers and surrendering completely to the warmth, a sensation made blissfully painful by knowing that giving in meant waking to a cold, dark room, body aching and stiff, the fire burned down to a few ginger embers. Now all of this is gone!

This cranberry color—it repulses me. It is overbright and public. What had been a glowing brick oven is now a cheerful bandstand. Where before the thick, bisque cornices framing the ceiling and windows had seemed stately and important, now they were white, like festoonery, as strained as a forced smile, or a stiff, starched bow. How could this happen? How could a world be gone in an instant? Why hadn't anyone consulted me?

Well, I was seven years old.

The purpose of the writing retreat was to encourage and support one another, so everyone nodded meaningfully—presumably as perplexed by the vapidity of the memory as I was—and then one woman burst out with, "The 1980s! That cranberry color is just so '80s!" And everyone laughed, myself included, though I actually didn't get what the 1980s had to do with it.

De Wolfe was far cannier than I. As an adult, she recognized that the wallpaper she found so offensive was designed by William Morris, whose work she frequently and enthusiastically derided in her syndicated newspaper column. Like Edith, she'd been mounting her own public attack against the overuse of ornament and fabric, the stultifying atmospheres that made living rooms feel more like tombs. In other words, she loathed the Victorian aesthetic because it evoked her own unhappy childhood.

Edith, too, was highly sensitized to her environment as a child. In her memoir she confides, "My photographic memory of rooms and houses—even those seen briefly, or at long intervals—was from my earliest years a source of inarticulate mystery, for I was always vaguely frightened by ugliness." Like de Wolfe's, her aversion to Victorianism was forged early on: "One of the most depressing impressions of my childhood is my recollection of the intolerable ugliness of New York City, of its untended streets and the narrow houses so lacking in external dignity, so crammed with smug and suffocating upholstery."

Until Edith and de Wolfe—and a whole raft of other women now known as the Lady Decorators—entered the field, architects were exclusively men, who designed houses inside and out, from the blueprint to the arrangement of the furniture. The publication of Edith's design manual wasn't a radical act exactly (and, of course, she shared credit with a male coauthor), but it did open the door for her peers to enter the public realm as professional tastemakers, even establishing their own decorating businesses.

One unintended result of this development was the gendering of the design world. Until only very recently, architecture and industrial design were considered male pursuits, as if all those slide rules and heavy metals were too tricky for the fairer sex, who were confined to the soft, fabric-filled realm of decorating. (Even today, only 19 percent of licensed architects are female.)

Consequently, the world of interiors has been denied the true respect it deserves, to actual, negative effect. My own initial scorn for home décor is the best testimony to this I know—and a variation on the kind of internalized sexism that is so often hard to detect. As the evolutionary psychologist Steven Pinker writes in

The Blank Slate, "The belief that human tastes are reversible cultural preferences has led social planners to write off people's enjoyment of ornament, natural light, and human scale and force millions of people to live in drab cement boxes." Ignoring our primal cravings comes at a cost.

Not until the turn of this current century did scientists begin paying attention to our unconscious relationships with our physical environments, confirming what Edith and de Wolfe and others like them had known all along. Studies suggest that high ceilings encourage creative thinking; that smooth, literally cool materials such as chrome and glass connote a sense of psychological coldness, possibly because they remind us of ice, whereas wood, which has a higher resting temperature than metal, evokes a feeling of warmth; that the angular forms common to high-modernist furniture pose the same threat to our animal brains as does a sharp rock or tree branch—something to be on the alert for, not relax into. Rooms painted red, a color we automatically associate with danger, make us better at paying attention to details (such as catching spelling errors), while those painted blue, a color we associate with wide-open vistas such as the sky and ocean, encourage creative problem solving.

In other words, with her bedroom suite, Edith created the perfect environment for her work: in the boudoir, her imagination turned inward; in the bedroom, it took flight.

And so I began to enjoy my job at the magazine. The office itself was a standard maze of gray cubicles, but the atmosphere was so far removed from the actual world that stepping off the elevator onto the eighteenth floor was like slipping into *I Dream of Jeannie*'s pink-and-purple bottle. Here, carpets and cushions,

not politicians or bankers or filmmakers or novelists, were paramount. Days passed in a froth of silks and Belgian linens; the
tiniest tassel was treated with gravity. It wasn't that life beyond
receded; rather, it was remodeled, renovated, everyday emotions
transmuted into material goods. When the stock market was
soaring, our hallways burst with joyous excess destined for photo
shoots: mountains of costly, hand-embroidered throw pillows;
$400 golden wastebaskets. When it tanked, the tides of luxury
receded, leaving behind an uptick in DIY resourcefulness and an
enthusiasm for glue guns.

Happy at work, and with D, for the first time in several years
I actually felt like celebrating my birthday; that summer, when I
turned thirty-four, I threw a party on the roof of D's (very nice)
apartment building in Tribeca, complete with hired bartenders,
custom cocktails, and catered hors d'oeuvres.

I began to think that maybe, finally, I was growing up.

But at my brother's wedding the following month, I blew any
semblance of maturity. I ruined the toast I was to make to the
newlyweds. I'd been working on it for months. I was so proud of
Christopher—as proud as a mother, almost—and felt so strongly
that I must be for him both his mother and his sister that when
I say "working on" the toast, what I really mean is constantly
panicking, writing and rewriting, trashing, and procrastinating,
so that by the day of the wedding I hadn't finished and was still
scribbling at the reception, and when I stood up and delivered it,
it was horrible. I made no sense. I rambled. I forgot to mention
his bride.

I didn't then and still don't want to think that I was subcon-
sciously sabotaging my (and their) experience because I couldn't
bear to be the only one left without a family of my own, but that
may be so.

The following month I went to Paris for the first time, with
D and his parents and two brothers, all of whom I adored, and

traipsed happily behind them from one museum to the next. They're incredibly open, generous people, funny and warm. *What wonderful in-laws they'd be*, I thought to myself.

And yet something was off. I'd been working so much, I hadn't even had time to think about or plan for this trip; I simply showed up and followed, which wasn't entirely stupid—D's parents know the city as well as their own house—but underscored my complete lack of agency. I still wasn't living my own life. All I did was stay late at the office, go out for dinner with D or a friend, drink one glass of wine too many, and afterward lie on the sofa, an empty husk. I'd been privately fretting over this fatigue. Sure, work was demanding, but there was something aggressive about how tired I'd become, almost as if I'd been drugged; I'd sleep through whole weekends if I could.

When, in Paris, I started stealing sleep like an addict—begging off breakfast so I could stay in bed, sneaking out for a five-minute nap in the lobby while everyone finished lunch—I could no longer deny that I'd been this way once before, also with a boyfriend, my first year of college; after six or so months together, when in his presence I'd be blindsided by the overwhelming urge to sleep. As soon as we broke up, the malaise vanished. Lesson learned, clean and simple: I'd been bored. Not because the boyfriend himself was boring, but because I was still too young and intellectually unformed to understand how much I craved a particular sort of probing, analytical conversation we didn't have together.

Not long after D and I returned to New York, I met up with some new friends at a bar after work, writers all, without him. As the night progressed, and our conversation gained momentum—among the four of us it seemed we'd read every book ever published—I felt a forgotten energy fizz up and down my arms and legs, like goose bumps, as well as a guilty awareness that I didn't want to call D and invite him to join us. I hardly knew these people, and yet the immediacy with which we shared references and ideas made me feel at home in a way that being with D never had. I didn't know if I'd ever gain entry to Edith's "Land of Letters," but I yearned to, and at the very least, I realized, I wanted someone who wanted to travel there with me.

For Thanksgiving, I flew to visit my old friend from college, Michael, now an English professor in Toronto. Wheeling my little roller suitcase through the airport I felt as light as Mary Poppins* and her magically bottomless carpetbag, as if I hadn't been on a plane at all but blown in by a breeze. All weekend I soared—as awake as I'd ever been—gusting from coffee shop to dinner party, energized by the nonstop talk that has characterized our friendship since our freshman year in college. The boyfriends come and go, but Michael is there whenever I need him. Of course I could not stop analyzing my predicament incessantly.

"I am beginning to think that D thinks marriage is next. Maybe I think marriage is next. Is marriage next? Do I marry him?" I said, probably multiple times.

"You absolutely do not have to marry anyone," he said.

"But I'm thirty-four," I said.

"Who cares?" he said.

"Wait," I said. "I'm asking the wrong question. What I mean is: How am I here again in this same place, just as I was with R?"

"You have no choice," he said. "Men think you're marriage material."

"That's a little self-congratulatory," I said. "Every man I get

---

* In 1934, when P. L. Travers introduced the fictional spinster nanny, modeled on her own never-married Aunt Ellie, she was in her mid-thirties and living with a woman; at forty she moved out on her own and adopted a baby boy.

involved with does not want to marry me. I'm not even sure D does. What I mean is, how have I once again put myself in a situation where marriage seems the implicit next step, one I'm ambivalent about taking?"

We were in his kitchen, putting on our shoes to go take his dog for a walk. "Or wait," I added. "Maybe 'marriage material' is kind of an insult! Who wants to be *marriage material*?"

"But you are marriage material," he said. "You can't deny that you strive for self-realization, and to be substantial, and being substantial is what makes someone marriageable. Nobody actually wants to marry a boring person, even if so many do. Didn't Jane Austen write in *Emma* something like, 'Men of sense, whatever you may choose to say, do not want silly wives'?

"The odd dilemma of the spinster," he continued professorially, "is, she's the most marriage-inspiring, and the less she wants it, the more coveted she becomes—at least until the moment it's too late!"

We laughed and then sank for a second into a mutual sulk. One of our ongoing arguments is whether, on the dating market, aging is worse for straight women or gay men.

"Also," he said, "no matter how hard you look for something else—some way of being in a committed relationship with a man that isn't marriage—there *is* nothing else. Not in the minds of most straight men, at least."

That part rang true. I'd noticed a pattern: usually if a man and I made it all the way through seven dates, we became girlfriend and boyfriend; at six months—the longest amount of time a person can remain on her/his best behavior, I've concluded from ample field research—there was a big fight, accusations of being misunderstood, etc.; if that didn't sink us, we'd have another three good months before the pressure started to mount, like a weather front, and we exploded—whether bang or whimper, game over.

After Thanksgiving, back in New York, as D scrolled through his phone, showing me pictures of his own holiday with his family, a photo of an antique diamond ring flashed past. I think. I pretended not to see it. Who knows? Maybe I really didn't.

That Christmas, his parents brought us to a luxurious eco-resort in Mexico. D and I had our own hacienda with a massive bed draped in white mosquito netting, as romantic as a honeymoon.

I was sick with a sense of duplicity. I didn't know why, but I just didn't want this—this being part of a family. It didn't make sense: I love my family. I loved D's. I envied my brother's whole-hearted commitment to his wife, and her certainty that she wanted children. I suspected (and still do) that I would love being a mother—which, I realized, as we trooped *en famille* down to the beach each afternoon, was part of the problem.

Shielded by an umbrella, I peered over the rim of *Middle-march* and watched as a woman my age hoisted her toddler onto her hip, the child's dimpled legs tawny from the sun, her hair a beautiful frenzy of caramel curls—the most ethereal of cherubs. My arms ached to hold the girl, feel that soft, plump cheek rest against my shoulder, let my nose graze the top of her head.

But the knowing was visceral: if I became a mother, I'd lose myself. I wouldn't become a "real" writer. This was irrational. The way my mother's freelance writing career made her so available to me was a firsthand lesson that someday I, too, could do the same; indeed, all around me were women who wrote and also had children, from friends to world-famous award-winning authors I read about in magazines. And yet still, for me, making such a significant decision seemed improbable. I'd be erased by pregnancy, sleep deprivation, teething rings, diapers; sippy cups, car seats, strollers, Legos; day care, other kids' birthday parties, pumpkin farms, bouncy houses; ballet recitals, soccer practice, summer camp, temper tantrums; all-consuming love and eternal worry ("Now my heart lives outside of me," a friend said about her small twins). In comparison, my current work schedule would be a cakewalk.

Meanwhile, watching D's parents, I saw that they embodied the very best of the traditional male-breadwinner model. D's mother had always worked as an interior designer, but only on projects she wanted, free to follow her creativity beyond the demands of the marketplace. They were obviously still very much in love and had an enviable closeness, a blend of mutual respect and shared adventure.

But still, I couldn't do it. I *wanted* to want a man who wanted to support me, along with all the possibilities such an arrangement suggests: being able to afford a nanny so I could write full-time and also raise children; traveling wherever we liked; maybe even fulfilling my adolescent dream of designing and building my own house, à la Edith (albeit different)—but I kept tripping up over that tiny construction, "my own." My own, my own.

That afternoon, after lunch, D and his brothers and I played in the pool like a pack of unhinged otters, dunking and bonking one another's heads with foam bats. The sky was clear; the sea spangled. Our laughter rang out. So much beauty—handed to me, a gift on a platter. Suddenly there I was again, back during my first year with R in Brooklyn Heights, smothered by the sensation of having been handed a prize I'd yet to earn.

Later, at the hacienda, I told D I didn't want to shower together and spent a long time in the bathroom washing my hair and combing through the conditioner. Was it possible, I wondered, that being self-supporting wasn't just a "goal" I wanted to achieve but a state of being that was integral to my motivation and sense of personal achievement? That, in my father's words, I needed the "pull" of financial necessity along with the "push" of my own drive to feel alive? Or, a variation on that: I needed to create my own security. Abandoning my struggle, and slipping into an easier life, meant abandoning myself.

It was a depressing thought, no matter how I looked at it. If true, it meant I might never have children, for the simple reason that I couldn't know when I'd be ready to take on the responsibility of caring for another human being. And even if I reached that point while still in my childbearing years, I couldn't guarantee I'd be able to provide the material support to which a child is entitled. After showering I put on my favorite red cotton dress for dinner— red, the color of danger.

"Always do what you are afraid to do," urged Ralph Waldo Emerson, according to landfills physical and digital, overflowing with greeting cards, posters, blogs, and Facebook posts. As with many a popular adage, the meaning changes when you return the quote to its context. From his 1841 essay "Heroism":

> Be true to your own act, and congratulate yourself if you have done something strange and extravagant, and broken the monotony of a decorous age. It was a high counsel that I once heard given to a young person, "Always do what you are afraid to do."

He doesn't elucidate. But the passage clearly celebrates fidelity to individuality and unconventionality, which is many degrees different from the equally famous "The only thing we have to fear is fear itself," as Franklin D. Roosevelt announced in his 1932 inaugural address (paraphrasing Francis Bacon). What does it mean that even I, a congenital optimist, detect a whiff of that infamous American will to prevail, against all odds, in that rousing, pleasingly counterintuitive, rather macho, and imminently quotable sentiment?

I prefer how Jane Addams put it (likely in direct response to the Emerson quote, which she'd recorded three years prior in her journal): "To do what you are afraid to do is to guide your life by fear. How much better not to be afraid to do what you believe in doing! Keep one main idea, and you will never be lost."

She wrote that around 1880, while an undergraduate at Rockford Female Seminary, for the student magazine. Her plan was to be a doctor, so she could live and work among the poor; instead, she had to undergo a spinal operation, suffered a nervous breakdown, dropped out of medical school, and spent much of her twenties in despair. But she'd meant what she wrote.

In 1888 Addams traveled to see Toynbee Hall, a Gothic complex in the East End of London that united men of all backgrounds to provide social and educational opportunities for the working classes. The next year, at age twenty-nine, she and a friend founded their own female-centered version in Chicago, called Hull-House. By 1920, there were almost five hundred settlement houses across the country, run predominantly by single women— those who had the most time to devote to the cause.

Addams never married or had children, but she launched the social-reform movement, essentially the precursor to the social-welfare programs started by the federal government in the 1930s. In 1931 she was the first American woman to win the Nobel Prize.

On the last day of the Mexico trip D's mother and I went for a long walk on the beach. She's tall and thin, with short, dyed-red hair, possibly the most serenely free-spirited person I've ever met.

"My husband is the most important thing in the world to me," she said.

We'd never spoken intimately; I liked that the walk was bringing this out of her. But I wasn't sure where she was headed.

She got right to the point. "Kate, I would love to have you as my daughter-in-law. D loves you. We all love you. But I want you to know that you should only marry someone if he is the most important thing in the world to you, more important than anyone or anything else."

It was the kindest thing she could have done for any of us.

Back in New York, D and I broke up.

I was very, very sad. But not frightened. I could be alone again.

And then, after the sadness had passed, I saw that I'd crossed into an entirely new country.

I wasn't alone again. My life was teeming with people: family, friends, colleagues. The tailor at the dry-cleaning shop who hemmed my dresses and skirts. My hairdresser, a gifted gossip. The college friends I'd kept close with even though we lived in different states and countries. The convivial widow who on warm afternoons sat on her stoop with a magazine and a glass of bourbon and drew me into a chat when I passed.

The following year, my brother and his wife would have their first daughter, and my heart would do exactly what people say happens, expand even further.

I started jokingly referring to my job as my "husband" (as in, my source of economic stability), an "antidepressant" (it was so demanding, I didn't have time for melancholy), and a full-time "vacation" (even with the long hours, it was far easier than writing freelance), all rolled into one. It even enabled me to go on actual vacations. That fall, when the man I'd just started dating went to Puerto Rico for work, I decided that sex in a tropical location while in the flush, first stages of a romance was well worth the expense, and I flew down to join him. That winter, I skipped out on Christmas by traveling to Argentina for a week with a new female friend, also single. We had so much fun, we called it "our honeymoon."

Now I wanted to make my studio apartment look as beautiful as it felt. I was flipping through a book about Charleston, the farmhouse that Virginia Woolf's sister, the painter Vanessa Bell, had rented in the English countryside a century before. It seemed to embody my fantasy life: sunlit rooms cozy with sagging bookshelves, oil portraits hung beside overstuffed chairs, and nearly every surface—walls, doors, windowsills—covered in her own hand-painted designs.

I was captivated by a specific corner—nubby lavender linen love seat, white paisleys hand-painted on lavender walls, French doors open onto a wildflower garden—and I submitted to the magazine's powers-that-be that we produce a feature about making over my tiny Brooklyn studio in its image. For a furious month a stylist sorted through fabrics and paint chips, even commissioned a replica love seat. My own piles of books and thrift-store treasures would round out the effect—everything but the French doors opening onto a wildflower garden.

The stylist and his team did the entire makeover in two days, while I was at the office. The night I returned home to the completed project, a low lamp was glowing on my desk, and Bach's cello suites warbled from my ancient boom box, hidden from view. I sank onto the love seat. The walls were covered with hand-painted paisleys. Dramatic curtains with a Bloomsbury-esque blue-and-purple floral print hung to the floor. I felt as if I'd just been pulled into a deep, warm embrace. A Technicolor fantasia of Woolf's famous "a room of one's own."

A few weeks after the feature was published, I started receiving e-mails from women I'd known growing up, mothers of friends, friends of my mother: "I was standing in line at the grocery store and saw your apartment in a magazine! You are *so* your mother's daughter!" And, "Good Lord, if your mother could only see what you've done—to think you have exactly her style!" I stared at their messages. My mother didn't have style. What in the world were they talking about?

I learned the answer a couple of years later, when the magazine sent me to New Orleans to write a feature about the home of an interior designer. I was thrilled; the novelty of traveling for work hadn't worn off—I'd never stayed in such nice hotels. Besides, New York was getting to me—all the endless late nights, the screeching subways. Even so, the Puritan in me kept guard; becoming accustomed to luxury seemed unwise.

Each afternoon, after finishing my research, I strolled through the various neighborhoods, marveling over the astonishing charm of it all: bright red geraniums erupting from clay pots; wisteria vines curling over a wrought-iron balcony; coral paint peeling from a weathered façade. But it wasn't until my last day that the low-running conversation I'd been having in my head finally made itself heard. "Oh, Mom would love those tall, narrow shutters," I'd say to myself, or, "Just look at those faded chintz curtains! Mom would die and go to heaven."

Did I actually laugh out loud? I wanted to. I couldn't believe it. Not only had my mother had a very specific sense of style, but I'd inherited it. Exactly. All this time, I thought I'd been perfecting my own "neo-Victorian bohemianism" (or so I'd come to think of it), but in fact I was channeling her and the lovely old house she'd furnished, trying to invoke its familiar comforts in each small apartment I moved to. The careworn antiques, the weakness for scrollwork, the floral prints. How had I never noticed this?

The explanation dawned slowly. When she was alive, I was still directing my aesthetic energies into my clothes. I was proud of our handsome home (not to mention proprietary of the living room walls) but completely blind to the effort that went into making it; hanging new curtains seemed a tedious, grown-up chore, like filing taxes. After she died, and my family life changed, the house became a mausoleum to my lost, happier childhood, one shrouded in grief, not a place I could experience with any objective distance.

It wasn't until I became an adult myself, living on my own, that I graduated into paying close attention to where I lived, analyzing and upgrading, eventually developing a domestic language, which felt far more natural to me, I suddenly realized, than fashion ever had. When you're insecure about your appearance, trying to make yourself look better is a fraught endeavor. The home is a blank canvas, or empty vessel—a place where the will toward beauty can be expressed unchecked, without the messy complications of the self.

Several months later I received a mysterious e-mail.

"Is this Nancy Bolick's daughter? I'm Margaret, the friend she wrote a romance novel with . . ."

"Romance novel?!" I typed back. "What romance novel?" My mother had written many newspaper and magazine articles, and several young-adult history books, but a romance novel? She didn't even read romance novels.

It turned out that over brunch one morning in the 1980s Margaret had suggested that they collaborate on "one of those stupid books that are selling so well," for fun. My mother confided to her that she had, in fact, already started writing one—this in itself blew my mind—so the two decided to pick up where she'd left off.

When the publisher asked for a "racier" rewrite, they gave it up. I asked if she could mail me the manuscript.

Several weeks later, there it was, stuffed into my building's tiny metal mailbox. I'd worked late, and on the walk home from the subway a thunderstorm had decimated my umbrella; I tugged gingerly on the package, trying not to get it wet. Once upstairs, I poured a bowl of cereal for dinner and sat down at my kitchen table. That night my apartment felt particularly empty and dark, in a way it didn't usually, rain driving against the windows.

Since my mother had died, I'd longed to hear her voice one last time—and here it was, an unexpected communiqué from the grave. Not only that, but I was about to encounter her fantasy life. Why else would a happily married mother of two embark on such an uncharacteristic project, if not to dream up an imaginary existence, a make-believe version of what might have been? "We put in a lot about our children and our lives," Margaret had said in her e-mail.

However gently I opened the envelope, it tore anyhow. Out came a thick stack of white paper yellowed by age. The font was pale grayish, from an old 1980s dot-matrix printer, and the title page read *Design for Love,* by Rena Hart (a pseudonym!). In disbelief I began to read, forcing myself to go as slowly as possible, fighting the desire to devour the entire thing in one fell swoop, so I could savor each precious paragraph, each spectral sentence, for as long as I could.

What I read astounded me. The book is first-rate Harlequin, replete with heaving bosoms and star-crossed lovers. Its plot, a complicated scenario involving a real-estate investor scheming to take over a sleepy New England town, is lifted straight from a community issue my mother had felt passionately about. But one thing in particular pulled back the curtains, not just on my mother's life but on my own: the book's heroine, Ivy Winter, is an unmarried interior decorator living alone in New York City.

A woman once told me that in the late 1930s, when her grandmother turned eighteen, her father, a lawyer, had turned to her
and said, "Darling, in the eyes of the law you are now a spinster."

For argument's sake, let's agree that today eighteen—voting
age in the United States, when most people finish high school, and
when consent is incontestably legal in all states—is the age when a
girl becomes a "single woman." In that case, my mother was single
for six of her fifty-two years, and Edith for twenty-nine.

For my mother, being single was primarily a fantasy, one so
powerful that well into her marriage she chose to explore it in her
only completed work of fiction (that I know of). For Edith, it was
a long-term reality that, perhaps, began as a fantasy.

Edith was seventy-two when her memoir came out in 1934.
I'd been particularly struck by a short passage about her never-
married aunt, Elizabeth Schermerhorn Jones. Edith remembered
her as "a ramrod-backed old lady compounded of steel and granite," who, as a consumptive child, had been locked in her bedroom
one October and not set free "till the following June, when she
emerged in perfect health, to live till seventy" (in fact, she died
when she was sixty-six).

In her early forties, Aunt Elizabeth bought eighty acres in the
Hudson Valley and commissioned the building of a twenty-three-
room, brick Norman Romanesque mansion on a bluff overlooking
the river. After dubbing it a "dour specimen of Hudson River
Gothic," Edith claims that "from the first" she was "obscurely
conscious of a queer resemblance between the granitic exterior
of Aunt Elizabeth and her grimly comfortable home, between her
battlemented caps and the turrets of Rhinecliff."

I seized this observation and used it to support my pet theory
that Edith didn't like single women.

By now I had for ammunition not only the preening, wretched Lily Bart, but also the knowledge that, though only a decade older than Neith, Edith was deaf to the politics of suffragists and New Women. I grew rather adamant about it, trying to convince people that the only reason Edith was famous and Neith obscure was because Edith wrote about the moneyed elite, and we never, ever tire of reading about rich people, no matter that hers lived more than a century ago.

I trust by now that you're wise to my reversals of opinion.

When I went back to Edith's books and looked at them again through the lens of my grudge, I saw that I'd been completely wrong. She wrote frequently about unmarried women—*I* was the one who'd been blinded by all the silk gowns and opera gloves.

Lily Bart's descent into a boardinghouse wasn't a punishment; among other reasons, it was how Edith engineered the story to include, front and center, the lives of single women who hadn't been born into privilege. Sure, where Lily is bold and glittering, Gerty Farish is meek and mousy, but it's Gerty who has a secure sense of self and manages to live alone with great grace and virtue. The poor, innocent spinsters Ann Eliza and Evelina of *Bunner Sisters*; Kate Clephane, who abandons her husband and infant daughter in *The Mother's Recompense*; Charlotte Lovell, the unmarried mother in *The Old Maid*—all of them are not only crucial to Edith's critique of the conspicuous consumption she grew up with, but also allow her to explore the lives of single women in the city.

Edith died before her Aunt Elizabeth's mansion became a metaphor for every lonely old spinster: by the 1950s, it was an abandoned ruin, and it remains one to this day.

At this point I'd been "single" in the strictest definition of the word for seventeen years, nine of which I'd spent being single and also fantasizing about being single, simultaneously.

At first this realization greatly depressed me. I'd been running in place.

But then I went back and counted the number of single female characters Edith had dreamed up between 1900, when she published her first book of fiction, *The Touchstone,* which features a famous widowed writer who was married only very briefly, and 1913, when she divorced Teddy. During that thirteen-year period she produced six novels, three novellas, and forty-three short stories. Including minor characters, that adds up to at least eighty-two single women (fifty-seven unmarried, twenty-two widowed, three divorced) and seventy-eight wives, one of which is having an affair, another who is separated, and two who are scheming to kill their husbands.

Who knows? Maybe just as Edith dreamed her new life into being by designing The Mount, she created these fictional single figures as a way to imagine herself beyond her own marriage, testing the waters, so to speak. What did they teach her?

I'd already decided what she had taught me. Maeve, the first of my five awakeners, had supplied an image and point of view that set my adulthood into motion. Neith had given me the words to think critically about marriage, and actually establish a life of my own. Edna had led me through those early, confusing years of sex as a single person.

What Edith taught me was this: to live happily alone requires a serious amount of intentional thought. It's not as simple as signing the lease on your own apartment and leaving it at that. You must figure out what you need to feel comfortable at home and in the world, no matter your means (indeed, by staying within your means), and arrange your life accordingly—a metaphorical architecture.

Some decisions I'd made intuitively: along with city life, I'd prioritized mobility (proximity to subways over parks), peace and quiet (an "uncool" neighborhood rather than a more lively area), and sociability (I was within walking distance of friends). To be able to afford these specific requirements, I had very little space and even less storage, zero conveniences (dishwasher, washer/dryer), and none of what I deemed "luxury" items (stereo, television, car), though I did eat out often and buy clothes.

Too, I'd cultivated an active social life that combined light connections with deep friendships. I was constantly engaged with other people and had a strong emotional support system.

But I'd failed in one crucial respect: on my quest to be self-supporting I'd overlooked those classic architectural principles, balance and proportion.

By 2008, the magazine was doing incredibly well. Only three years old, we'd won several industry awards and sold nearly one million copies each month, to an overwhelmingly female readership. I often wondered who all these women were. In the late 1800s and early 1900s, home décor offered a way for idle society wives to professionalize themselves and enter the public sphere, where they transferred their values to the middle class via advice books and newspaper columns, literally spreading the gospel of home décor, popularizing ideas of taste and of the home as a marker of taste, a means of expressing and even forming the self. In the 1950s, as the postwar tidal wave of products and appliances helped usher modernism into the American home, home décor provided creatively frustrated housewives with an expressive outlet.

How does home décor serve us in the twenty-first century, now that women are flooding workplaces and universities in unprecedented numbers? Do we flip through interiors magazines as a way of longing for an idealized home, a vision we've largely left behind?

Or is something more pernicious at work? Is the airbrushed dreamscape of perfect surfaces the Victorian domestic prison by another name, a glass castle of unachievable aspiration to which we think we'll gain entry if we stay late at the office, work enough weekends—in short make enough money to buy all those beautiful things we never have time to enjoy? Where is the line between a true appreciation for surfaces and superficiality?

Or so I asked myself as I created these domestic illusions. By now I'd been promoted twice and had my own office with an enormous window overlooking a towering electronic billboard in Times Square; pulling down the shade muted but didn't block the frenetically blinking digital displays. I liked being "successful" for all the reasons anyone would—the comfort of a big, steady salary; incredible benefits; an expense account; authority. But I couldn't shake the sensation that I was living out someone else's version of success, not my own. Like many corporate executives the world over, I fantasized constantly about quitting.

This, then, was the most important lesson Edith had to teach me: the trade-off I'd made in order to live alone—that I would be an editor-writer and, therefore, have less time to devote to writing that mattered to me—was a sham. Like Edith, I, too, had to break whatever chains were holding me and actually start writing for real.

8

The Social Visionary

Charlotte Perkins Gilman, circa 1900

SOMETIMES YOU DON'T HAVE TO FIND THE COURAGE TO BREAK
whatever bonds are holding you; the ropes simply loosen and fall
from your ankles and wrists, and you stand up from the railroad
track to which you'd been tied, reborn. Or so it seemed at the
tail end of January 2009, when my boss announced to the staff
that the magazine was dead, effective immediately, victim of the
recession.

The following week I was snuggled on my green velvet sofa, steaming mug of tea at my elbow, reading a novel. The ceilings of my apartment soared with possibility. My bookshelves were troves of abandoned volumes waiting to be rediscovered, convivial with knickknacks: cheap blue china horse, antique silver vial of smelling salts, tiny plastic gorilla. Finally I was free to write whatever I wanted.

Instead, I fell back into the freelance grind and dashed out every night to see friends, go on dates. By July I still hadn't gotten a writing project off the ground. My friend Karen intervened.

"I'm sending you into a 'convent,'" she said. "A metaphorical convent. No dates, no parties, no events where men might possibly be. Your job is to stay home and concentrate on starting a writing project. Three weeks."

Karen is a visual artist who creates extraordinary sculptures and installations. My college friend Michael had introduced us several years before, and initially I'd been intimidated by her willowy height and dusky beauty, but ten minutes into the conversation her warmth and emotional acuity overwhelmed surface impressions, and I drew her close in my mind and didn't let go.

"It's a pretty classic notion that a frequent dater should take a pause for inner development," she explained.

We were on the telephone, she working in her art studio, me puttering around my apartment. Interpersonally speaking, I'm like a round-the-clock beat reporter, always chasing a story, always curious to hear what someone has to say. Sometimes it felt as if I couldn't walk down the street without winding up on a date. Karen was trying to make me see that this openness to experience could also be a hazard, distracting me from myself. In effect, she was advising me to build a few walls. I thought of Edith's line in *The Decoration of Houses*: "While the main purpose of a door is to admit, its secondary purpose is to exclude."

Only two days into my "cloistering" I agreed to see a movie

with a man I'd recently dated, as "just friends." Karen shot me down: "Totally against convent rules." I obeyed her and didn't go.

Five days in, I snuck out to a dinner party. Afterward I confessed to my Mother Superior and admitted I'd even felt a spark with the host; at one point our eyes had lingered for one-quarter of a split second longer than necessary.

"You're married to God/your project right now!" she chided. "Still, ooh, I love that flash moment, when you just *know* there's a connection."

Nine days in, I reported I'd been e-mailing with an old boyfriend—which didn't count, I argued, because I wasn't actually seeing him in person.

"I'm entertained you believe you aren't breaking convent regulations," she sighed. "As your Mother Superior, I encourage you to remind yourself of your vows, but I acknowledge that being a nun is not your true calling."

I made it all of two weeks before uncloistering myself.

Autumn skittered by like a leaf, or so I trust, because next thing I knew, it was winter.

I forgot to make a payment and lost my health insurance; I struggled to pay my bills. By the close of the year I'd fallen into the worst depression I'd known. It took everything I had to finish an assignment and e-mail it to the editor. Afterward I'd crawl onto the sofa—the only article of furniture, I'd noticed, with the same dimensions as a coffin—and sleep. And sleep. My bookshelves loomed menacingly, overcrowded morgues of forgotten ideas and dusty knickknacks ("modern litter," Edith Wharton called them). Why did I collect so much junk? What was with all this infernal clutter?

Few realizations are as demoralizing as knowing that the

only thing standing between you and what you want is yourself, I thought to myself, then cringed. When had I started talking to myself like an inspirational poster?

To anyone who dared ask (e.g., my highly concerned brother and father), I insisted that, no, I would not look for another full-time job, because then I'd *really* never get a writing project off the ground.

One night I had a dream so vivid, it seemed to be shouting. The next day I recited it to my therapist:

I wake up in a stranger's bedroom. I don't know how I got there. It's impeccably decorated in dark blue floral everything—wallpaper, curtains, bedspread, pillows, those horrible tissue-box covers you hide the regular tissue box in. It's all very high-end, custom-made. Awful.

To be in a room made entirely of somebody else's decisions, a room I have absolutely nothing to do with, to just sit there looking around and hating everything I'm looking at, is shockingly liberating. I am elated. Then it dawns on me that Willy . . .

Here I interrupted myself to remind my therapist that Willy was my childhood friend who now lived and worked as a photographer on the Lower East Side, the one who'd hooked me up with the magazine. She is rail thin, with chin-length hair she dyes platinum, and bright cornflower-blue eyes that suddenly seemed not unrelated to the floral wallpaper.

Willy is somewhere else in this house, which is actually a thirteenth-century villa on the outskirts of a hamlet in Italy. We're there on a magazine assignment: I'm writing a story, she's shooting photos.

While still in bed I close my eyes and envision my apartment in Brooklyn, and everything—my beloved books and knickknacks, my treasured silver candelabra, the green velvet sofa I bought off Craigslist—is covered in canvas tarps, the drapes drawn tightly across the windows. For the first time in my life I am overcome with the sensation of not ever wanting to go home.

For the first time in my life, I realize I don't have to.

I get out of the bed and find my cell phone in my suitcase and call my brother and tell him to go to my apartment and take anything he wants and leave the rest on the sidewalk. It is so unlike me to have figured out overseas cell phone coverage; I am very proud of myself.

He says, "What?" very alarmed.

I say, "Oh, don't worry—in Brooklyn, stuff vanishes the minute you put it outside. City people are vultures."

He says no, what he objects to is basically erasing my entire existence.

I say, "Think of all the free stuff you'll get! Besides, you know you can visit me in Italy whenever you want."

Then I walk downstairs and find Willy, and we get into a Fiat, and I drive us down a narrow road toward a collection of spires and towers in the distance—the hamlet.

We pass a massive white billboard with the words *When all is lost, I remain*—biblical and oracular, like an advertisement for The Lord Almighty, Inc.—written in huge black Gothic letters, and I say out loud with surprising force, "That is bullshit."

Which is when I realize that up until that very moment I'd believed if not in God, then in that billboard. News stories about rich people going bankrupt and killing themselves—as if they were nothing but the sum of their possessions and being stripped of them was tantamount to death—had always saddened me. I'd think, pityingly, "All that matters is you are alive. The rest is gravy."

But now, driving past the billboard, I know that losing everything *is* death, and that it's a good death, a death that I crave, and I don't want anyone to save me.

I keep driving. I drive through a forest. And then the trees thin out and give way to a vast, wide snowfield, and as I pass by, I'm acutely aware of both the massive, hard sheet of ice on top and the small, tender blades of grass beneath, and that when spring comes, there will be a glorious green meadow.

I stopped my monologue.

"So corny, right? Hello, incredibly obvious dream," I said, afraid, as usual, of boring my therapist. Listening to (or reading) someone recount a dream is like listening to someone describe, frame by frame, a movie you will never see.

"What do you think it means?" she asked.

"That it's time I give up on life as I know it and start a new one," I said. "That because I'm a freelancer, I can live anywhere I want. I don't have to stay in Brooklyn."

When I said this out loud, it didn't feel dull and obvious. It felt terrifying.

"Do you know Edna St. Vincent Millay's poem 'Renascence'?" she asked, then leaned forward and started to recite.

The combination of dark blue floral wallpaper with Willy's cornflower-blue eyes and yellow hair had reminded me of something. Back home that night, I searched my bookshelves. There it was: a paperback copy of Charlotte Perkins Gilman's short story "The Yellow Wall-paper."

The piece first appeared in the relatively short-lived literary periodical *The New England Magazine* in January 1892. The original version opens with a pen-and-ink illustration of a young

woman sitting in a rocking chair beside a barred window. She's
wearing a long dress with a fitted bodice and puffed shoulders,
and her hair is smoothed neatly into a bun. There's a pad of paper
on her lap, a pen in her hand. The caption tells us what she's
writing: "I am sitting by the Window in this Atrocious Nursery."

Our unnamed heroine and her well-intentioned if madden-
ingly patronizing physician husband, John, have rented a colonial
mansion for three months, to aid her recovery from a nervous
breakdown after the birth of their first child.

For the couple's bedroom, she'd wanted the one downstairs
that opened onto the piazza, but "John would not hear of it" and insisted they take the nursery at the top of the house. The windows
are barred, presumably so children won't fall out. The wallpaper
is torn off in great patches, and as for what remains, "I never saw
a worse paper in my life. One of those sprawling flamboyant patterns committing every artistic sin." She continues:

> It is dull enough to confuse the eye in following, pronounced
> enough to constantly irritate and provoke study, and when you
> follow the lame uncertain curves for a little distance they sud-
> denly commit suicide—plunge off at outrageous angles, destroy
> themselves in unheard of contradictions.
>
> The color is repellent, almost revolting; a smoldering un-
> clean yellow, strangely faded by the slow-turning sunlight. It
> is a dull yet lurid orange in some places, a sickly sulphur tint
> in others.

When she protests, John takes her in his arms and calls her
"a blessed little goose."

Aside from the wallpaper, she actually likes the room, which
sounds not unlike Edith Wharton's—big and airy, with views of
the garden and bay. Though, in truth, she's Edith's inverse: a
defenseless renter, not a lordly owner, confined to a bed that's

inexplicably nailed to the floor, longing to write, but forbidden to, on doctor's orders.

Things only get worse. She begins to suspect that the wallpaper has a consciousness, and knows full well its vicious influence: "There is a recurrent spot where the pattern lolls like a broken neck, and two bulbous eyes stare at you upside down."

Angry, she declares, "I never saw so much expression in an inanimate thing before, and we all know how much expression they have!" To soothe herself, she indulges wistful remembrances of inanimate objects past. "What a kindly wink the knobs of our big, old bureau used to have," she muses, and there was that one chair in particular that "always seemed like a strong friend."

Before long she detects the shape of a woman trapped in the pattern, stooped and creeping about, shaking at it, as if trying to get out.

Our heroine becomes fixated on this figure. She must free her. She will free her. And so she does. But the conclusion is left intentionally vague. By freeing the woman in the wall, did our heroine liberate herself, or go irretrievably mad?

The closing illustration in *The New England Magazine* is provocatively enigmatic. John is splayed on the floor, distraught, among strips of torn wallpaper. His wife leans over his prostrate body, her hair loosened now and falling forward like a curtain. Whether she's consoling him, or just double-checking to confirm that he's unconscious before she makes a break for it, is unclear.

One night over Thai takeout at my apartment Willy mentioned that she was sick of living on the Lower East Side and could use some extra cash besides. From some dim, forgotten corner of my mind I felt a lightbulb fizz awake.

"Please," I said. "Sublet out your place at a profit. Stay here. Check my mail or something. Burn it down."

I had a knife in my boot: Newburyport.

That night I bought an Amtrak ticket. In a month I'd be thirty-eight. Exactly a decade since I'd moved to New York. Ten years—a tight, round noose of a number. On the train, I tried to take stock of what I'd gained and lost in ten years' time.

By any reasonable measure, slinking back to my childhood home was a form of failure. There are those who say big cities warp otherwise ordinary citizens into callow hedonists. We never grow up. We're too selfish, too picky, on constant lookout for someone more attractive or successful than whomever we're already with. We're incapable of making the compromises necessary to sharing ourselves with a partner. As with those nineteenth-century women who left abusive marriages, we're told we're unable to accept reality for what it is.

When I stepped off the train in Boston and saw my father waiting, his curly hair that had stayed dark for so long now completely gray, I knew I'd made the right decision. Those measures of adulthood were someone else's, not mine.

As we turned onto our street, my heart caught in my throat, and I thought of Edna Millay's poem "Ashes of Life":

Life goes on forever like the gnawing of a mouse,—
And to-morrow and to-morrow and to-morrow and to-morrow
There's this little street and this little house.

Edith Wharton created her home in her own image. Maeve Brennan never had a home of her own. Charlotte Perkins Gilman simply absconded with the concept altogether. The sort of person who knew from a very young age exactly what she wanted to do with her life, Charlotte had a will so ferocious that even bad luck couldn't weaken it.

Not long after she was born, in 1860 (just two years before Edith Wharton), her father started to make himself scarce, and eventually took off for good, leaving her fragile, unresourceful mother to raise two children alone, on very little money; over the next eighteen years they moved among rooming houses, relatives' homes, and even a "cooperative household," for a total of nineteen times in all, eventually settling in Providence, Rhode Island. Rather than focus on these deprivations, Charlotte responded with characteristic pragmatism: she took from her weak, unloving mother the example of exactly how not to be, and from her absent father access to one of New England's most distinguished families.

Among her earliest memories was a visit to the "wonder house" that her father's aunt, Harriet Beecher Stowe, had built in Hartford, Connecticut, with the proceeds from her bestselling anti-slavery novel, *Uncle Tom's Cabin*. Stowe and her sisters—the prominent suffragist Isabella Beecher Hooker, and the never-married Catharine Beecher, author of what's been called America's first complete guide to housekeeping (when keeping house was as demanding as a full-time job)—were the lights by which the young girl guided herself. In 1855, anticipating Betty Friedan by more than a century, Catharine had pronounced domestic despair a nationwide epidemic. As she wrote about marriage in her book *Letters to the People on Health and Happiness*:

> How many young hearts have revealed the fact, that what they had been trained to imagine the highest earthly felicity, was but the beginning of care, disappointment, and sorrow, and often led to the extremity of mental and physical suffering.

At seventeen Charlotte declared in her diary that she would never be confined to the home as a mere wife and mother. She was going to devote her life to public service.

Her biographer Cynthia J. Davis considers the ages between sixteen and twenty to represent Charlotte's "declaration of independence." She writes, "The love, guidance, and sense of belonging she had yearned for futilely in her personal life became the governing principles of her avowedly impersonal religion of public service."

By now Charlotte was tall and strong, with long, curly brown hair. She began a course of self-improvement by teaching herself discipline. First she created arbitrary exercises—for instance, "get out of bed at thirteen minutes to seven." Once she'd mastered those, she turned to cultivating thoughtfulness, tact, and honesty, along with more corporal virtues. After studying physiology and hygiene, she adopted a daily exercise routine—gymnastics, an hour of brisk walking, running a seven-minute mile on her toes, and twenty-five repetitions of five different ways to lift two-pound weights—augmented with a cold sponge bath, early to bed, and open windows while sleeping. She swore off caffeine and corsets and for the rest of her life wore only comfortable clothes.

In 1878 she enrolled in the inaugural class of the Rhode Island School of Design, and the following year she was credentialed to teach art. Like Neith, Edna, and Edith at this age, she was also writing poetry; in 1880 her first publication, "To D.G."—the initials stand not for a person, but for dandelion greens—appeared in the *New England Journal of Education*. By twenty-one, she'd resolved to never marry. She'd fallen into passionate, sexless love with her friend Martha Luther and decided that this close, fulfilling friendship was all she needed. As she wrote to her beloved in 1881:

I am really getting glad not to marry. . . . If I let that business alone, and go on in my own way; what I gain in individual strength and development of personal power of character, *myself as a self,* you know, not merely as a woman, or that useful animal a wife and mother, will, I think, make up, and more than make up in usefulness and effect, for the other happiness that part of me would enjoy.

Not only would a future together allow them to reconcile the irreconcilable poles of love and work, but to extend their happiness to the social body as a whole. In another letter to Martha she wrote:

And bye & bye if we both persist in scorning matrimony, what joy to be, besides perfectly happy ourselves, a burning and a shining light to all our neighbors, a place where all delightful people congregate, a house wherein young and guileless aspirants for literary or various fame shall believe and tremble. Houp la! We'll be happy anyway.

Unfortunately, Martha had different intentions. Not long after these letters she became engaged (to a man), forcing a devastated Charlotte to find a new outlet for her formidable energies—which, of course, she did, more than admirably.

She spearheaded the founding of a women's fitness center in Providence, the Sanitary Gymnasium for Ladies and Children. She painted greeting cards and sold them at a profit. Sometimes, coming home late on a winter night, she would climb atop a boulder in a vacant lot and "exult in the white glittering silence, deeply commiserating [with] all those timid women who never know the wonder and beauty of being alone at night under the stars."

Around this time, she wrote about her desire not to marry in an unpublished piece called "An Anchor to Windward." Her reasons include her love of freedom, her longing for a home of her own, her desire to change the world, and her refusal to be absorbed by "that extended self—a family." Inside the cover of her 1882 journal she declared "work" her "watchword" for the year, and denounced "love and happiness" with a resounding "NO!"

Ten days later she met a handsome painter, Charles Walter Stetson, who proposed to her before three weeks were out.

This was perhaps the only time in her life that Charlotte diverged from her own compass, and she learned her lesson well. For a full two years she deflected her suitor, but their physical chemistry proved too electric for her to deny. They married on May 2, 1884, jumped into bed, and happily stayed there for quite a while. Ten months later she gave birth to a daughter, Katharine.

Immediately, Charlotte fell into a debilitating depression. She couldn't move or read or think. Eventually, having no idea what else to do, she traveled without Katharine to the home of a friend in Pasadena, California, in the hope that the sun would lift her spirits. It did. So much so that she returned to Rhode Island a healthy woman—only to be immediately felled again. It was this long period of postpartum depression, and her disastrous "rest cure," that she drew on to write "The Yellow Wall-paper," a condemnation of sexist medical practices and women's confinement to the domestic sphere.

In 1888, after four years of marriage, she convinced Walter that they needed to officially separate. She was twenty-eight. She'd devoted the last decade to two all-consuming love affairs that, according to Cynthia Davis, "had nearly broken her heart and health." Her thirties, she resolved, would be different.

The salubrious effects of her decision were immediate. Prior to 1890, the year she turned thirty, she'd published quite a lot (including her first book, an 1888 collection of drawings called *Art Gems for the Home and Fireside,* under the byline Mrs. Charles Walter Stetson). But between 1890 and 1891 she doubled that output and then some, publishing sixty-seven works of nonfiction, fiction, drama, and poetry.

When "The Yellow Wall-paper" appeared in 1892, it became a sensation and made Charlotte a public figure. The following May, she took stock of her life. She was thirty-three. With any luck she had forty more years left before she died. As she had as a teenager, she made a list of her priorities in her diary and re-solved anew to pursue them. In 1894 she finalized her divorce and sent her nine-year-old daughter to live part-time with her father and the woman he was about to marry, Charlotte's own childhood best friend.

When the nation got wind of her decision to leave her family, it erupted in outraged newspaper articles and op-eds. She didn't let it bother her. Instead, she used her celebrity to travel around the country advancing her ideas, a one-woman reform movement with a specific emphasis on "material feminism"—an effort to change sexist cultural standards through redefining the actual architecture of the home.

Her ideas were an expansion on and popularization of the "cooperative housekeeping movement" spearheaded in 1868 when Melusina Fay Peirce published a series of articles in *The Atlantic Monthly* encouraging women to form housekeeping cooperatives and seek reimbursement from the husbands who clearly profited by their labors. Charlotte found this theoretically appealing but practically unworkable, and in her copious writings and lectures advocated for "getting the kitchen out of the house, not more cooks in the kitchen," as Davis so succinctly puts it.

You don't need to live in a single-family house and drive a four-door sedan—designed to hold two parents and two chil-dren—to know how doomed were her efforts. America's allergy to socialism, conviction that bigger is always better, and patriarchal insistence that a woman's identity as mother and nurturer re-mains bound to the kitchen proved to be intractable. Since 1960 the typical age at which women marry has risen from twenty-one to twenty-seven (and for many of those who pursue higher education that number climbs into their early thirties), family size has shrunk to the lowest it's ever been, and 3.2 million people live alone, but we still inhabit an architectural landscape made for other people, in another time, and which was problematic—for women, at least—even then.

In a sense, Charlotte's ingenuity was realized by big cities, where even though most apartments have kitchens, a multitude of restaurants take the onus off food preparation, and emphasize, if not a communal way of living, then at least a way of life that revolves around public spaces—sidewalks, subways, buses, parks— and deemphasizes the centrality of the domestic sphere.

Once in Newburyport I established a routine. In the mornings I'd wake in my old bedroom on the third floor, walk downstairs to make coffee and oatmeal, and sneak back up to what had been my mother's office, on the second floor, before my father's first client arrived. He and his longtime paralegal are something of an Abbott and Costello; it was comforting to hear their repartee wafting upstairs as I worked. At lunchtime, my father and I would meet in the kitchen to joke around and slice tomatoes for sandwiches or fork sardines onto saltines.

When he knocked off work at six o'clock, I'd force myself to stop, too, and spend the evening making dinner and reading. Once the weather got, and stayed, hot I'd drive across the bridge to Plum Island and down the long, bumpy road that cuts through the Parker River National Wildlife Refuge, between golden dunes and bright green salt marshes. At the very southern tip I'd park, walk down to the water, dive in, rush back to my towel—the Atlantic Ocean was reliably freezing—wrap it around myself, and sit for a while, watching the low, lapping waves collapse into long ruffles of foam. By now the daytime beachgoers had already packed up and headed home for dinner, so it was just me and a few stray fishermen standing sentry over their fishing poles.

On the road between Plum Island and downtown is a big "American four-square" house—a popular style at the turn of the last century—known by locals as the Pink House. It's a pale pink, three steps below bubble gum, just above ballet shoe, on a spot of dry ground by the saltmarsh, with no other houses around. When I was a child, it was a mainstay of my nightmares—the Pink House, a dark stormy sky, and a great horned owl, that solitary night hunter with its sulfurous eyes, perched at the very top, on the widow's walk, scowling.

Somewhere along the way the family that owned it had moved away, and I'd been surprised to see how badly it had fallen into disrepair—paint peeling, a few windows boarded up. I could see straight through its empty rooms to the sky beyond. The place was practically a ruin, as if it really did belong in a nightmare, though now a grown-up version: a mirage, a siren, a foreboding metaphor.

She—and she was a she, obviously, with her demure paint job and gabled widow's walk—was what it looked like, I decided, to cut yourself off entirely from the world, let yourself go, and become your truest, most alone self. A vision of what I could become if I wasn't careful. Or of what I couldn't become if I was too careful. In other words: attraction at its most ambivalent.

But after a few days I couldn't deny that catching sight of those haggard pink shingles gave me the warm glow of happening upon a long-familiar face. Maybe the house was so cheap, I could scrape up enough money to buy it. The Pink House could be Grey Gardens to my "Little Edie" Bouvier Beale. House-rich and cash-poor, I'd wrap cashmere sweaters around my head, wear my skirts upside down, and putter happily, dusting my cherished knickknacks. What in the city felt like failure had begun to seem more like freedom.

Driving off the island each evening, I'd make sure to give the house one last glance in the rearview mirror, as if nodding goodbye to a neighbor. Back home I'd make a salad, drink a glass or two of wine, and read *Moby-Dick*. I'd never known such unbroken solitude.

In July Karen came up from New York. The night of my birthday we drove out to the beach, and she surprised me with a flower-themed picnic: flower-shaped potatoes on homemade pizza; flower-shaped cucumbers tossed in vinegar; banana cake on a bed of pink roses. How she'd managed to throw this together without my noticing was beyond me.

We reclined on a blanket, our artful Tupperware feast arrayed before us, sharing a bottle of Sancerre. She was going through a down period, too—a relationship had just ended; work was hard to find—and we languished in our shared frustrations. There was never enough time for long, sprawling visits like this in the city. Listening to her describe the challenges of being an artist, I remembered my ancient ambition to be a poet, and I wondered if my extended foray into nonfiction—book criticism, personal essays, author interviews, celebrity profiles, consumer journalism—wasn't merely a way to support myself, but also a crutch, a place to hide. Or was it my fixation on supporting myself that served as a shield?

As we talked, the sun sank into the sea, dragging behind it a radiant red flame, a curtain drawing closed at the end of a play, and the chill that had been creeping across the sand swept up our legs and through our hair. We packed up our feast, turned the blanket into a cloak for two, and, bound warmly together, walked back to the car, the very last theatergoers, leaving behind an empty, windswept stage.

In September 1898 Charlotte returned to New York from a lecture tour in England with only one dollar in her secret pocket— nothing more.

At this point, thirty-eight years old, she'd been living on her own for a decade, and she was in the middle of a five-year period of such intense travel that she didn't even have a permanent residence. She took great pride in her nomadic status, believing it made her "better able to judge dispassionately and to take a more long-range view of human affairs than is natural to more stationary people." Whenever she had to list her address on a form or in a visitors' book she wrote, *At Large.* In an essay, she declared "A Woman-at-Large" to be a new category of occupation "most essential to the workings of advanced civilization"—yet one that received no payment or recognition.

Earlier that year she'd published *Women and Economics,* to overwhelming acclaim. It was translated into seven languages, compared to John Stuart Mill's *The Subjection of Women.* Drawing on sociology and history, the book argues that women's secondary status, and economic dependence on men, are culturally enforced, not—as prevailing wisdom went—the result of biological inferiority.

Motherhood, she wrote, is "the common duty and the common glory of womanhood," but confining women to this role alone stunts women's creative and personal growth; they need professional lives, as well. Shared kitchens in city apartment buildings would help women balance family and work, and provide social support for those who chose to stay at home. Eventually these changes would result in "better motherhood and fatherhood, better babyhood and childhood, better food, better homes, better society."

By now she'd fallen in love again, this time with her first cousin, George Houghton Gilman. For two more years she continued to live and travel alone, until marrying and setting up house with him in 1900. Here was a woman with the rare capacity to be so true to her own compass that she could break the rules she made for herself without compromising her ideals.

The twelve years Charlotte spent on her own between marriages pushed her to realize her own intellectual and creative potential. It was by forgoing the demands made on a wife and mother that she was able to cultivate herself—and, once she was ready, fall in love again, this time prepared to rise to the demands of coupledom. (And she never stopped being a mother; though she and her second husband never had children, her daughter from her first marriage often lived with them, and the two women remained close.)

In 1904 she explained her changing attitude toward marriage in an essay called "The Refusal to Marry." When she was young, she writes, she'd idealized the women who, "fully convinced of the need for economic independence, trained in specialized labor and loving it, and keenly aware of the difficulties of married life, both mentionable and unmentionable, have cut the knot by simply refusing to marry." Now, happily married, she's decided that duty to the world actually necessitates "a fully developed, normal personal life"—i.e., sexual intimacy.

Of the many differences between her era and our own, one is particularly crucial: sex. Charlotte came of age at a time when it was believed women didn't like to have sex, and even if they did, the only place to do it was within a marriage. For her to experience her own definition of "a fully developed, normal personal life"—that is, a loving, sexual relationship with a man, one conducted openly, recognized by her peers and society—she really did have to get married.

Today, of course, women don't need to be married to have sex, or to buy a house, or to pass down an inheritance. Marriage is a constantly evolving idea and practice that will, likely, continue to change. But in the meantime, it remains our culture's definition of the highest form of interpersonal commitment, and because of that we'll keep on doing it for as long as we fall in love.

It's important to remember, however, that the widespread practice of marrying for love—not responsibility to family and community—is only about two hundred years old. Women have been pursuing professional careers for half that time, but in significant numbers only over the past forty years. In many ways, the decision of whether and whom and when to marry is more complex than ever. Yet we make our personal calculations, such as they are, according to ideas about what makes a good marriage so outdated that even Charlotte was questioning them a century ago.

Charlotte's second marriage was very happy. George supported her in everything she did, which included not only over a dozen more books but also a monthly journal, *The Forerunner,* which she maintained from 1909 to 1916, writing the entirety of nearly every issue (enough to fill twenty-eight long books, she once claimed).

It was here that she published perhaps my favorite of her works, her satirical utopian novel *Herland,* exactly one hundred years ago, in 1915.

The story goes like this: Long ago and far away, a country lost all its men to war and natural disaster—when, on the brink of extinction, a miracle occurred. One of the few remaining women bore a daughter, through parthenogenesis (virgin birth), then four more. Each of her five daughters in turn bore five daughters. And so on.

Two thousand years later, when three American men on a scientific expedition—Terry, a male-chauvinist playboy; Jeff, a sentimental doctor; the feminist-minded narrator, Vandyck, a sociologist—stumble across this fabled land, roughly the size of Holland, it has a population of three million women.

Much wisecracking ensues. The book's comedy turns on the trio's assumptions about women being upended, and the jokes hold up, somewhat sadly; one would hope that, a century on, gender stereotypes would sound a little more old-fashioned. For instance, Terry believes there are two kinds of women, "Desirable and Undesirable. . . . The last [sic] was a large class, but negligible—he had never thought about them at all."

Unfortunately for him, in Herland the women couldn't care less what he thinks. Athletic, strong, fearless, rational, unadorned, they are everything he believes a woman isn't. They keep their hair short and wear a simple, loose uniform of several light tunics, one of them covered in pockets (not a feature of women's clothing in the early 1900s), layered over a modified union suit; when it's time for her daily exercise, a woman simply peels off the tunics.

The country is beautiful and the society itself a complex yet harmonious sisterhood: communal, peaceful, and free of filth, criminals, kings, and aristocrats, even bad ideas. "When we get a thing like that into our minds, it's like—oh, like red pepper in your eyes," one woman explains. Education is the highest art, and motherhood sacred. Most laws are revised every twenty years. The food is simple and healthful (no red meat) and the means of production completely self-sustaining. All the trees bear edible fruit.

The architecture features high ceilings and lofty windows, and though Herland is a cooperative nation, its citizens have a strong sense of personal privacy, and "not the faintest idea of that *'solitude a deux'* we are so fond of," Vandyck reports. Instead, they have what he calls the "two rooms and a bath" theory down pat; every child has her own bedroom, "and one of the marks of coming of age was the addition of an outer room in which to receive friends. . . . It seemed to be recognized that we should breathe easier if able to free our minds in real seclusion." The houses are kitchen-less, naturally.

Most fascinating to me, however, is how, after several centuries of bearing five children apiece, the women resolved the threat of overpopulation. Though they prioritized mothering over all activities, they decided that not everyone had to give birth. By learning to isolate the onset of pregnancy—"a period of utter exaltation—the whole being uplifted and filled with a concentrated desire for that child"—those who wanted to could defer it by engaging in physical and mental activity, and "solace her longing" by caring for existing babies. As one woman, Somel, tells Vandyck, "We soon grew to see that mother-love has more than one channel of expression."

Vandyck is appalled. "We have much that is bitter and hard in our life at home . . . but this seems to me piteous beyond words—a whole nation of starving mothers!"

Somel smiles and says, "We each go without a certain range of personal joy, but remember—we each have a million children to love and serve—*our* children."

She is far wiser than we who've forgotten that our country's celebrated "unalienable rights" are life, liberty, and the *pursuit* of happiness. Every life, even in America, goes without a certain range of personal joy of some variety or another.

In 1932, age seventy-two, Charlotte was diagnosed with inoperable breast cancer, and in 1934 George died unexpectedly. After his death, she flew to Pasadena, California, where she was taken care of by her daughter and friends. Charlotte had vowed, in her early thirties, after nursing her mother through her death, never to inflict such an ordeal on her child, and before the year was out she decided it was finally time to take her own life.

On August 17, 1935, Charlotte Perkins Gilman covered her mouth with a handkerchief soaked in chloroform—the ultimate act of self-determination.

Or maybe I won't buy the Pink House, I decided.

When you find yourself at yet another crossroads, sorting out your best next step, it's as useful to know what you don't want as what you do. Yes, I was still speaking to myself in the language of inspirational posters. Imagination is not boundless; we all have limitations.

But I wanted to engage with the world, not retreat from it. That's why I'd chosen journalism to begin with. Being self-supporting was the furthest thing from a shield—it was my foundation and also my liberty.

And cities don't warp otherwise ordinary citizens. Arguably, by now it's the other way around. Over the past several decades an ever-swelling demographic of single people has remade the city in its own image, a seeming utopia of twenty-four-hour bars and hotels and restaurants and shops and spas springing up to suit our every whim, to protect us from loneliness. No wonder studies show us that single people are happier in urban areas.

Only now, in Newburyport, geographically incapable of meeting up with every last person for drinks or dinner or lunch or coffee, could I see how enslaved I'd been to my social schedule, how freighted by an outsize sense of interpersonal obligation, just a few degrees away from a Victorian socialite paying her endless rounds of calls.

In order to find and do work I found meaningful, I had to radically rethink how I spent my time, and my money. I couldn't bear to tally up all the hours I toiled, particularly on meaningless assignments, and where that income went: not just rent and bills and student loans, or even clothes and haircuts and cosmetics, but the countless nights out at restaurants and bars, tipsily hailing taxis instead of taking the subway, all to the same end—keeping my social life in constant motion.

Charlotte showed me that we become adults by learning how to be responsible to ourselves, whether or not we're married or have children. I thought again of those classic architectural principles, balance and proportion.

In August I returned to Brooklyn and brought my new solitude with me. I went out less and focused more on the friendships that meant the most to me. I took an editing job on the condition I could work on my own writing from home one day a week. When an apartment opened up in my building, I convinced Willy to take it. Like me, she was still single. I thought we'd be even happier with our own neo-boardinghouse. I called it "The Home for Lively Spinsters."

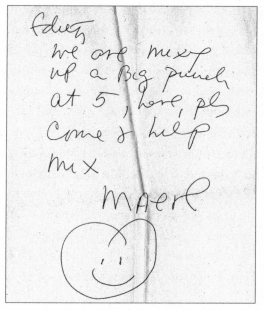

Note from Maeve Brennan to Edith Konecky, 1972

THE QUIET CONVIVIALITY OF A HOTEL BAR AT DUSK, THE ROOM NOT yet full of patrons, the bartender liable to top off my vodka and seltzer because the night is young. Shielded by a book and low candle, near enough others to eavesdrop, far enough to not get involved. And upstairs, someone is tidying my room, smoothing the crisp pillowcases, wiping down the sink, leaving behind a fresh stack of white towels. Folded neatly in a drawer are a few sweaters and skirts, two dresses hanging in the narrow closet—all that could fit in a single suitcase, just enough to get by, nothing less, nothing more.

It was January 2014, and I'd checked into a hotel overlooking Washington Square Park, where Maeve Brennan had once lived, to get a taste of hotel living. Charlotte Perkins Gilman's idea of "A Woman-at-Large" had returned me to Maeve. I'd never been able to shake the suspicion that her tragic demise was almost *too* tragic, too faithful to the age-old script that demands that a single woman be punished for her sins. Did her life really fall apart after she published "The Springs of Affection" in 1972? Or did Maeve, like Charlotte, simply veer in an unexpected direction, finding pleasure and sustenance in a different kind of living?

Of the many hotels she called home, this is one of the few remaining. Its fortunes have risen and fallen and risen again, along with those of Greenwich Village. It opened in 1902 as a handsome residential hotel called the Hotel Earle, grew into Art Deco grandeur, and by the '50s fell into disrepair—the perfect haven for the latest counterculture. In 1964, Bob Dylan and Joan Baez lived in room 305 (in her song "Diamonds and Rust" she recalls "that crummy hotel").* The Byrds' Roger McGuinn took room 702. In the 1970s it was cleaned up and in 1986 rechristened with its current name, the Washington Square Hotel. Today the clientele is

---

* It was around this time that Paul McCartney and John Lennon created "Eleanor Rigby," about pop's most famous spinster, originally called "Miss Daisy Hawkins," perhaps in reference—conscious or not—to Sadie Hawkins, the spinster in Al Capp's *Li'l Abner* comic strip. In 1937, Sadie's father gathered all the bachelors in Dogpatch and organized what Capp called a Sadie Hawkins Day footrace; she got to marry whomever she caught (an inversion of the mythical Atalanta, who reluctantly agreed to wed whatever man could outrun her). The concept inspired real-life Sadie Hawkins Dances—where girls invite the boys— across the country. As for the heartbreaking Eleanor Rigby: the song opens with her in a church, picking up rice after a wedding, and waiting at the window, "wearing the face that she keeps in a jar by the door / Who is it for?" and ends with her burial, to which "Nobody came."

largely international; over breakfast that morning I'd overheard at least four different languages.

The room was perfect—quiet, simple—and the food excellent. After one night I wanted to stay forever. Instead, when a snowstorm blew in, I extended my reservation from two nights to four, knowing that waking to a city blanketed in white would justify the expense, and it did. I spent the first day of the storm in bed reading, looking out the window, languishing in the knowledge that I was seeing the park as Maeve had in 1960, after ending her marriage and returning to the city.

She'd done what all of us—from the chambermaid wheeling the vacuum cleaner down the hall to the bar-back drying the highball glasses and placing them on the shelf—are supposed to do: she had married. And it hadn't worked out. In those days, being unmarried was "no small thing for a woman over forty," Angela Bourke reminds us in her biography. Maeve was forty-two, a woman between countercultures, too young for the last and too old for the one blooming around her, though I doubt she'd have joined in anyhow. Her unconventionality never extended to bohemianism.

But she wasn't back where she'd started; she'd simply arrived where she'd left off, this time stronger and smarter and maybe even stripped of illusions. Which is a place we all must reach, like it or not.

During the twelve years she'd lived alone in the city before her marriage, she'd fashioned her own apprenticeship. She'd taught herself how to write and to see, to catch the details that make a story sing. She'd learned the subtle choreography of working with editors, how to allow another person into your own muddled, unspooling process and let him or her guide you without changing your course.

In that regard she was especially fortunate. Several months prior I'd visited the author and *New Yorker* writer Janet Malcolm at her home in Manhattan. Malcolm hardly knew Maeve, who was seventeen years older than she, but her late husband, Gardner Botsford, was one of Maeve's most important editors (the two were exact contemporaries). She gave me a large envelope of Maeve's letters to Botsford, dating from the early and mid-1960s, after she'd left the hotel and was spending winters alone in East Hampton.

Drawing on my own experience, I wondered if Maeve's devotion to "surface" details had made her something of a perfectionist when it came to filing copy—good practice when writing short pieces, but antithetical to more probing and meandering endeavors, which require working through several rounds of rough drafts. For a woman who, at her professional heights, was known for pinning a fresh carnation to her lapel every day, filing unfinished work must have felt like the literary equivalent of going out for dinner at a nice restaurant while forgetting to wear shoes.

Typewritten on thin sheaves of pale blue and yellow paper, Maeve's letters to Botsford are long and chatty, brimming with observations of people they both know, anecdotes about her entourage of cats and Bluebell, her faithful Labrador retriever, as well as her reactions to books she's reading, thoughts about stories and reviews she's working on, updates on her progress. They reveal an astoundingly productive intimacy—that of the narrator's trust in her reader's interest, the implied agreement that she can be, well, as long-winded as she wants, both parties knowing that seeds for stories travel on such currents of air.

I was reminded of a line in Malcolm's celebrated book *The Journalist and the Murderer*: "A correspondence is a kind of love affair. . . . It is with our own epistolary persona that we fall in love, rather than with that of our pen pal." Maeve's letters to Botsford *are* their relationship, a space where she could create, inhabit, and celebrate an identity that nurtured her in her solitude and fueled her writing process, and that, unlike her marriage, allowed her to flourish.

When it had occurred to me in 2013 that Maeve's niece, Yvonne Jerrold, must still be alive, I wasn't sure what to do. Angela Bourke had already interviewed Jerrold for the biography, and I couldn't imagine she had much more to say on the topic. Surely she wanted to be left well enough alone.

It's generally understood that Maeve suffered from schizophrenia, though Bourke never uses that term in her biography. (When I called to ask her why, she explained that her academic training makes her fastidious about not going beyond sources, and she'd never found one to confirm the diagnosis. Besides, she said, after the Vietnam War there were huge advances in psychopharmacology and people were "throwing labels around freely." She thought a label that was being used then might not even be understood the same way today.)

Symptoms of schizophrenia usually start between the ages of sixteen and thirty; it's very uncommon to become schizophrenic after age forty-five. As those of us who have never experienced or witnessed schizophrenia firsthand know from popular media, it's among the most world-annihilating of mental disorders, involving hearing voices and other false sensory perceptions, delusions, mental incoherence. The majority of people who have schizophrenia struggle to take care of themselves, work, keep friendships, or maintain romantic attachments.

Unsurprisingly, the disease is widely mythologized. When Elyn Saks, a law professor and author of a memoir about her lifelong attempt to control schizophrenic symptoms with psychoanalysis, was diagnosed in her late twenties with "chronic paranoid schizophrenia with acute exacerbation," she immediately thought of the "years of books and movies that presented people like me as hopelessly evil or hopelessly doomed." In her memoir, she describes how in an instant she foresaw a life of violence and delusion. "Maybe I'd end my life in an institution; maybe I'd *live* my life in an institution. Or become homeless, a bag lady whose family could no longer care for her," she writes. "I'd be that wild-eyed character on the city sidewalk that all the nice baby-carriage-pushing mommies shrink away from. *Get away from the crazy lady.* I'd love no one; no one would love me."

My heart broke when I read that line. I'd been trying to understand why it is that when women express their anxieties about the future—their "feared selves," as Hazel Markus and Paula Nurius termed it—they often go straight to the crazy bag lady (and her "sister," the cat lady). Often it's said in jest, but the crack is too pervasive to not be consequential. Why is *this* of all fates more terrifying than any other?

At first I thought it was simply that the specter of the crazy bag lady has been branded so deeply into the collective female consciousness that we're stuck with her. Now I realized I was wrong. What is haunting about the bag lady is not only that she is left to wander the streets, cold and hungry, but that she's living proof of what it means to not be loved. Her apparition will endure as long as women consider the love of a man the most supreme of all social validations.

I couldn't decide which was worse: that Maeve actually did become a schizophrenic bag lady and was never treated effectively, or that she'd remained sane but somehow, for some reason, allowed her life to go so completely off the rails.

And yet, how much of her "story" is reality, and how much is a projection of what all of us who aspire to a better life fear? Certainly she'd fallen from a glamorous height, failed in the most traditional sense. But did that necessarily mean she'd been unhappy?

For a while I contentedly held on to this question, taking comfort in the possibility it presented, afraid to risk digging deeper, only to discover once and for all that I was completely wrong, and Maeve really did end up miserable and alone.

Eventually, of course, curiosity won out.

Yvonne Jerrold, Maeve's niece, turned out to be very easy to find: she has her own website. In all of two minutes I learned that she lives in Cambridge, England, where, after a career as an architect and garden designer, she now writes novels and makes stone carvings. I read a 2008 clipping from her local newspaper, in which she explains that her rather hilarious-sounding second novel, *A Case of Wild Justice?*, about a group of elderly neighbors who turn themselves into crime-fighting suicide bombers, was inspired by the outrage she felt after her eighty-nine-year-old mother—Maeve's sister Deirdre—endured a series of burglaries. The accompanying author photo showed a woman with a kind expression and short, wispy blond hair. In January 2013 I sent her an e-mail with the subject line "Your Aunt Maeve."

Before I knew it, I was sitting at my desk in Brooklyn, astonished to be talking on the phone with someone who was actually related to Maeve Brennan.

Jerrold's primary memories of Maeve are necessarily those of a child, and sporadic, at that. Jerrold was born in Washington, DC, a couple of years before Maeve moved to New York, but in 1950 her father died, and her mother brought the family back to Dublin, where Maeve made infrequent visits.

I asked if her aunt had had an influence on her life anyhow.

"Quite a lot!" she said. "Probably because I had secret ideas about wanting to be a writer. I found her such an attractive, interesting person. Everybody did—she just *was*."

It pleased me to hear this. I hoped my nieces might say something similar about me someday, if anyone should ask. By now my brother and his wife had two small daughters, and I was already looking ahead to many happy decades as an aunt.

But there I was again, comparing myself to Maeve, a person I'd never met, a long habit that now felt more specious than ever as Jerrold drew a portrait that both did and didn't match the one I'd been carrying now for fifteen years. Talking about a person is entirely different than reading about them. And listening to someone who knew that person talk about her is yet more different.

She started with Maeve's physical self. "She was neat, slim, well-dressed, disciplined, elegant, controlled—in a ballerina sort of way, like a teacher, or a librarian." This I could tell from photographs. When she described her "enormous grin" and green eyes—"the twinkliest eyes you could imagine"—I realized I'd never seen Maeve in color.

"Her wit was the most important thing," she added. "She laughed all the time. When she wasn't sitting smoking and watching people, she was making wry ironic observations about life and people, and joking about herself and others with obvious glee. She was interested in most things, and came up with some crazy ideas." She described her humor as "cerebral and sophisticated and mischievous and self-deprecating."

What about Maeve's romantic life?

"She had lovers and affairs, and her heart was broken from time to time. She did things she never would have dreamt of in Ireland. But she did not come across as a sensual person. She did not act in a sexy way. She was most unsexy. When she was in Ireland, she appeared modest and demure, as any convent-educated Irish woman normally would in the 1950s. Nowadays women are sexy all over the place!"

We laughed. So true!

"She never talked about wanting to have children. I believe she wanted solitude and cats. She was crazy about animals. I think she didn't find married life particularly congenial. She was very undomesticated and always had home help. I can't imagine she made a conscious decision about how her life would go, apart from her early ambition to write, which I think never left her. That was her focus. She carried an enormous black patent-leather purse around with her. I asked why it was so big and she said it was to carry whatever she was writing at the moment."

I asked what Maeve's relatives thought about her.

"Her Irish relations in Wexford found her strange and exotic," she said. "She drank, she smoked. She was very thin, wearing slim, elegant, New York City clothes, and high heels. She didn't drive, so she'd hire a driver and go down to see her cousins in Wexford, causing excitement among the local children. Nobody had a car in those days."

Reading Bourke's biography, Jerrold had been surprised to get the impression that Maeve was actually very sad. "I asked my mother about this, and she said that yes, Maeve was quite a sad person. As a child I never saw this. I saw her cross, furious, irritated. But never, ever sad."

Well, was she lonely? I asked.

"She was a loner, which was understandable," Jerrold said. "You're a writer—you know. When you're a writer, you don't want to waste time or energy on people who require you to be social. She never sought that comfort. She sought independence, experience, and observation. She wanted to experience the world."

I didn't confess that my Achilles' heel is my sociability. This wasn't about me. Or was it?

"She didn't need people. Writing was the center of her life. Everything else was peripheral. Ultimately, at a writer's center, there's a hard core."

I thought suddenly of a photo shoot I'd been the subject of not long before, in which the photographer kept making me scowl, and I kept resisting. "I'm not a scowler—that's just not how I walk around the world," I'd said. "How about when you're sitting down at your desk writing?" he'd asked. "That's the person I'm trying to capture."

How was I supposed to know what I look like when I'm writing? Because I couldn't picture it, I stood there in front of the camera and imagined I was actually sitting at my desk, staring into the computer screen, and I felt the muscles around my eyes tighten, and those around my mouth relax—if not a scowl, exactly, definitely not an inviting countenance. Yes, I realized. There is a hard core at my center, and a great deal of my personality is constructed around not ever letting anybody see it. Even *I* don't "see" it—I'm acquainted only with my blank expression in the bathroom mirror as I wash my face in the morning, my toothy smile in a snapshot, and the extremely rare glimpse in a mirror of my top lip tugged into an involuntary sneer by the effort of lifting a weight at the gym, the sight of which never ceases to shock me.

"But I don't think she had a general loneliness," Jerrold continued. "Her working life was full of people, mostly writing colleagues. Whenever she wanted to, she'd go to the office. Other times she would stay at her house in Long Island for weeks and weeks to write."

She explained that Maeve was generous to a fault. "You couldn't stop her giving things away. She was not at all materialistic, and believed things should belong to the people who most valued them."

She also had extraordinary presence and energy, Jerrold added. "I couldn't keep up with her intensity, her enthusiasms. She could make you feel inadequate. People like that do wear other people out," she said. "I think there are actually two kinds of people: one draws all their energy internally and is giving out personality all the time, and the other draws their energy from other people and is always taking. The takers are exhausting to the givers."

Maeve was a giver. *What kind am I,* I wondered. (*Kate, this is not about you.*)

But I already knew the answer. More than a few people have told me I wear them out. Several years ago a dear friend confessed that she "couldn't keep up with" my enthusiasms. "You have so many of them," she said, "that I can no longer tell which ones are real and which are fleeting."

Are "givers," in Jerrold's terms, more likely to live alone, in part because they're just "too much" for other people?

Or does her equation actually describe something else—the two faces of the single woman? Home alone, she lives for herself, drawing on her own internal resources. Among others, she enacts a kind of performance, playing to an audience, whether for the sake of it, or because she's waiting to be plucked off the stage and brought home by a man.

Soon Jerrold was theorizing that her own mother, growing up in the shadow of her precocious, dominant older sister, never really became herself.

Jerrold's mother had made all the "right" decisions for a woman, yet when only thirty-one, she found herself a widowed mother of four. It's not surprising, then, that Maeve was an object of pity and possibly even envy—she had made the "wrong" decisions, yet lived quite well, and it must have been tempting on some level to want to punish her for having done so.

And yet for Jerrold, Maeve was an example of how to be successfully untraditional. Perhaps if it weren't for her aunt, all these years later she wouldn't have become a writer herself.

Sometimes, when I'm interviewing someone, and I get so caught up in the conversation that I lose track of what to ask, I resort to the lamest question of all: Is there something I'm not asking that I should? By and large the answer is no, and rightly so. But it was as if Jerrold had been waiting for someone to ask exactly that.

"I'll tell you one thing that people have not picked up on: Maeve grew up with more knowledge of the Irish troubles than my mother did, but all the family had mental scars from the violence of the time," she said. "They'd grown up in poverty. Every now and then their father was dragged off to yet another prison. They grew up frightened. And they turned against politics."

Their new life in Washington, she explained, had been peaceful and posh. The sisters were expected to act as ladies there.

"Some writers come out of tempestuous countries and write about it for the rest of their lives. This particular family was displaced by war, but Maeve never mentioned politics or the Irish war of independence in her writing."

I asked her about the family rift caused by the publication of "The Springs of Affection" in 1972. She fell silent. Then: "There were a lot of bad feelings because of Maeve's false and unkind portrayal of her aunt. The family was very hurt," she said finally. "Maeve seemed to have moved such a long way from her roots; I don't think she'd have done it if she was in Ireland. I think it was partly due to her grief over the death of her father when she was far away in New York, and partly due to the influence of her editor Maxwell, and partly due to the fashion at the time in *The New Yorker* for biographical short stories.

"I think it was a bad moment for Maeve when she returned to Ireland in the 1970s. She may have harbored a little feeling that someday she could come back, and instead she realized she'd gone too far, that through her own actions she'd burned all her boats. She was already ill by then."

She paused again. "The trouble with Maeve was, she was volatile. As she began to lose her grip on reality, she alienated all her friends and colleagues. By the time she died alone in a nursing home, she'd alienated so many people that everyone felt sad and guilty.

"I couldn't afford to go to the funeral," she continued. "Nobody from our side of the family went. She was close to her brother to some extent, and his sons arranged it. They, and my mother, all said don't bury her, it will become a pilgrimage place. Her ashes were scattered in the ocean. Very unsentimental."

I was quiet.

As if reading my thoughts, Jerrold said, "People tend to romanticize her, but to me she's a person, not an icon or myth. You know, I was in New York recently, at a reading event for Maeve, and I met someone who'd known her at the end of her life."

"What?" I said.

"Here we'd all thought she'd lost all of her friends. But it turns out after that—after she'd burned all her boats—she'd gone to an artist's colony and met a lovely woman named Edith Konecky. If Edith hadn't heard about the event, and shown up at the pub, I would never have known that Maeve had found a friend during some of her most troubled years."

My heart sped up. There is no mention of Edith Konecky in the biography.

"How's this?" she offered. "I'll send her an e-mail and see if she's up to talking to you."

After I hung up with Maeve's niece, she e-mailed Edith Konecky, and Konecky e-mailed me, writing, "I knew her as well as one can know someone who is going mad, and I think I may have been the last person she trusted."

Now here I was in downtown Manhattan on a cold February afternoon in 2013, walking from the subway to her apartment. The winteriness felt appropriate. Maeve loved snow and rain, and living by the ocean in the off-season, when the beaches were empty. She loved so many things—cats, dogs, roses, people—that sometimes I wonder if she chose to be alone to best enjoy them all.

When I knocked on Konecky's apartment door, a dark-haired, middle-aged woman answered—Konecky's widowed niece, who'd started living there part-time that very week. She took my coat as her aunt approached. Tall and white-haired, with a mischievous glint in her eye, Konecky radiated charisma. Had her hands not trembled as she reached to get ice for our Scotch and sodas, I wouldn't have believed she'd just turned ninety.

I offered to manage the ice myself, and she led us into a spacious, book-lined living room, where she settled into a rocking chair and I sank into a plush, orange-striped sofa that bore an uncanny resemblance to the marmalade cat that now climbed into her lap. Konecky has published six books; the most recent, a novel called *Love and Money,* came out in 2011.

I asked when she'd first met Maeve.

"Nineteen seventy-two," she said. Just a few months after Maeve published "The Springs of Affection." Konecky was five years younger, fifty. "We were at the MacDowell Colony, in New Hampshire. I walked into the dining room, and there was a woman sitting at a table with a brown paper bag on her head, so of course I went over and sat there."

"I'd have done the same!" I laughed, delighted and astonished. MacDowell was the artists' colony I'd gone to in 2006, the first time I'd tried to write about Maeve. I'd had no idea that she'd been there, too.

"She explained she'd just come from the beauty parlor and her hair wasn't dry," Konecky continued. "I was fascinated by her—her Irish accent and quick wit. Cats weren't allowed, but she was there with at least five of them.

"Everything Maeve did was crazy." She laughed. "She was very busy feeding and cleaning up after the cats all the time. One day she went downtown and found a little kitten in the snow. She picked it up, put it in her coat, and went around to all the shops to ask whose it was. Nobody claimed it. For a while, I kept finding it in my bedroom—I'd pick it up and return it to Maeve's."

One night Konecky went to bed and found the cat curled up adorably on her blankets. She asked Maeve if she should just keep it. Maeve said, "That cat needs a person, and you need a cat! I've been putting her on your bed every night."

Konecky chuckled. "I'd never had cats. I never thought I'd like them. Maeve said that everyone should have a cat named Minnie. And so I named it Minnie, and that's how I came to cats."

I tried to make eye contact with the cat in Konecky's lap and decided that, four decades on, the probability of her being one and the same Minnie was highly unlikely.

When she mentioned the name Elaine Dundy, my slack grasp on time loosened even further. I'd interviewed Dundy in 2007 about her 1958 novel, *The Dud Avocado,* considered the first-ever instance of what we now call "chick lit." In it, the plucky American protagonist, Sally Jay Gorce, says about women, "It just isn't our century." So I'd asked Dundy, at the time eighty-five, what she thought about the evolution of available heroines over the course of her lifetime. She told me that in 1964 she and a friend were so fed up with their era's "passive and put-upon" heroines that they decided to produce a magazine about it. "We published it in what you would call 'menstrual red,'" she said. "So I think I was ahead of everyone in saying that women are getting a very bad deal." Dundy died the year after we spoke, in 2008.

One night at MacDowell, Maeve and Konecky and Dundy got very drunk. "Dundy was wearing a brown sweater, and Maeve *hated* that particular shade of brown, so when Dundy passed out, Maeve took the sweater and announced, 'She'll never see that one again!'"

I was in heaven listening to Konecky talk—memories, stories, gossip.

Another time, Konecky looked at Maeve with all her cats and said, "What are you? A woman who writes or a woman who keeps cats?"

Maeve said, "I'm putting them down, and you'll drive me."

"Why not just set them free?" Konecky asked.

"It would be a terrible thing to think about them cold and lost," Maeve explained. "I'd much rather think of them floating on a cloud." And so she brought them to a vet and had them all killed.

"That," Konecky said, "is how I knew she was a good Catholic." Then she added: "She was mad by then, and getting madder."

One evening back in the city Maeve invited several women over for drinks in a bar she'd set up in her living room. At some point, a man walked in, an odd fellow from the colony whom Maeve obviously couldn't stand. She yelled at him to get out. He did. After he left, Konecky warned Maeve to be careful, because that man was clearly "schizo." Maeve said, "I am, too!"

For a while, Maeve slept in one of Konecky's bedrooms.

"What was she like as a houseguest?" I asked.

Konecky mused. "She wasn't like a guest. She was always rather critical of me. Why wasn't I writing? Why hadn't I finished that book? Why was I involved with that woman?" (Konecky was married until her forties, when she was seduced by a woman at a different artists' colony and realized she was bisexual.)

Maeve was undeniably complicated to be around, but she was clearly a devoted, generous friend, always encouraging Konecky to fight her insecurities and write. In 1976, when Konecky finally published her first book, an excellent coming-of-age novel called *Allegra Maud Goldman,* Maeve provided a blurb: "The only thing wrong with Edith's novel is that it's too short."

———◄▬———

Thirteen years later, in 1989, when Konecky published her second novel, *A Place at the Table,* she and Maeve were no longer in touch. The book closes with a heartrending chapter in which the protagonist, Rachel, thinks she's spotted her old friend Deirdre in the East Village. "I don't know why I looked a second time, bag ladies are such a common sight," she says. But she does look—"dressed in layers of filthy rags, she is running clumsily on broken shoes in pursuit of a stray cat"—and when the woman disappears down the steps to the L train, Rachel nervously follows her onto the subway and finds a seat directly across from her:

> The fingernails are bitten to the quick, the hands are dirty and veined, but they are Deirdre's hands, disproportionately large and strong for the rest of her. . . . There is no sign of recognition. . . . Her teeth must be gone, I think. . . . Her teeth, the inky black of her hair, probably her spirit, all gone.

Rachel silently studies her for several stops, until out of nowhere Deirdre says, "You've lost weight, Rachel." The conversation that follows is disjointed, jarring. At some point Deirdre says, "Why are you following me? What are you doing here?"

> "Is it morbid curiosity?" Then, her voice rising to a scream, really frightening me, she asks, "Am I that fate worse than death?"
>
> I stare at her.
>
> "Is that what it is? Are you using me to face your own fears? Or to eva-a-a-de them?"
>
> I am too shaken to respond. *Is* it that I need to know the worst that can happen? *Is* this the worst that can happen? . . .
>
> *"Answer* me, Rachel." She spreads her arms wide, a theatrical gesture. She was never given to theatrical gestures. "I am calling to you from the black abyss that you have always known

was there," she chants, like a witch, like a wraith, "the abyss that you have always skirted so glibly. Am I your demon, your doppelganger, your dark side?"

"I think so. Maybe," I say. "Yes."

She sighs. "Well, I am not," she says in her normal voice.

The spell has broken. They talk amicably until they reach Canarsie, the end of the line ("Cheap symbolism," Deirdre mutters), and the train doubles back. Deirdre rummages in the dirty bags at her feet, producing a bottle of wine and two smudged plastic tumblers. They toast each other's health, inquire after mutual friends, family, their work. When Deirdre says she doesn't write anymore because there's nothing more to write about, Rachel thinks to herself how much there is for her to write about: "Confessions of a New York Bagperson, Living Off the Land, The Woman Who Threw It All Away, Slouching Toward Canarsie, Waiting for Godot, Queen Lear."

As the train passes under the East River Deirdre says, "I watch and I listen . . . and I think about what I have seen and heard. . . . Yes. That is what I do. The really frightening thing in life, I think, lies in our capacity for inattentiveness to it."

"Maybe she's right," Rachel muses to herself. "Maybe that's why we do it, why we write, why we live. Because we're interested. Curious. Attentive. Because we're children who've never acquired blinders."

Back at Fourteenth Street Rachel gets off the train knowing that she'll never see her old friend again.

The book is fiction, yet the scene is so intense, it feels real. I asked Konecky if it had actually happened.

"I saw a woman chasing a cat outside the subway at Fourteenth Street and First Avenue," she said. "She was shabby. A bag lady. It could've been Maeve. I hadn't heard from her in a while. So I imagined it was her and followed her down into the subway— but from there on out it's fiction. She hadn't been put away yet."

The cat slunk off her lap and wandered down the hall.

"She kept looking for a place that felt like home," Konecky said, "and never found it."

After Konecky and I had finished our cocktails and eaten dinner at the Japanese restaurant across the street, she sent me home with a legal-size manila folder of Maeve memorabilia: twelve airmail letters, all sent to Konecky from Ireland; eight scraps of paper with quick little notes, presumably from their time to- gether at MacDowell; a slim, dove-gray envelope from the old *New Yorker* offices on West Forty-Third Street, firmly stapled all around the edges. *It was in the pocket of my gorgeous lime green coat,* is scrawled across the back with a turquoise ballpoint pen in Maeve's distinctive looped cursive. Whatever the improvised package once held—a key? an earring?—is long gone.

Two pages torn from a spiral-bound calendar, dated January 1975, are jotted full of quotations and thoughts. On the twentieth, she paraphrases a line from Albert Camus's essay "Rebellion and Art": "Oh, if only one living creature had definite shape." Beneath that is "Edith Konecky (Rubin) is the Phoenix." On the twenty-seventh is the cryptic yet intuitively logical equation:

Mirror—Need—Feeling
Window—Mind—Observation

There are also typewritten transcriptions from Edith Konecky's own diary. On February 13, 1974, she wrote:

Maeve's call tonight from NY. . . . [Her] advice to me: "Make
a list of everything you did today before you go to sleep and
then write down what you're going to do tomorrow. Go to the
supermarket and burn off some of that nervous energy. . . . Get
up and do something tomorrow. Shine your shoes."

I was touched to see evidence of Maeve's almost motherly
concern for Konecky, and I was deeply heartened by the breezy
ease of her tone, the shorthand of two friends who see each other
frequently. It was a completely different side of Maeve than the
one I'd seen in her letters to Gardner Botsford.

Botsford had existed for Maeve as a sort of beneficent, almost idealized parental presence—a man who took care of her and
asked in return nothing but what she wanted to give, her writing.
Konecky was a peer. On paper, at least, Maeve confided in her
less than she did her editor, but it's obvious that the two women
had a very deep and well-maintained connection, which took root
in the soil of their actual, lived, everyday lives, in the dining
hall and small cabins of an artists' colony in the New Hampshire
woods, the stuffy living rooms of overheated city apartments in
winter, day trips out to the beach, dinners at Midtown restaurants. Whereas with Botsford the correspondence was the relationship, with Konecky it was merely part of a life spent sharing
other activities.

Living alone forces people to figure out how to manage their
emotional needs. My father likes to joke that those who talk way
too much "suffer from undelivered discourse"—as in, they spend
so much time not speaking that when they get the chance, they
can't stop. It's a slightly cruel way of thinking about the truly
lonely, but useful for others. It inspired me to diversify my port-
folio of attachments, so to speak, parceling out different aspects
of myself to different people, partly so I wouldn't overwhelm any
one person with the fire hose of my "undelivered discourse," but

also to protect myself from leaning too heavily on a buttress that couldn't and shouldn't sustain my full weight.

Maeve was long supported and protected by her *New Yorker* colleagues, but after she "burned all her boats," as her niece had put it, and spun further and further away from the professional sphere, she entered a sisterhood of writers who understood first-hand her daily challenges—if not her illness exactly, at least the struggle to be a woman who also writes. I began to realize this after reading the following, which appears a little farther down in Konecky's diary entry about Maeve's phone call from that February night in 1974:

> Then call from Tillie [Olsen]. Tillie sounding tired, mournful, stammering with fatigue. Maeve sounding high, funny, unself-pitying. But Maeve, I fear, is teetering on the brink. Fragile. Tillie takes better care, protects herself. Both so solitary, re-clusive. Maeve needier.

Tille Olsen was also a writer, as well as something of a sooth-sayer about the ways in which the demands of domesticity can limit women's literary production. In her book *Silences,* published in 1978, she asks: "What *are* creation's needs for full functioning?" Her answer: "Wholly surrendered and dedicated lives; time as needed for the work; totality of self."

I liked knowing that Maeve and Tillie Olsen had been friends. After several decades of enjoying very few female friendships, not to mention her geographical and emotional alienation from her family, befriending women who took their writing as seriously as she did must have felt to Maeve like a miracle. Finally, she'd found her people—who were also lucky to be found, and they knew it.

Possibly because of the long-ago closeness she'd once shared with her sister, Maeve was skilled at being a good friend, gener-

ous, fun, supportive. In Konecky's folder of memorabilia are several letters she wrote to Maeve long after she died. In February
2003 she wrote, "I wish I could ask you now how you like being
dead," and on the next page, "You told me once that you never
really cared for sex, that you only had it out of pity for them (the
men who were your lovers, husband) because they wanted it so
much, poor things." There is a passage of Maeve's, and beneath it,
"Maeve, you wrote this to Tillie Olsen, who treasured it, and had
it up on her studio wall. I copied it, and it's now on the [bulletin]
board over my desk." The passage reads:

I have been trying to think of the word to say to you that would
never fail to lift you up when you are too tired or too sad [to]
not be downcast. But I can think only of a reminder—you are
all it has. You are all your work has. It has nobody else and
never had anybody else. If you deny it hands and a voice, it will
continue as it is, alive, but speechless and without hands. You
know it has eyes and can see you, and you know how hopefully
it watches you. But I am speaking of a soul that is timid but
that longs to be known. When you are so sad that you "cannot work" there is always danger fear will enter in and begin
withering around. A good way to remain on guard is to go to
the window and watch the birds for an hour or two or three.
It is very comforting to see their beaks opening and shutting.

This is *real* friendship—the kind that takes another's soul as
seriously as one's own. Aristotle considered it the highest order
of love, *philia,* or "friendship love," in which tending to somebody
else's welfare is central to our own flourishing.

Maeve's advice to Tillie Olsen to stand at the window and watch the birds opening and shutting their beaks made me think of the introduction she'd written in 1969 to *The Long-Winded Lady,* her collected *New Yorker* columns. The essay is very short and worth reading in its entirety, particularly for her description of New York City, which ranks up there with E. B. White's deservedly famous line, "On any person who desires such queer prizes, New York will bestow the gift of loneliness and the gift of privacy." He wrote that in 1948. Twenty-one years later, Maeve entered the annals with: "These days I think of New York as the capsized city. Half-capsized, anyway, with the inhabitants hanging on, most of them still able to laugh as they cling to the island that is their life's predicament."

What the birds and their beaks reminded me of was something more universal. Later in the essay she says that looking back at the forty-seven columns she'd written between 1953 and 1968, she sees that The Long-Winded Lady isn't interested in "the strange or exotic ways of people," but instead "the ordinary ways, when something that is familiar to her shows." She continues:

> [The Long-Winded Lady] is drawn to what she recognizes, or half-recognizes, and these forty-seven pieces are the record of forty-seven moments of recognition. Somebody said, "We are real only in moments of kindness." Moments of kindness, moments of recognition—if there is a difference, it is a faint one.

The kindness she's talking about is different than the Bible's "love is patient and kind," and the Torah's *mitzvah,* and even the secular bumper-sticker encouragement to "Practice random acts of kindness and senseless acts of beauty," which casts doing something nice for someone else as rather arbitrary and pranklike.

What Maeve suggests here is that a flash of recognition—of

the observed by the observer, or between two people—has the ordinary transcendence of a bird opening and shutting its beak. It reveals her deep appreciation for ephemerality, the small, often overlooked moments that are our day-to-day existence.

Judged according to traditional definitions of love and well-being, Maeve's ceaseless switching among apartments and hotels and writing colonies and friends' summer cottages in the off-season seems self-destructive. Had she stayed in one place and set down roots, we think to ourselves, she wouldn't have ended up dying alone in a nursing home. Looked at another way, however, through the lens of her own fascination with "moments of recognition," she was arranging her life exactly as she wanted it. For Maeve, what sociologists call "strong ties"—the judgmental eyes of her sister and relatives; Ireland's excessively repressive, sexist culture—were asphyxiating; maintaining them might have spared her from dying alone (a fate none of us can guarantee evading), but would have definitely held her back while she lived. In New York City, surrounded by a constantly changing cast of colleagues and lovers, doormen and bartenders, chambermaids and taxi drivers, as well as, in late middle age, female friends, she was able to live amid a meteor shower of "weak ties" that sustained her everyday without encroaching on the freedom she needed to continue to thrive as a writer. They were her material, and she her own, too.

After meeting Edith Konecky, I decided I might as well call Richard Rupp, the professor who'd found Maeve in the nursing home, to hear him tell the story. Toward the end of our conversation he said something I couldn't let go of: "She had a good life up there, but it was a miserable life because she was unlucky in love."

Over the years I've noticed that only men use this phrase—"unlucky in love"—in reference exclusively to unmarried women, as if they can't possibly comprehend that contentment or even happiness is possible without the centrality of a man. Even my father said it to me once, with all good intentions, after a breakup. I told him that I was sad for sure that the relationship hadn't worked out, but that in fact I considered myself lucky in love: I'd had the pleasure of falling in love several times, with men who loved me in return. Just because one or the other of those relationships hadn't lasted my entire life didn't detract from what I'd gained. Edna Millay summed it up rather nicely in her sonnet "I Shall Forget You Presently, My Dear":

I would indeed that love were longer-lived,
And vows were not so brittle as they are,
But so it is, and nature has contrived
To struggle on without a break thus far,—
Whether or not we find what we are seeking
Is idle, biologically speaking.

Clearly Maeve's mental health contributed to her downfall. But I wasn't convinced being "unlucky in love" had all that much to do with it.

Are Women People Yet?

Ragged Island, Casco Bay, Maine

By now you've surely noticed that of my five "awakeners" only three—Neith Boyce, Edna Millay, and Maeve Brennan—ever met the official definition of spinster.

I don't accept *all* the blame for this. When I attached myself to Neith and Edna, I didn't know they'd eventually "join the vast majority," as Neith so memorably put it. I'd been dimly aware from the first that Maeve had married, briefly, but her writing persona was so solitary that I managed to forget this until Angela Bourke published her biography. Besides, two open marriages and one unsatisfying interregnum with an alcoholic don't really represent marriage as I'd ever thought of it. Edith Wharton chose me, not the other way around, so her marriage doesn't count.

Charlotte Perkins Gilman represents a category all her own. Her ability to think clearly and deliberately about each stage of her life* taught me the most about the long-ago fantasy that set my adult life into motion: the spinster wish.

In my early twenties, the "spinster wish" was my private shorthand for the novel pleasures of being alone. As I grew older, and felt more strongly the cultural expectation of marriage, the words became more like a thought experiment, a way to imagine in detail what it would look like to never settle down. The word *wish* is crucial. A wish is a longing, not a plan of action. It was perhaps precisely because I found so much meaning and satisfaction in my relationships that I conjured such an escapist fantasy, not because I didn't want such relationships, but because I also wanted to find other avenues of meaning and identity.

Only now, looking back, do I see that this thought experiment ultimately doubled as positive reinforcement; by continuing to wonder about and converse, internally, with "ambiguous women"—the scholar Carolyn Heilbrun's wonderful term for those who choose not to center their lives around a man—I became one.

It wasn't until I researched this book and came to a more

---

* Charlotte preferred the word *living* to *life*. "*Life* is a verb, not a noun," she once wrote. "Life is living; living is doing." The same might be said for the word *love*.

comprehensive understanding of the largely unwritten history of the "ambiguous woman," that I truly fell in love with the word *spinster* itself. To explain why, I must briefly share two more history lessons.

———◄█▬———

The first lesson predates the lives and times of my five awakeners. As I mentioned at the beginning of this book, in early America spinsters were usually outcasts, pushed to the edges of society by circumstance, where they often endured painful isolation and scorn.

This began to change during the American Revolutionary period, when the fervor for social and political independence inspired by our new Constitution ignited the minds of not a few thinking women to question the "conjugal imperative," becoming what I think of as "radical spinsters"—quiet outsiders with a mission.

According to historian Lee Chambers-Schiller, among small pockets of New Englanders born between 1780 and 1840 arose what she calls a "Cult of Single Blessedness"*—unmarried women who chose and reveled in their status. Like the far more prominent Cult of Domesticity it wasn't an actual cult; rather, it was a way certain women (and there weren't all that many of them) thought of themselves in relation to the social order— specifically, as those women who chose to remain celibate rather than compromise their integrity by marrying merely for social or economic gain. By rejecting "the self-abnegation inherent in domesticity," they engaged in the "cultivation of the self," upholding

---

* Chambers-Schiller borrowed the term from Shakespeare, who used it, humorously, in *A Midsummer Night's Dream,* to refer to the state of being unmarried.

the single life "as both a socially and personally valuable state," and "through the choice against marriage, articulated the values of female independence."

Many of the era's most influential thinkers—most famously America's first female public intellectual, Margaret Fuller, the great suffragist Susan B. Anthony,* and the popular novelist Louisa May Alcott—remained single for most if not all of their lives. In 1984, when Chambers-Schiller published the first-ever historical study of these pioneers, she pulled her title, *Liberty, a Better Husband,* from an entry in Alcott's diary, written on Valentine's Day 1868, in which the never-married novelist mentions an article she'd just finished writing, titled "Happy Women." "I put in my list all the busy, useful, independent spinsters I know," notes Alcott, "for liberty is a better husband than love to many of us."

I like to think that these writers and activists influenced the group of unmarried seamstresses who petitioned the Massachusetts State Legislature to give them their own village in the wake of the Civil War. The women argued that because they far outnumbered men in the region, and therefore couldn't marry, the state should, in effect, step up and be their husband. They requested "a tract of good cultivated land" divided into lots ranging from a half acre to five acres, each with "a good (but the cheapest possible) house." Every woman would be provided with "rations, tools, seeds, and instructions in gardening" until she became self-supporting, at which point she'd pay off her debt and become sole proprietress of her domain, which she could leave to a female heir in the event of her death.

Such a reasonable, modest, even considerate request! Not surprisingly, the legislature didn't respond. But the proposal bril-

---

* In 1896 the newspaperwoman Nellie Bly asked Susan B. Anthony if she'd ever been in love. Her answer: "Bless you, Nellie, I've been in love a thousand times! But I never loved any one so much that I thought it would last. In fact, I never felt I could give up my life of freedom to become a man's housekeeper."

liantly highlights the plight of an underclass of poor widows and would-be wives who had no choice but to go it alone—and yet, even more tellingly, responded with self-respect and ingenuity.

The second (and final) history lesson is about a centuries-long phenomenon known among demographers and historians as the "demographic transition"—a long, massive decline in family size that took place in the United States between 1800 and 1940.

Throughout the 1600s and 1700s, it was common for a woman to give birth nine months after her wedding and go on to get pregnant every two years, until she reached the end of her fertility or died (whichever came first). Even with high infant-mortality rates, the enormous risks presented by both pregnancy and childbirth, the fact that some women never married, others were infertile, and still others developed secondary infertility, the average "completed" family—those with mothers who survived to age fifty—had 8.02 children.

Recently women's historian Kathryn Sklar showed me a graph, so I could see for myself: a straight line marches steadily at the 8.02-mark across two centuries—until the early 1800s, when it begins a sharp plummet and steadily declines over the next 120 years. By 1900, the average had dropped to 4 children per family. It sank further during the Great Depression, to 3, then rebounded in the late 1940s and 1950s. What we think of now as the mid-century Baby Boom really just put us back where we'd been in 1900—to an average of 4 children per family. In the 1970s and 1980s family size shrank to its lowest ever—between 1 and 2 children—and has hovered there ever since.

We still don't know how to fully explain this radical shift. My first guess was migration to the cities, but Sklar explained that fertility has always been low in urban centers—I was shocked to learn that fertility decline was actually *driven* by rural areas. She said that demographers point to the importance of families and women within families wanting to control their economic futures in new ways. Some even argue that this "industrious" attitude, which preceded the Industrial Revolution, made the Industrial Revolution possible.

In her fascinating paper "Victorian Women and Domestic Life," Sklar argues that the transformation from large to smaller families happened because for the first time in American history women of all classes and races were consciously exerting control over their own bodies and the reproductive process. This "widespread adoption of family limitation," combined with all the other radical changes taking place in America between 1830 and 1880— the transportation and communications revolutions, the abolition of slavery, and the separation of public and private life, to name a few—actually "constituted change in human history on the scale of the Neolithic Revolution."

Which is to say: It was the first time women as a group (as opposed to scattered individuals) had ever exerted control over their own bodies and the reproductive process. The first time women were acting on the idea that they were people first, women second.

Sklar uses as one of her case studies Charlotte Perkins Gilman's great-aunt, Harriet Beecher Stowe. Harriet married Calvin Stowe in 1836, when she was twenty-four. By 1843 she had five children, including a pair of twins. Their marriage was a good one. But the next summer, in 1844, Calvin left home to travel for work, as he did every year, and in the series of letters they exchanged while he was away, a stalemate emerges.

He is very forthcoming about his attraction to her. "Every desire I have, mental and physical, is completely satisfied and filled up, and leaves me nothing more to ask for. My enjoyment with you is not weakened by time nor blunted with age, and every reunion after separation is just as much of a honeymoon as was the first month after the wedding," he writes. "Yet we are not as happy as we might be."

This oblique reference is to their sexual life. In her own way, Harriet has been making it clear that she's had enough of the demands of wifedom. "I am sick of the smell of sour milk and sour meat, and sour everything, and then the clothes *will* not dry, and no wet thing does, and everything smells mouldy; and altogether I feel as if I never [want] to eat again." In another letter she writes, "I feel no life, no energy, no appetite . . . in fact, I am becoming quite ethereal."

What she doesn't state outright is the memory of her own mother, who gave birth to eleven children before dying at forty-one. Harriet would not allow herself the same fate. Her method of contraception was sexual abstinence. In the spring of 1846 she fled to Brattleboro, Vermont, for a water cure, and stayed for ten months. Almost immediately upon her return home, Calvin did the same, staying away for fifteen months. In this way, for six years—1843 to 1849—Harriet avoided pregnancy. In 1848 and 1850, when she was thirty-seven and thirty-nine, she gave birth twice more, thereby omitting, as Sklar puts it, two to three children that her mother did not.

No doubt her sister Catharine approved. In her wildly popular *Treatise on Domestic Economy,* first published in 1841 and reprinted every year until 1856, she wrote that the most important fact in a woman's life was whether or not she controlled it, for "there is nothing, which so distinctly marks the difference between weak and strong minds, as the fact, whether they control circumstances, or circumstances control them."

As the numbers show without a shadow of a doubt, Harriet Beecher Stowe and her husband were part of a national trend toward family planning that affected all classes and groups. The Victorian era has gone down in the popular imagination as a century-long frigidity-fest. In fact, Sklar suggests, the so-called "passionlessness" we attribute to Victorian women was their ingenious means of shutting down their own libidos, and those of their husbands, in order to abstain from sex at a time when birth control was unreliable and/or simply physically uncomfortable (e.g., sheep intestine).

More than a century has passed. Today we tell girls to grow up to be or do whatever they want. But the cultural pressure to become a mother remains very strong; rare is she who doesn't at least occasionally succumb to the nagging fear that if she remains childless, she'll live to regret it.

Charlotte Perkins Gilman's adolescent declaration to her beloved Martha Luther, then, remains among the most prescient things she ever wrote. Here is the passage I quoted earlier, this time with the salient phrase in bolded letters:

> I am really getting glad not to marry. . . . If I let that business alone, and go on in my own way; what I gain in individual strength and development of personal power of character, ***myself as a self*, you know, not merely as a woman, or that useful animal a wife and mother,** will, I think, make up, and more than make up in usefulness and effect, for the other happiness that part of me would enjoy.

While researching this book taught me the true value of the spinster, writing it made me see that the question I'd long posed to myself—whether to be married or to be single—is a false binary. The space in which I've always wanted to live—indeed, where I have spent my adulthood—isn't between those two poles, but beyond it. The choice between being married versus being single doesn't even belong here in the twenty-first century.

The question now is something else entirely: Are women people yet? By which I mean: Are we finally ready for a young woman to set out on the long road of her life as a human being who inhabits but isn't limited by her gender? We've been evolving toward this new question ever since America was founded, albeit excruciatingly slowly and with many stops and starts along the way. Until the answer is an undeniable yes, a girl actually can't grow up like a boy, free to consider the long scope of her life as her own distinct self.

I grant that a wholesale reclamation of the word *spinster* is a tall order. My aim is more modest: to offer it up as shorthand for holding on to that in you which is independent and self-sufficient, whether you're single or coupled.

If you're single, whether never-married, divorced, or widowed, you can carry the word *spinster* like a talisman, a constant reminder that you're in very good company—indeed, part of a long and noble tradition of women past and present living on their own terms.

If you find yourself unhappily coupled, you can use the word *spinster* to conjure a time when you weren't, and to recall that being alone is often far preferable to being in a bad relationship. Figuring out how to reclaim that happier self can offer a road map out.

For the happily coupled, particularly those balancing work and children, *spinster* can be code for remembering to take time out for yourself. And if you've never learned how to be alone in a way that feels fruitful and energizing, there's no time like the present. As the never-married Sarah Orne Jewett wrote in her 1896 novella *The Country of the Pointed Firs,* which remains one of the best books about the many varieties of the single experience:

There are paths trodden to the shrines of solitude the world over,—the world cannot forget them, try as it may; the feet of the young find them out because of curiosity and dim foreboding; while the old bring hearts full of remembrance.

Tomorrow morning, Willy, S, and I are driving north to Newburyport, and from there up the coast of Maine.

By now I've known Willy for thirty-seven years. These days she's seeing a sculptor who lives in Queens (he has a deadline, so he can't join us).

I met S in 2012, through friends. For our first date he brought me to see *Richard III* at the Brooklyn Academy of Music. For our second, he brought me to the US debut of Philip Glass's Ninth Symphony at Carnegie Hall. For our third, he met me at my office near Columbus Circle for afternoon coffee in Central Park; walking back, he took my hand and held it, and when we parted, we kissed for so long that I knew right then there wouldn't be anyone but him for a while.

He lives in Brooklyn, too, though forty minutes and two subway lines away. He's a freelance writer, seven years younger than Willy and me, tall and lean with dark brown hair, and when I say he's brilliant what I mean is that he has an uncommonly moral intelligence, and that talking with him feels like wandering through a library of books I've never read (and some that I have), where there's room enough for my own thoughts to roam. Sometimes I think he has a little bit in him of every man I've ever loved, and other times I think I've never met anyone like him. He's so unusual and honest—so much so that, to my occasional dismay, he is rarely romantic, though he did once say the most romantic thing anyone has ever said to me: that he liked the idea of having a child with me because he admires so much the kind of woman I am, and wants to see me raise a daughter in my own image. I have no idea if that will actually happen. Our age difference seems to have stripped away conventional expectations; for the first time I don't feel pressured to be ready for something I'm not. Every so often we get into a fight that makes me think we've reached the end, which can be unsettling, but even so I prefer this uncertainty to false comfort.

The three of us will spend a night in Newburyport, and then we'll drive two hours to Harpswell, Maine, where we'll ask a fisherman to ferry us out to Ragged Island, the one Edna Millay and Eugen Boissevain bought in 1933. It's at the outermost edge of Casco Bay, about eighty acres, with only one house, and no electricity or plumbing. After Edna died, it was bought by a couple in their early fifties, and through friends I was able to locate one of their grandchildren, today an editor at *The New York Times*.

"It's rough living there, not for everyone," he'd said fondly when we spoke on the phone. "Wood stove. Kerosene lamps. Propane fridge." He described walking a path through the woods to the well, filling up five-gallon water buckets, and "humping them back down to the house."

While we talked, we both logged on to Google Earth so he could give me a virtual tour. The island is only hospitable during the summer months. According to locals, Edna spent most of that time in the nude, wandering around in what felt to her to be utter privacy, oblivious to the lobstermen offshore hauling their traps onto their boats, who could see her, plain as day.

"Hah," I said. "Just like her poetry. All of these so-called private things made public."

She swam laps in the nude, too. Seen from the sky above, the swimming cove is shaped almost exactly like a heart.

Preparing for our pilgrimage, I'd thought of the poet Mary Oliver, who was fifteen when Edna died in 1950. The morning after her high school graduation, she drove from her parents' home, in Ohio, to Steepletop, Edna's estate in central New York, where she became friendly with Edna's sister Norma and stuck around. "I was seventeen; I was enthralled by everything, and more or less lived there for the next six or seven years, running around the 800 acres like a child," Oliver later wrote.

As with my first visit to Edna's house in Newburyport, I won't know why I want to see Ragged Island until I get there. I suppose Willy and S and I will spend an hour or so walking around, then boat back to shore, drive to Portland, on the other side of the bay, and take the ferry out to Cushing Island, where Willy's family owns a house. This is the island my family used to vacation on when I was small, when Willy and I and the other children would sprint in our bathing suits across wide green lawns and down to the beach, where, if the tide was low, I'd break away to a long isthmus of rocks and tidal pools to "play Karana" (which in adulthood I misremembered as "Karenina," that other outcast woman).

On this late-summer day we'll bring our groceries over on the ferry. Maybe we'll steam lobsters in a pot and dip the meat into shallow dishes of melted butter and share among us a couple of bottles of wine. Afterward we'll sit on the porch and talk in the deepening silence.

Maybe Willy will tell us stories about Margot Schuyler, her spinster great-aunt, who also summered on this island and formed a lifelong friendship with Edna after their disastrous one-night stand in Paris in 1922, when Edna was there writing for *Vanity Fair*. Margot had a tattoo on her inner thigh—a pair of birds perched on a pair of hands; the "Schuyler Family Crest," she called it—and another, of a black widow spider, on her shoulder.

Willy will definitely give S and me the master bedroom, with its high, pitched ceiling—she's very generous that way—and take for herself the smaller bedroom at the other end of the house. S will fall asleep before I do, as he always does, and I'll probably lie awake thinking mulishly or perhaps accurately about how I can't possibly let go of these five awakeners of mine after all; they're too much a part of me. I'll start to hatch a plan to visit East Hampton to see if I can find the little shingled cottage by the sea that Maeve Brennan lived in for a while, the one she described in a short story as "absurd" but that, "in spite of all it lacked, and for all its temporary air . . . had an air of gaiety about it, and even welcome," and, like her, was "good-hearted in spite of itself."

In the morning we'll be woken early by the birds, chattering at one another in the treetops all around and above us, their intricate conversation a delicate lace coverlet being draped over a long, shining breakfast table, readying the day to begin.

One evening not long after Mary Oliver moved from Edna Millay's estate to Greenwich Village, she went back to visit Norma and found her sitting in the kitchen with a photographer named Molly Malone Cook. "I took one look and fell, hook and tumble," Oliver wrote decades later, in a photo book about her and Cook's more than forty years in love together.

In 1990, the year I graduated from high school, Oliver wrote a poem called "The Summer Day." She ends it by asking a question that electrified me when I first read it in 1992, and that, when my mother died four years later, I absorbed into my bloodstream, like an unspoken mantra:

Tell me, what is it you plan to do
with your one wild and precious life?

Works Cited and Consulted

Ackerman, J. M., C. C. Nocera, and J. A. Bargh. "Incidental Haptic Sensations Influence Social Judgments and Decisions," *Science,* June 22, 2010, vol. 328, no. 5987.

Allaback, Sarah. *The First American Women Architects* (University of Illinois Press, 2008).

Austen, Jane. *Emma* (John Murray, 1815).

Beauvoir, Simone de. *Memoirs of a Dutiful Daughter* (Gallimard, 1958).

———. *The Second Sex* (Gallimard, 1949).

Beecher, Catharine. *A Treatise on Domestic Economy* (Harper & Brothers, 1841).

———. *Letters to the People on Health and Happiness* (Harper & Brothers, 1856).

Bines, Joan P. *Words They Lived By: Colonial New England Speech, Then and Now* (Eye of the Beholder, 2013).

Botsford, Gardner. *A Life of Privilege, Mostly* (St. Martin's Press, 2003).

Bourke, Angela. *Maeve Brennan: Homesick at "The New Yorker": An Irish Writer in Exile* (Counterpoint, 2004).

Boyce, Neith. *The Bond* (Duffield & Co., 1908).

Boyd, Nancy. *Distressing Dialogues* (Harper & Brothers, 1924).

Brennan, Maeve. *The Long-Winded Lady: Notes from "The New Yorker"* (William Morrow, 1969).

Brown, Gillian. *Domestic Individualism: Imagining Self in Nineteenth-Century America* (University of California Press, 1990).

Callahan, Michael. "Sorority on E. 63rd St.," *Vanity Fair*, April 2010.

Carter, Susan B., Roger L. Ransom, and Richard Sutch. "Family Matters: The Life-Cycle Transition and the Unparalleled Antebellum American Fertility Decline," in Guinnane, Timothy W., Sundstrom, William A., and Whatley, Warren C., eds. *History Matters: Essays on Economic Growth, Technology, and Demographic Change* (Stanford University Press, 2003).

Ceplair, Larry, ed. *Charlotte Perkins Gilman: A Nonfiction Reader* (Columbia University Press, 1991).

Chambers-Schiller, Lee Virginia. *Liberty, a Better Husband: Single Women in America: The Generations of 1780–1840* (Yale University Press, 1984).

Collins, Gail. *America's Women: 400 Years of Dolls, Drudges, Helpmates, and Heroines* (William Morrow, 2003).

Coontz, Stephanie. *A Strange Stirring: The Feminine Mystique and American Women at the Dawn of the 1960s* (Basic Books, 2011).

———. *Marriage, a History: From Obedience to Intimacy, or How Love Conquered Marriage*, (Viking Press, 2005).

Davis, Cynthia J. *Charlotte Perkins Gilman: A Biography* (Stanford University Press, 2010).

Davis, Katharine Bement. "A Study of the Sex Life of the Normal Married Woman," *Journal of Social Hygiene*, March 1923, vol. IX, no. 3.

Dazkir, Sibel S., and Marilyn R. Read. "Furniture Forms and Their Influence on Our Emotional Responses Toward Interior Environments," *Environment and Behavior*, September 2012, vol. 44, no. 5.

DeBoer-Langworthy, Carol. *The Modern World of Neith Boyce: Autobiography and Diaries* (University of New Mexico Press, 2003).

De Paulo, Bella. *Singled Out: How Singles Are Stereotyped, Stigmatized, and Ignored, and Still Live Happily Ever After* (St. Martin's Press, 2006).

Didion, Joan. *Play It as It Lays* (Farrar, Straus & Giroux, 1970).

Doan, Laura L., ed. *Old Maids to Radical Spinsters: Unmarried Women in the Twentieth-Century Novel* (University of Illinois Press, 1991).

Draper, Dorothy. *Entertaining Is Fun! How to Be a Popular Hostess* (Doubleday, 1948).

Dublin, Thomas. *Women at Work: The Transformation of Work and Community* (Columbia University Press, 1979).

Dundy, Elaine. *The Dud Avocado* (E. P. Dutton & Co., 1958).

Eastman, Max. *Great Companions: Critical Memoirs of Some Famous Friends* (Farrar, Straus & Cudahy, 1959).

Ehrenreich, Barbara, and Deirdre English. *Witches, Midwives, and Nurses: A History of Women Healers*, second edition (The Feminist Press at CUNY, 1973, 2010).

Eliot, George. *Middlemarch: A Study of Provincial Life* (William Blackwood and Sons, 1871).

Epstein, Daniel Mark. *What Lips My Lips Have Kissed: The Loves and Poems of Edna St. Vincent Millay* (Henry Holt, 2001).

Foley Doyle, Jean. *Life in Newburyport, 1900–1950* (Peter E. Randall Publisher LLC, 2007).

Freedman, Diane P., ed. *Millay at 100: A Critical Reappraisal* (Southern Illinois University Press, 1995).

Friedan, Betty. *The Feminine Mystique* (W. W. Norton, 1963).

Fuller, Margaret. *Woman in the Nineteenth Century* (Greeley & McElrath, 1845).

Gay, Peter. *Modernism: The Lure of Heresy* (W. W. Norton, 2007).

———. *The Bourgeois Experience: Victoria to Freud: Education of the Senses* (Oxford University Press, 1984).

Gill, Brendan. *Here at "The New Yorker"* (Random House, 1975).

Gilman, Charlotte Perkins. *The Living of Charlotte Perkins Gilman: An Autobiography* (D. Appleton-Century, 1935).

———. *Women and Economics* (Small, Maynard & Co., 1898).

Gissing, George. *New Grub Street* (Smith, Elder & Co., 1891).

Goldman-Price, Irene, ed. *My Dear Governess: The Letters of Edith Wharton to Anna Bahlmann* (Yale University Press, 2012).

Gornick, Vivian. *Approaching Eye Level* (Beacon Press, 1997).

Granovetter, Mark S. "The Strength of Weak Ties," *American Journal of Sociology*, May 1973, vol. 78, no. 6.

Grimm, Robert Thornton, Jr. "Forerunners for a Domestic Revolution: Jane Addams, Charlotte Perkins Gilman, and the Ideology of Childhood, 1900–1916," *Illinois Historical Journal*, Spring 1997, vol. 90, no. 1.

Hawthorne, Mary. "A Traveller in Residence," *London Review of Books*, November 13, 1997, vol. 19, no. 22.

———. "Observer," *The New Yorker*, December 28, 1998.

Hayden, Dolores. *The Grand Domestic Revolution* (MIT Press, 1981).

Heilbrun, Carolyn G. *Writing a Woman's Life* (W. W. Norton, 1988).

Hess, Judye, and Padma Catell. "Dual Dwelling Duos: An Alternative for Long-Term Relationships," *Journal of Couples Therapy*, 2001, vol. 10, nos. 3/4.

Israel, Betsy. *The Bachelor Girl: The Secret History of Single Women* (William Morrow/Harper Collins, 2002).

Jackson, Shirley. *We Have Always Lived in the Castle* (Viking Press, 1962).

James, Henry. *The Bostonians* (Macmillan, 1886).

———. *The Portrait of a Lady* (Houghton Mifflin, 1881).

Jerrold, Yvonne. *A Case of Wild Justice?* (Troubador Publishing Ltd., 2008).

Jewett, Sarah Orne. *The Country of the Pointed Firs* (Houghton Mifflin & Co., 1896).

Kazin, Alfred. "Brooklyn Bridge," *Harper's Bazaar*, 1946.

Kessler, Carol Farley. *Charlotte Perkins Gilman: Her Progress Toward Utopia with Selected Writings* (Syracuse University Press, 1995).

Kessler-Harris, Alice. *In Pursuit of Equity: Women, Men, and the Quest for Economic Citizenship in 20th-Century America* (Oxford University Press, 2001).

———. *Out to Work: A History of Wage-Earning Women in the United States* (Oxford University Press, 2003).

Keyser, Catherine. *Playing Smart: New York Women Writers and Modern Magazine Culture* (Rutgers University Press, 2010).

Knight, Denise D., ed. *The Abridged Diaries of Charlotte Perkins Gilman* (University Press of Virginia, 1998).

Konecky, Edith. *A Place at the Table* (Hamilton Stone Editions, 1989).

———. *Allegra Maud Goldman* (Harper & Row, 1976).

———. *Love and Money* (Hamilton Stone Editions, 2011).

Kroeger, Brooke. *Fannie: The Talent for Success of Writer Fannie Hurst* (Times Books, 1999).

———. *Nellie Bly: Daredevil, Reporter, Feminist* (Times Books, 1994).

Kundera, Milan. *Immortality*, translated by Peter Kussi (Grove Weidenfeld, 1991).

Larson Research + Strategy. "The 2013 Allianz Women, Money, and Power Study," 2012.

Lee, Hermione. *Edith Wharton* (Alfred A. Knopf, 2007).

Lerner, Gerda. *The Creation of Feminist Consciousness: From the Middle Ages to Eighteen-Seventy* (Oxford University Press, 1993).

Lesko, Barbara S. *The Great Goddesses of Egypt* (University of Oklahoma Press, 1999).

Lessing, Doris. *Prisons We Choose to Live Inside* (Harper Perennial, 1987).

Lynch-Brennan, Margaret. *The Irish Bridget: Irish Immigrant Women in Domestic Service in America, 1840–1930* (Syracuse University Press, 2009).

MacBain, Jenny. *The Salem Witch Trials: A Primary Source History of the Witchcraft Trials in Salem, Massachusetts* (Rosen Publishing Group, 2003).

Mariani, Paul L. *Lost Puritan: A Life of Robert Lowell* (W. W. Norton, 1994).

Markus, Hazel, and Nurius, Paula. "Possible Selves," *American Psychologist*, September 1986, vol. 41, no. 9.

Marshall, Megan. *Margaret Fuller: A New American Life* (Mariner Books/Houghton Mifflin Harcourt, 2013).

McCarthy, Mary. *Intellectual Memoirs: New York, 1936–1938* (Harcourt Brace Jovanovich, 1992).

Mehta, Ravi, and Rui (Juliet) Zhu. "Blue or Red? Exploring the Effect of Color on Cognitive Task Performances," *Science*, February 27, 2009, vol. 323, no. 5918.

——. "The Influence of Ceiling Height: The Effect of Priming on the Type of Processing That People Use," *Journal of Consumer Research*, August 2007, vol. 34.

Middlebrook, Diana Wood. *Anne Sexton: A Biography* (Houghton Mifflin, 1991).

Milan, Anne, and Alice Peters. "Couples Living Apart," *Canadian Social Trends*, Summer 2003, no. 69.

Milford, Nancy. *Savage Beauty: The Life of Edna St. Vincent Millay* (Random House, 2001).

Miller, Brett C. *Elizabeth Bishop: Life and the Memory of It* (University of California Press, 1995).

Miller, Nina. *Making Love Modern: The Intimate Public Worlds of New York's Literary Women* (Oxford University Press, 1999).

Mitchell, Margaret. *Gone with the Wind* (Scribner Book Company, 1936).

Monroe, Harriet. "Edna St. Vincent Millay," *Poetry*, August 1924.

Nehring, Cristina. *A Vindication of Love: Reclaiming Romance for the Twenty-First Century* (Harper Perennial, 2009).

O'Dell, Scott. *Island of the Blue Dolphins* (Dell Publishing, 1960).

Oliver, Mary, and Molly Malone Cook. *Our World* (Beacon Press, 2007).

Olsen, Tillie. *Silences* (The Feminist Press at CUNY, 1978).

Picardie, Justine. *Chanel: Her Life* (Steidl, 2011).

Pinker, Steven. *The Blank Slate: The Modern Denial of Human Nature* (Viking Press, 2002).

Plath, Sylvia. *The Bell Jar* (Heinemann, 1963).

Ray, Benjamin C. Salem Witch Trials Documentary Archive, University of Virginia (http://salem.lib.virginia.edu/home.html).

Rayne, Mrs. M. L. *What Can a Woman Do* (Eagle Publishing Co., 1893).

Robinson, Harriet H. "Early Factory Labor in New England," in Massachusetts Bureau of Statistics of Labor, *Fourteenth Annual Report* (Boston: Wright & Potter, 1883).

Rosenthal, Naomi Braun. *Spinster Tales and Womanly Possibilities* (SUNY Press, 2002).

Rowbotham, Sheila. *Dreamers of a New Day: Women Who Invented the Twentieth Century* (Verso, 2010).

Saks, Elyn R. *The Center Cannot Hold: My Journey Through Madness* (Hyperion, 2007).

Sandoval-Strausz, A. K. *Hotel: An American History* (Yale University Press, 2007).

Showalter, Elaine, ed. *These Modern Women: Autobiographical Essays from the Twenties* (The Feminist Press at CUNY, 1989).

Siegal, Reva B. "'The Rule of Love': Wife Beating as Prerogative and Privacy," *Yale Law School Faculty Scholarship Series*, 1996.

Sklar, Kathryn Kish. "Victorian Women and Domestic Life," in Sklar, Kathryn Kish, and Dublin, Thomas, eds., *Women and Power in American History*, third edition (Prentice Hall, 2009).

Sochen, June. *The New Woman: Feminism in Greenwich Village, 1910–1920* (Quadrangle Books, 1972).

Stansell, Christine. *American Moderns: Bohemian New York and the Creation of a New Century* (Metropolitan Books, 2000).

Strohm, Charles Q., Judith A. Seltzer, Susan D. Cochran, and Vickie M. Mays. "'Living Apart Together': Relationships in the United States," *Demographic Research*, August 13, 2009, vol. 21.

Trimberger, Ellen Kay, ed. *Intimate Warriors: Portraits of a Modern Marriage, 1899–1944* (The Feminist Press at CUNY, 1991).

Wagner-Martin, Linda. *Sylvia Plath: A Biography* (Simon & Schuster, 1987).

Wetzel, James R. "American Families: 75 Years of Change," *Monthly Labor Review*, March 1990.

Wetzsteon, Ross. *Republic of Dreams: Greenwich Village: The American Bohemian, 1910–1960* (Simon & Schuster, 2002).

Wharton, Edith. *A Backward Glance: An Autobiography* (D. Appleton-Century, 1934).

———. *The House of Mirth* (Charles Scribner's Sons, 1905).

Wharton, Edith, and Ogden Codman. *The Decoration of Houses* (B. T. Batsford, 1897).

Wilkins, Mary Eleanor. *A New England Nun and Other Stories* (Harper & Brothers, 1891).

Wilson, Edmund. *The Shores of Light: A Literary Chronicle of the Twenties and Thirties* (Farrar, Straus & Young, 1952).

Wolfe, Elsie de. *After All* (Harper and Brothers, 1935).

Wolff, Cynthia Griffin. *A Feast of Words: The Triumph of Edith Wharton* (Oxford University Press, 1977).

Woolf, Virginia. *A Room of One's Own* (The Hogarth Press, 1929).

———. *To the Lighthouse* (Harcourt Brace, 1927).

Further Reading: Spinsters Through the Years

Adams, Margaret. *Single Blessedness: A Generous and Unapologetic Celebration of Unmarried Life in a Married Society* (Penguin Books, 1976).

Ashton-Warner, Sylvia. *Spinster: A Novel* (Simon & Schuster, 1959).

Cobb, Michael. *Single: Arguments for the Uncoupled* (New York University Press, 2012).

Edwards, Marie, and Eleanor Hoover. *The Challenge of Being Single: For Divorced, Widowed, Separated, and Never Married Men and Women* (A Signet Book, 1974).

Hillis, Marjorie. *Live Alone and Like It: A Guide for the Extra Woman* (Bobbs-Merrill Company, 1936).

Peterson, Nancy L. *Our Lives for Ourselves: Women Who Have Never Married* (G. P. Putnam & Sons, 1981).

Reed, Myrtle. *The Spinster Book* (G. P. Putnam's Sons, 1902).

Sarton, May. *Journal of a Solitude* (W. W. Norton, 1973).

Simon, Barbara Levy. *Never Married Women* (Temple University Press, 1987).

Acknowledgments

Spinster began at the MacDowell Colony in 2006, fell dormant for five years, and came roaring back to life in the wake of an article Scott Stossel asked me to write for the November 2011 issue of *The Atlantic*. For that assignment, and for the experience of working so closely with a genuine virtuoso, I will always be grateful.

Scott opened the door for me to publish this book, but without the archival research done by biographers and historians my essaying would be impossible. I am deeply indebted to the work of Angela Bourke, Lee Chambers-Schiller, Cynthia J. Davis, Carol DeBoer-Langworthy, Alice Kessler-Harris, Brooke Kroeger, Hermione Lee, Gerda Lerner, Nancy Milford, Christine Stansell, and Kathryn K. Sklar.

Special thanks to those who agreed to be interviewed and/or provided source material: Yvonne Jerrold, Edith Konecky, Hazel Markus, Janet Malcolm, Richard Rupp, and Sam Sifton. Also to those who answered crucial questions at key moments: Caleb Crain, Bella DePaulo, Dan and Marcia Edson, Susan Hertz, Stefanie Shattuck-Hufnagel, Karen Karbinger, Jack Kelley, Eric Klinenberg, Brian O'Keefe, and Victor Tine.

The remarkable Susan Wissler, director of The Mount, gave me a winter writing residency (and my own summer interview series). Working with her, Ross Jolly, Rebekah McDougal, and Kelsey Mullen relieved the solitude of book writing and brought me closer to Edith Wharton. I am especially grateful to Anne Schuyler for her research.

I need to thank some teachers: Pete Moss, Susie Linfield, and the late Ellen Willis. Likewise, some early editors and bosses: Toby Lester, Cullen Murphy, and Dara Caponigro.

As I (mostly) left magazine journalism behind to write this book, my dear friend Courtney Hodell took my hand and led me through this domain she knows so well, reading my first draft and many drafts subsequent, offering vital critiques, and answering my endless questions about process and best practices. I'd have drowned without her.

A few others helped keep me afloat. Karen Azoulay, Ali Bolick, Christopher Bolick, Doug Bolick, Michael Cobb, Malcolm Gladwell, Toby Lester, Courtney Lynch, Molly Pulda, Gary Sernovitz, and Dan Smith took time to read this manuscript and provide invaluable feedback. Conversations along the way with Ruth Altchek, Martha Almy, Carolyn Clement, Johanna Conterio, Alexandra Jacobs, Maria Maggenti, Gillian MacKenzie, Thomas Meaney, Ryan Nally, Jenny Nordberg, Willy Somma, Catherine Steindler, and Rebecca Traister inspired and sustained me. Erika Troseth Martinez cheered me on from afar.

Thanks to Karen Azoulay (again!) for assisting with photos, Eileen Reynolds for gathering early research, and Elizabeth Gumport for her fastidious checking of facts. Emily Drabinski e-mailed me academic articles whenever I asked, and the Washington Square Hotel put me up for two nights so I could live the Maeve Brennan life.

Tina Bennett is everything I could want in an agent: tough, honorable, learned, wise, and fearless; her edits were instrumental.

As for Crown: The magnetic Molly Stern saw the potential for this project like no other publisher. Vanessa Mobley is the kind of editor reputed to no longer exist: generous with her time, skilled at knowing when and how to push, able to make the weak parts strong. Claire Potter made everything difficult easy. I greatly benefited from the talents of Chris Brand, Elizabeth Rendfleisch, and Terry Deal.

Seth Colter Walls had the misfortune of meeting me at the exact moment I embarked on this book, though I was fortunate. His erudition elevated my thinking; his conceptual and creative suggestions helped me find my own direction; his humor and emotional support brightened the dark season of doubt.

Whenever I call my father in the middle of his workday and ask if he's too busy to talk, he says, "Never too busy for you." This lesson in always being available to the people you care about is one my brother learned well. They have seen me through everything, and my love for them is boundless.

ABOUT THE AUTHOR

KATE BOLICK is a contributing editor to *The Atlantic*.
She was previously the executive editor of *Domino* magazine. She lives in New York.